Thinking Fair

Rules for Reason in Science and Religion

Lucas John Mix

ISBN: 1515153282
ISBN-13: 978-1515153283

Dedicated to the Hill Society.

Thank you for questioning…

absolutely everything.

TABLE OF CONTENTS

CHAPTER 1
The Ground We Walk

Sometimes you have to wander a bit. When I started graduate school, it took me six months to find the shortest path to the chapel from my dorm room. People joke about the difficulty of finding God at Harvard, but finding Memorial Church is not that hard. It has a large white spire and sits in the middle of Harvard Yard. Still, every second counts when you want to rise as late as possible and still attend morning prayers. Efficiency mattered to me, but I couldn't be efficient until after I'd been adventurous. Wandering between the massive brick buildings I stumbled across hidden art, ran into interesting people, and learned far more about the university than I would have had I started with a map.

I care about thinking clearly. I am passionate about finding the shortest distance from data to conclusions. And yet reasoning, too, requires exploration. We may be on completely different paths, or on the same path with different destinations. Studying biology, comparative religion, and martial arts, I have encountered a variety of reasoning styles. I have wandered the mental landscape and found that the shortest path is seldom the most obvious. Most paths I would not walk again, but a surprising number have proven useful. Beauty showed up in surprising places and I often found something I would need later on.

We forget that the wisdom of the ages started as wisdom of the moment. The Age of Reason required an Age of Discovery. Reason must be more than getting from point A to point B. It should challenge us to understand the ground we're covering. It should show us things we never looked for and teach us about the people we meet.

After Harvard, and after attending seminary in California, I moved to Tucson, to work at the University of Arizona. I taught evolutionary biology and religious studies, but my primary job was as chaplain to the students. Every week, I would spend three hours just sitting on a hill in the middle of campus talking with students about how they, and I, thought about the world. Frequently, we spoke about knowledge and belief. Why do people think the the things they do? And how can they continue to think them? I could give you examples, but I'm sure you can come up with better ones on your own: things you find obvious but others don't, or just the opposite. I wanted to help them understand one another and how different people think differently. I wanted to help them think clearly about how they would put together their own picture of the world in light of all the new things they were learning. We called it the Hill Society and each of us discovered something new on a regular basis.

The Hill people sprawled leisurely across the landscape, both literal and figurative. Sometimes it could be hard to tell what exactly we were talking about, but we managed to spend a good deal of time on science, and religion, and ethics, and reality, and all those issues Westerners have become afraid to talk about. We're good at paired monologues – talking at each other – but lousy at sharing, listening, and coming to consensus. Whether symptom or cause, the breakdown has everything to do with our inability to understand how others think. Too often we assume others must be on the same path we are and dawdling, if not actively stalling, when they do not reach the same conclusions we do. The Hill Society rarely reached consensus, but we found every year that we understood each other better and we understood ourselves better. All that sprawling showed us the lay of the land.

Conversation taught us to appreciate one another's goals as well as our premises, not just the conclusions we reached but the reasons we reached them. We found we could walk our own paths more efficiently, collide less often, and even help each other on occasion. And it was fun.

I miss my time on the Hill and I know others do as well. This book is an attempt to continue that conversation. I write to all the people that need a Hill, but mostly college students, struggling to find their place in the world, trying to make the most of the wisdom (and not-so wisdom) thrown at them every day. This is how I try to reason clearly. This is how I think about the things that are important to me: truth, value, and friendship.

SCIENCE AND RELIGION

Most mornings at Harvard, I walked back from Memorial Church to my office in the Museum of Natural History. Two approximately equal paths exist. One leads directly between physics and chemistry. The other veers between sociology and European studies.[1] The positioning is oddly appropriate.

There is a gap between modern biology and modern Christianity. I don't find it particularly difficult or significantly larger than other gaps – say between science and the humanities – but crossing the distance takes effort. And it requires choices about exactly how you will go. I write with a keen awareness of the anxiety this causes and the desire many have to make the distance shorter, or to avoid certain paths altogether. Some even ask that whole departments be shut down. They don't think people should be going there in the first place. This saddens me.

My research deals with the space between. It deals with those parts of biology and theology that face each other and the tricky land grabs, disputed territories, and no man's lands that occasionally arise. I am employed in both, do research in both, and genuinely love the people and work in both places. Friends frequently ask me how I manage it. What's going on in my head? This book is also for them. The roads from science to religion and back again have become familiar to me. Walk with me and take in the sights.

THINKING OUT LOUD

I have to say, from the very beginning, that I expect you to think for yourself. We have fallen into the habit of speaking about reason, religion, and science (alone and together) with a need to persuade. We keep score, asking whether a point has been made, an argument won. I aim for something different. I will be happiest if you read this as a mental memoir, a reflection on how I think, rather than a prescription for how you should.

Thinking in public can be a scary business. We associate personal worth with intelligence, knowledge, and wisdom. Ask

[1] Wonderfully, William James covers the same ground in his 1884 essay on free will, "The Dilemma of Determinism." He reflects on the choice to walk home by way of Oxford Street or Divinity Avenue, the same paths I mention.

anyone with mental health issues; we can be cruel and dismissive when we think others do not think clearly. We are quick to judge others' concepts of truth, because we are constantly working on our own. And so, often we are silent about those areas of our own reasoning that seem problematic. We fail to share them and ask for advice, fearing that others will think us crazy. If a fully rational way of thinking about the world exists, I have yet to find it. The world is messy and all of us form messy pictures of it.

There are two kinds of ignorance: hidden and revealed. The first is much less painful, but only the second can be fixed. We think better when we talk these things through, when we try with humility and sincerity to genuinely share how we make sense of the world. I'm thinking in front of you with the hopes that you will find some of it helpful, some of it beautiful, and some of it entertaining. I only ask that you return the favor by thinking for yourself – out loud. This Hill thing works because we cover more ground as a group than we could as individuals.

Thinking Together

Thinking clearly may not be a competition, but it can be a game. We should talk with one another about what our expectations are, what things we have in common, and what the rules should be. Often we find in discussion that others are playing by different rules, and that can be deeply frustrating. If I'm playing poker and you're playing pinochle, we both have a hand of cards, but I doubt we'll have much fun. Nor would it mean much for either of us to claim we'd won. And yet this happens daily in "debates." A more appropriate metaphor might involve my trying to build a wall while you try to pave a road using the same stones. A common theme throughout the book will be communities in science and religion that come together to form conclusions. They make progress on common goals by communicating, setting an agenda, and creating common standards.

This rule making can be seen as limiting. Indeed, it has limits, particularly when you ask that the players play only one game and always one game. Luckily that doesn't happen as often as it used to. In the 21st century most of us belong to multiple communities. That can be wonderful; it allows us to pursue different ends with different people. It can be awful; we need to renegotiate with each group.

Above all, it can be confusing when we mistake one group for another, or expect every group to behave like the one we like best. Let us assume as we wander that we will run into strange and wonderful games that defy expectation. I'm curious to see what the geeks with tablets are doing together that has them so excited. And I'm interested, if slightly daunted, by what the jocks are doing with the Frisbee. Reasoning should be no different. There will turn out to be some common rules – everyone on the quad speaks English – but we won't know until we investigate. Who would join a game without first making sure they knew how to play?

This book presents some rules for common reason. They are, I admit, my rules. I have done my best to share not only my version, but also the versions of friends and competitors I have met along the way. Of course you will see them through my eyes. Call it house rules and remember I expect you to walk away with exactly those concepts that inform you, and nothing more. Ask whether my picture lines up with what you know or explains the behavior of others. Ask what you consider as given and what is up for interpretation.

I'll start by introducing a wide variety of tools we use to understand the world. What rules do we use when we play games of logic, reason, and evidence? What strategies work and how do they work? You might have noticed that almost no one in college plays tic-tac-toe. There's a reason for that. It may be consistent, but it has ceased to be fun and useful. The outcome is too easy to predict. Thinking games work the same way. If some of them seem too simple, bear with me. They introduce some very interesting aspects of game play that will be useful later on. More to the point, you may discover that others grew up playing them quite differently.

Next I introduce modern science. Over the last thousand years, humans have gotten good at a particular reasoning game that starts by setting up a very specific court – a type of thing to be talked about and a way of talking – then reasons from observations to a model of the physical universe. Clear rules and immense productivity have made science one of the most successful reasoning games. In recent years, some thinkers have even suggested that it should be enough for us, that nothing exists beyond the bounds of the scientific field. I'm not convinced. I wrap up the section with a few thoughts about numbers, values, and people: areas where science has trouble producing the kinds of answers we want.

The third section introduces religion, which turns out to be a poorly defined amalgam of reasoning games and countless other activities. It encompasses Christianity, Islam, and Judaism, but also Hinduism, Buddhism, and other traditions less familiar to Western thinkers. I share my own thoughts on how religions use reasoning games within broader frameworks of philosophy, practice, and politics. I also talk about how God, souls, and communities inform Christian reasoning games, why they seem both necessary and useful.

The three areas – reason, science, and religion – come together as a plan for self-improvement, my plan for learning and growing. In thinking about thinking for myself I came up with some concrete suggestions, not only to improve the accuracy of my thoughts, but the quality of my behavior. I want to be knowledgeable, but also wise – correct, but also fruitful. Our mental maps can never be fully separated from what we do with them. Thinking clearly requires curiosity, diligence, and love when approaching the world. It takes work and a profound care for the things we think about. We cannot separate our knowledge from our character and our communities.

From the beginning of history, these three aspects of humanity have interacted – what we think, what we do, and with whom we do it. The terms of "the science-religion dialogue" are very new, but the questions have been with us forever. How do we think clearly about the world? How do we see it plainly and understand the way it works? Modern science arose as a particular school of thought within European and North American culture, heavily influenced by the creeds, ethics, and social structures of Judaism, Christianity, and Islam. The scientific picture, likewise, had a profound impact on how those religions looked at the world. Sometimes they embraced science and sometimes they pushed against it, but increasingly they used scientific words and ideas. In the twenty-first century a basic understanding of the reasoning games popular in each helps immensely when we try to understand culture, politics, or simply the opinions of our neighbors.

We must appreciate not only what people think but why they think the way they do. Beyond asking whether they are reasonable or correct, we must ask how their beliefs work for them. I hope this book will help you do just that. Largely, I have aimed at providing something provocative, but accessible to all. There are pointers to academic philosophy, theology, and science, but my goal is only to give you a taste of the many different ways people look at the world. Whether you are conservative or liberal, theistic or atheistic, an expert or a novice, you will recognize and sympathize with me at some points and find me alien and annoying at others. With luck, you will find the foreign thoughts less foreign and see the familiar thoughts in a new light.

A Word of Warning

Knowledge and belief shape us. From religious creeds to scientific theories, we identify with the thoughts – and systems of thought – we hold dear. Those systems affect the choices we make about life and death, industry and environment, liberty and community. Thinking about thinking will challenge you. It will ask you to try out new perspectives, new reasoning games, and new conclusions.

As with a new pair of glasses, you can try out many different lenses, but at the end of the day only one or two will work for you. The others will probably give you a headache if you wear them for too long. Perhaps only one fits your personality, your history, and your understanding, but you cannot find the best fit until you've tried on at least a few. Some people walk away from this kind of discussion thinking that multiple perspectives are equally good. Others, including myself, think there really is a single reality out there. The best pair of glasses must be the one that shows it plain and clear. Still, it is good to know what the options are. Whichever lenses you end up with yourself, knowing about the others will help you understand your neighbors. This experience will allow you to see how other people see the world. You will know them better, communicate better, and perhaps even show them a thing or two. They, in turn, can help you see more clearly.

This is not a textbook. I need to be very clear on that. I present this as an exercise in thinking broadly, sympathetically, and systematically about how you view the world. I want you to experience different ways of thinking and reflect on what it would mean to do them well. I have not been thorough in citing the latest academic research in philosophy. Indeed, I must confess I find much modern analytic philosophy clouds rather than clarifies the central questions. This comes not from a bias against philosophy or modern research; I find the thoughts of modern philosophers invaluable. It comes instead from a recognition that some ways of thinking have worked historically. Good ideas can take a century or two to catch on and the really bad ideas usually get weeded out after 50 years or so. Ideas last because they work for people: not just a few people, but large numbers of people. So I veer toward philosophies that have stood the test of time.

Different people reason differently about the world. They have thoughts and beliefs that work for them. Realizing that can eliminate much hostility and fear.

☙ ✦ ❧

The way I think is not the only way to think, nor is it the best way to think, but it works for me. With luck, some of it will work for you as well. Thinking clearly turns out to be a very personal and personalized thing, but we can get better at it. We can learn to appreciate how our thinking shapes the decisions we make, the actions we take, and the communities we form. This book reveals something about how those pieces fit together in my life, as a scientist and as a Christian, but essentially as another person trying to figure it all out.

We each have a tendency to project our ways of reasoning onto others and then become upset when they fail to conform to our expectations. I'd like to relax some of that tension by exploring, in public, the ideas and experiences that underpin my own thinking. Science, among many other ways of reasoning, attempts to be explicit about the ground rules in a way that can short-circuit this miscommunication. So I will take a close look at science and some of the reasons I think it has been immensely successful. Theology, too, can be explicit, not only about how we play the game of reason, but how we play the larger game of life. By setting out how Christian theology works for me, I hope to show you a particular path from science to theology and back again. Many other paths exist as well, and many other theologies, but we must start somewhere.

Our reasoning has such a profound impact on how we see ourselves that we often become insecure when our ground rules are questioned. And yet it is only by asking these questions that we learn to talk meaningfully with other people. Reactionaries in both religion and science have set up a strict divide between the two so that they won't have to do this hard work. They hope that by being uncritical of their own ground rules, others will agree with them by default. But there are no default answers. History, philosophy, and science show us clearly that we really do have a variety of ways for thinking critically about the world.

REASON

CHAPTER 2
What Matters

We must begin with some basic questions about the world and how we deal with it. Philosophers put this kind of thinking in a box called metaphysics. Metaphysics has taken on a number of meanings over the years, but by and large it deals with questions about fundamental reality and how we come to know things. Some philosophers object to metaphysics in the first place because it seems to assume some level of reality beyond what we approach with our senses. Plato said we know things from memory, while Descartes claimed we know things by reason alone. Some modern thinkers, influenced by the success of scientific reasoning and experiments, wonder whether another level of thought should be necessary at all. Why should we question what we know? We simply know things by observation, don't we? Metaphysics pokes into the assumptions we make before observing and how those expectations shape what we see.

Even the word "metaphysics" can be problematic. It comes from a collection of works by the great philosopher Aristotle (384-322 BCE) who wrote extensively on what we see and how we think about it. In a collection known simply as *Physics*, he covered the physical world and the principles of motion. A number of other works, including *Categories*, dealt with Aristotle's understanding of understanding itself. How do we come to know? What types of knowledge are there? These works were compiled by a helpful scribe at least a century after Aristotle's death in a book entitled *Metaphysics*, meaning literally "after the physics" or "next to the physics." Originally this only indicated that these were further writings by Aristotle. Perhaps *Metaphysics* covered more complicated material than that in *Physics*, but it wasn't necessarily dealing with a single unified subject. Importantly, it discussed what was – or what Aristotle thought was – fundamentally, really real. This element of *Metaphysics* has had a profound impact on our later understanding of the word.

During the Middle Ages, metaphysics came to mean the study of "being *as* being," that is, what we mean when we say something exists. What is "reality" such that it means something to call an object real? Other ancient philosophers such as Plato (429?–347 BCE) and Plotinus (204/5–270 CE) claimed that the idea of something was more real than the observed thing. No white object is truly white. It is only imperfectly white, so whiteness *as* whiteness – whiteness insofar as it is white – must be more real, more perfect than any example of whiteness. We do not find the idea intuitive today because we are deeply invested in a view of the world where individual things are unquestionably real. Their "thingness" comes from our ability to touch and taste them – an idea that caught on dramatically with the Enlightenment and the scientific revolution. Ancient philosophers, on the other hand, distrusted physical things because they were imperfect and subject to change.[2]

Medieval philosophers (including scientists and theologians) also wanted answers to this question of what is real. At that time, the most popular answer, now called *realism*, said that broad categories are real while the things we taste and touch are only poor copies. A real, perfect whiteness exists in theory. The things we call white are never as pure as they could be. They are never perfect in their whiteness, but a perfect whiteness must exist. After all, how else would we be able to judge the imperfections in the tangible whites. The broad categories, called *universal substances* (e.g., "human" and "city") are real. The observable *individual particulars* like Mahatma Gandhi or Baltimore are not real in and of themselves; they are only real insofar as they participate in the universals. Universals exist fully while particulars are only images, as though the thing itself cast a shadow onto the wall.

The realists eventually lost out to the *nominalists*, who said that universals are only names. The nominalists flipped the whole model on its head, arguing that only particular objects are real. For them, universals represent categories we impose on nature. Gandhi and

[2] Heraclitus was concerned that everything in the physical world changes. "You cannot step in the same river twice." Because physical things move and change, Plato worried that we could never achieve perfect, unchangeable knowledge by studying them. On a similar vein, some philosophers argued that all of our senses are fallible; therefore, all knowledge obtained from the senses must also be fallible.

Einstein are real; the term "human" is only a name we use to lump them together. Universals are nothing more than collections of particular, real things.

Whether you agree with the realists or the nominalists – and even if the debate sounds like nonsense – you can see that the world has now been divided into two parts. On the one side are particulars, on the other universals. Philosophers were arguing about which ones are more important and about which ones count when we talk about reality. And, because metaphysics dealt with the question of non-physical things, the word picked up a third meaning. Metaphysical came to mean "beyond the physical." For the realists, it meant things more substantial than the physical. For the nominalists, it meant less substantial. Either way, a divide came into being between two very different claims about reality. Observation of particulars came to be associated with "physics" while reasoning about the universals was associated with "metaphysics." I put the two words in quotes, because that is not the way I use them. Neither do most philosophers use them this way. Having said that, many people have fallen into equating "metaphysics" with claims that some things are more real than physical things.[3]

Metaphysics became super-physics, the category that held the natural and beyond. It judged which things belonged in which camp. Metaphysics was believed to transcend physical science and thus the word took on its most common modern meaning – "greater than physics" or "beyond physics." We even see the prefix *meta-* loaned out to other words with that newer meaning: meta-language, meta-analysis, meta-narrative. I often hear people talk this way when they deal with questions in science and religion: they use metaphysical to mean transcendent or supernatural. Just as for the medieval philosophers, this can be used as an endorsement or an attack. It might be a "serious metaphysical commitment" or just "metaphysical mumbo jumbo."

I would like to talk about metaphysics, but I think I will have to be a little more precise. I do not wish to throw it out entirely, because it says something interesting. We're talking about what is real in a very immediate sort of way. Metaphysics, for me at least, conveys the idea that we are talking about how I come to think about the

[3] I have included a glossary in the back of the book with words, such as metaphysics, for which the definition may be unfamiliar.

world and what sorts of things deserve attention in the discussion. These questions need to be asked and need to be asked carefully. At the same time, I think the word "supernatural" conveys "beyond the physical" or "beyond natural laws" successfully. Let us leave transcending nature to "supernatural" and give a more limited definition to metaphysics. When I speak of metaphysics, I will be talking about one of two questions. The first, "What is real?" forms a branch of philosophy called ontology. The second, "How do we know things?" forms another branch, epistemology.[4]

Ontology deals with the fundamental reality of things: whether they can exist in and of themselves or only participate in the existence of something else. This can sound complicated, but it need not be so. When I ask whether a soul exists, that's ontology. When I ask whether the soul is the essence of a human, that's ontology. Likewise, when I claim that only material things exist, that's ontology. What is real? Ontology deals with abstract questions about the nature of existence, but it is terribly important in concrete questions about what we consider worthy of our attention. The question of what constitutes a person, for example, has a big impact on how we treat people. It lies at the heart of ethical debates about abortion, slavery, child abuse, disabilities, and war, to name just a few examples.

I have found the computer science definition most useful. There, ontology refers to the set of terms that may be used in a given language and the rules for using it. A multiplication sign ("×"), for example makes sense in math as an operation that can be performed between two numbers. Some computer languages will allow you to multiply variables with an "x". Others use an asterisk ("*"). Two programs can communicate if their ontologies match, if they use the same symbol or can translate from one to another. Humans have much more complicated languages, but we still need small units of meaning with which to communicate.[5] It makes a difference what

[4] I should note that this is a slightly odd use of "metaphysics", which often only includes ontology in current usage. Modern philosophers tend to keep epistemology and ontology in separate boxes, claiming one is secondary to or dependent on the other. Note that the argument can go both ways. I might ask about knowledge by thinking of my relationship with other real things. That puts the reality question first. On the other hand, I might ask about reality by asking how my experiences shape my ideas about existence. That puts the knowledge question first.

sorts of units and relationships you can say and imagine. It matters how you think of units like atoms, forces, souls, and spirits. Are they real? If they are, what properties do they have?

Epistemology forms the second branch of metaphysics; it deals with *how* we know *what* we know. How do we decide which things are real? How do we come to know things about them? How do we form belief? Once again, we can talk philosophically about empiricism and confidence or we can ask very simple everyday questions. How do I know that the sun will rise tomorrow? How do I know which toothpaste to buy or which route to take to work? Epistemology is all about generating knowledge.

As we explore the interaction of science and religion, it will be important to keep an eye on metaphysics. Tensions arise when two people are making different assumptions about reality and knowledge. Both the scientist and the theologian within me are invested in these questions. Neither will yield the fields of ontology and epistemology to the other because they both impact the way we think and have profound implications for knowledge and belief. Both observation and faith inform my understanding of what constitutes a human being. Both tell me something important about how I come to know and understand the world. So when I look at the interaction of science and religion, I will want to ask particularly pointed questions about what metaphysical assumptions have been made.

How do scientific and religious views of reality line up? The question can be answered only by looking at the metaphysical commitments in both. After assessing a variety of popular epistemologies (ways of knowing), I will turn to descriptions of science and religion, both from academic study and from personal experience. In particular, I want to look at how people use the various epistemologies in discerning the nature of reality. What do the words mean and how do

---

[5] Some have made the much more controversial claim that even thoughts must use these units. Others claim that the units of meaning are constrained by society, evolution, or neurology. Such claims exist at the boundary of epistemology and ontology and demonstrate how they intertwine. I do not commit to them here. I am only stating that we always communicate and often think using basic rules of this kind.

they shape our understanding? The purpose of this first section of the book will be to define terms and say precisely where our conversation will take place. After that, I begin to narrow the field of interaction. Where do conflicts arise and what should we expect from our discussion? Science and religion overlap in their approach to reality and we need to ask precisely how. It will be a matter of ontology and epistemology. What things are real and what things are worth talking about? What is the nature of our knowing and how does it affect our actions?

Before we can answer questions about how the universe was created or whether animals have souls, we must cover some very basic ground. What can be known about reality and how do we come to know it? Do we know things as individuals or only as groups? How do our ethics affect our understanding? If we are capable of finding truth about nature – and I would say emphatically that we are – then we must weigh the truth of science against other ideas about truth. We must build a picture of the world that gives us confidence about nature but also shapes our convictions about how we should behave. Science and religion both have interesting, even indispensable, things to say.

CHAPTER 3
The Nature of Reason

How do we come to know about the world around us? Introductory textbooks on science often start with a statement of the scientific method, while basic religious texts start with a statement about revelation. The New Testament and the Qur'an both open with passages on the relationship between humans and God. They establish a framework within which to think about the world and what you are about to hear. As we attempt to explore where religion and science collide (and sometimes collude), we should start with the question of knowledge – epistemology.

Both science and religion involve ways of thinking. Scientists reason using observation and hypothesis, a process known as the scientific method. For our purposes, one might say that science appeals to a single epistemology – a single way of looking at the world. Some diversity exists, but a clear sense of how we understand reality prevails. We have power over the world around us: the power of our senses to observe, the power of our hands to shape, the power of our voices to communicate, and the power of our minds to comprehend. Scientists use this power to weave understanding by recording and discussing observations, then setting up tests that confirm or deny our hypotheses. The process happens over and over again until we build up confidence in statements about the natural world.

Religious authorities, on the other hand, are not so limited in their worldview. Religions, being diverse, incorporate a wide range of epistemologies, some more rigorous than others. Ardent atheists in the twenty-first century have suggested that perhaps religious leaders don't reason at all – that instead they use authority and power to come to conclusions. This could not be further from the truth. Some small sects, called personality cults, do rest their knowledge heavily on the words and thoughts of a single person. Most religions, however, have intensive and carefully argued systems of thought.

They build traditions out of the thoughts and practices of thousands, if not millions, of believers.

Much of what we think of as modern, scientific thought arose among Western theologians and philosophers in the Middle East and Europe. They struggled to grasp how humans come to understand God and nature. Ideas we take for granted – like the intelligibility of the universe and the importance of trusting our senses over our preconceived notions – were developed in their philosophy.

Modernity, indeed every age of history, can be recognized by common assumptions about how people reason and what they consider reasonable. Our own reliance on the scientific method was forged in the medieval debates about realism and nominalism. At the same time, ancient religious establishments such as the Roman Catholic Church struggle with contemporary culture, because they retain epistemologies that were compelling to previous generations, but perhaps not to the world today. We are faced with a world where it seems increasingly difficult to come to a consensus about reason, particularly when so many are determined to ignore any alternatives to their own "epistemology" or way of thinking. We must look then at specific worldviews and specific epistemologies if we are to make sense of how science and religion operate.

I think we all suffer from a somewhat provincial notion that we may only come to understanding through a single method of learning and discerning – despite the fact that we never agree on what that one method is. Some have blamed this single mindedness on the scientific establishment and a sense of materialist reductionism that flattens out the world. It goes deeper than that. Others have blamed it on a modernist belief that one perspective must be best, that it should and will replace all the others. That comes closer to the truth, but still misses some important pieces of the problem. We need to go back to the Enlightenment and even further into the Middle Ages and seriously question the "hopes that our world is built on." What assumptions underlie our ability to know things at all? And how do those assumptions affect the models we create?

Discussion requires common ground and common assumptions about how we reach conclusions. Here, I'm narrowing my focus to comparative epistemology – how people come to understand nature and the physical world. Can we get a better grasp of both science and religion by asking how people see the world and their ability to understand it?

DIFFERENT WAYS OF THINKING

What makes a statement reasonable? I cannot recall how many times I've heard people say that an argument is (or is not) reasonable without questioning what makes it so. Atheist scientists dismiss believers as unthinking and superstitious. Meanwhile, science-doubting believers ask how scientists can fail to see a truth that is so clearly evident. Both sides of that divide fall into the trap of believing that reason reflects a single, correct way of looking at the world. Both sides assume that people who do not agree with them must be uninformed, unintelligent, or just unwilling to change.

You may not fall into either of those camps, but I suspect you too have found yourself in a similar situation. All of us have a tendency to assume that others think in the same way we do. If a statement sounds unreasonable to us, then there must be no reasonable way to make the argument. Even after years of studying different ways of thinking, I still catch myself judging other people's reasoning without stopping to ask why. How we think is one of our most basic mental processes. Nonetheless, variation appears between people. Two very intelligent people working with the same full set of information can come to two very different conclusions. That can be frustrating and even painful until we realize that they think differently.

This does not mean that all ways of thinking are desirable or even reasonable. I am not making the ontological claim (about what is). I am not saying that no single truth or best picture exists. That would be *relativism*, and it has never appealed to me. I am making an epistemological claim (about how we know). All of us understand the world imperfectly – or so both science and Christianity claim.[6] Humility is considered a virtue by nearly everyone. I am asking you to embrace the idea that different people might have different parts of the truth and think critically about how you decide whether they are right or wrong.

---

[6] Islam, Buddhism, and Judaism, just a to name a few other religions, also claim that we have imperfect knowledge.

Understanding takes work. Whether we like it or not, knowledge rarely appears fully formed in our heads. I would like to leave the door open for revelation, though a more careful treatment must wait until chapter thirteen. For the moment, let us say that if instant understanding does occur, it does so very infrequently. By and large, people use other methods for coming to know things about the world. All of those ways of understanding are subject to the conditioning and biases of our knowledge and context. As you read about each of the ways of understanding, start by asking simple questions about them. When would this work? How would this work? Who do I know that thinks this way?

Axioms

"We hold these truths to be self-evident…"

Every system of thought, every method of reasoning rests on certain fundamental premises. Those premises *may* be considered self-evident, as we see in the reasoning of Rene Descartes (1596-1650). Alternatively, they can be viewed as provisional starting points in the process of reasoning. Everything has to start somewhere. Axioms are our primary thoughts about reality, from which we launch reason.

Descartes' famous statement "I think therefore I am" forces the reader to reflect on the nature of grammar. At the surface level, we could say that thought implies the existence of a thinker, but there is a deeper level to this remark. When you make the statement "I think" you have unconsciously already formed an idea about the existence of an "I." Augustine of Hippo (354–430) says it more viscerally in *The City of God*, when he speaks of human nature.[7] He says that he exists and asks, "If I am mistaken about that, who is mistaken?"

Neither Descartes' statement nor Augustine's really functions as an argument, *per se*. Both shake the reader into recognizing something that she has already presumed. For example, you are reading this book therefore you exist. This particular postulate, the idea that something exists which can observe, reflect, and reason, will be very important for science, both for concepts of objectivity – I am different from the object I observe – and for empiricism – my

[7] Book 11, chapter 26

observations tell me something about the world. Christians consider the idea of personal existence central, but people in other religions do not. Buddhism, Hinduism, and Taoism all share doubts about the meaning of "self," though they may embrace some functional or temporary concept of identity.[8] In these cases also, a statement about individual identity can shock the reader into a new understanding. It reveals ideas we have, but rarely reflect on.

Classically, Descartes and others were reaching for something certain, something unquestionable. They wanted a solid rock upon which to build their structures of thought, and assumed there must be such foundations. Philosophers call this *foundationalism* – the idea that some certain, self-evident foundations for reasoning exist and can be discovered. An alternative, called *coherentism,* attempts to make coherent wholes without foundations. Over the last century, or perhaps a little longer, philosophers have developed schools of thought that are less certain about how the process works. More recent attempts to understand the world have been self-consciously provisional. They begin with statements – I would still consider them axioms – which are neither self-evident nor necessarily true. Rather they are useful. By naming and recognizing these statements at the outset, you can choose to accept or reject them later on. For this group of philosophers, a system of reasoning is more like a sweater, woven together from many different threads. If you reason carefully, you can remove individual premises later on. This is a difficult procedure and I'll talk about it more below.

It is important to note that the value of an axiom comes from the conclusions it supports. In both systems, the removal of an axiom has consequences. If you remove a foundation, the building will surely fall. Pulling a stray thread need not dismantle the entire sweater, but it can have profound effects. It may even unravel a significant portion. Axioms are those things you believe without appeal to some further argument or authority. They create a starting point for reason. I think they work best (provide for the most rational arguments) when they are transparent. If you remove them, you must also remove all the things you have come to think because of them. This dependence – this connection of premise to conclusion – plays a central role in the proper use of axioms.

---

[8] See *Prajñāpāramitā, Chandogya Upanishad,* and the *Tao Te Ching,* respectively, for examples.

Where do axioms come from? It would be tempting to say that many religious axioms come from revelation, but that would be a mistake. Revelation involves a particular appeal to authority, to God or another transcendent reality. Revelation is different. Axioms come before observation, before logic, and likewise they condition our ability to receive revelation. For instance, one cannot claim God has spoken without first thinking God exists.[9] Most of our axioms are held unconsciously. Others we recognize, but consider self-evident. Often we simply cannot conceive of thinking differently. We might think of Plato's idea of memory or Aquinas' sense of Natural Law, which tells us we know intrinsically what is right. Both of these make some appeal to why we should understand things before processing that knowledge in any particular way.

One should be extremely careful when claiming that a statement is axiomatic. When we say it of ourselves, it can be an excuse to avoid deeper investigation of our own worldview. When we say it of others, it can be a rhetorical stand-in for "unreasonable belief." Faith, for example, is not just an appeal to authority. It means trust in an already established idea or person. Discovering an axiom should be tremendously uncomfortable, because it says something about the person holding it. It will almost always seem to be out of your control.[10]

---

[9] Interestingly, one might claim "God has spoken" or more pertinently "Buddha said" without claiming God or Buddha as an ultimate, independent, or even rationally coherent entity. The title (both God and Buddha are titles, rather than names) and the concept of speech might be literal or figurative. The key here is to recognize that both cases require axioms. The literal requires us to think there is a Buddha to speak. The figurative requires us to hold some other picture that "Buddha said" evokes. The alternate picture would be the axiom in the second case. We are always allowed to say, "I didn't mean it in that sense," but we must then ask, "In what sense did I mean it?"

[10] Coherentists believe that our knowledge is assembled by trying to reconcile a variety of basic beliefs. As I mentioned earlier, these beliefs may be quite consciously provisional. My experience has been that most of these beliefs are unconscious, even for the most self-reflective of us. Further, when they are conscious, we will still feel compelled to provisionally accept one alternative or another – personal agency or determinism, comprehensibility or skepticism – despite being unsatisfied with both (and the whole range of possibilities in between). Some questions in metaphysics simply require operational answers, even when we know the questions are poorly framed.

The existence of self, the existence of nature, and the existence of God (if accepted) are generally taken as axioms. Arguments for "axiomatic" claims come in one of two forms: necessity and hidden reasoning. Necessary axioms seem unavoidable. Hidden reasoning axioms cover up deeper chains of reasoning, ones you can not or have not articulated. Ask yourself, "Is the arguer simply trying to reveal my preconceptions or am I being asked to rely on some other line of proof?" In the first case, I need to think more closely about myself and why I make the assumptions I do. In the second case, I need to trace the line of reasoning to its true source.

Axioms often appear irrefutable, which can be both a blessing and a curse. As Thomas Jefferson writes in *The Declaration of Independence*, "We hold these truths to be self-evident, that all men are created equal…" If you agree, as many Enlightenment thinkers did, that all people have equal rights, then the statement truly is self-evident. It you do not agree, the statement cannot convince you. Axioms make strong points in arguments when your opponents hold them. You can draw on the common assumptions to push in a given direction. Axioms make for very weak arguments when speaking to people from different cultures, people who may not share your premises. The biggest problem comes from their invisibility. How often do you question the existence of self? How often do you think about whether humans are all equal or about whether your form of reasoning works? Cross-cultural discussions quickly turn into train wrecks when we are unaware of the axioms that unite or divide us.

Conversion

We change our axioms not as a result of arguments, but in reaction to experience. In general we think of this as a conversion experience. Having experienced something profound, the thinker switches basic premises and begins to see the world in a new way. That conversion cannot be forced or compelled by argument, but they become more likely in certain environments. The silent retreat and the spirit quest both attempt to create enough space for believers to encounter themselves, God, and nature more fully than they have before. This encounter provokes them to question their axioms and may lead to a fundamental shift. Science teachers do this as well. One of the hardest and most rewarding tasks of a grade school science teacher is to convince the student that science works, that this type of reasoning can reveal new and interesting things about the world, and that the student can do it herself. No amount of argument can convince her. Indeed, philosophers of science regularly argue about exactly why science works. Instead, burgeoning scientists must recognize a faculty within themselves to process data and come to conclusions. That is a conversion experience, or as Buddhists say, an empowerment.

I have said that axioms may be used as a cover for poorly understood reasoning. Axioms may also be used as a defense against change. One of the most popular axioms in modern culture has to do with determinism, the idea that all events are forced by previous events. "If you only knew the full set of circumstances, down to the position of the last electron, you could predict exactly what would happen next." What if human behavior were like that? What if your every decision was not the result of personal choice, but a mechanical response to the environment? Karl Marx and countless others have used this argument to convince people to act, or not to act. After all, the outcome has already been determined by fate, by God, by the laws of nature, or by some other force.

It's a provocative theory, and all sorts of physical and biological arguments can be made for why humans might be conditioned to act in certain ways. At the core, however, belief in will is axiomatic to every system of reasoning. Every time you appeal to "truth," you're really asking someone to *choose* a particular opinion over another "false" one because it corresponds to reality. There is nothing in nature that compels you to prefer reality and good models of it. Rather, you must accept some power over the outcome, over your state of mind, in order to be convinced (or convicted) that some proposition is "true." If humans do not have will, if all of our actions are predetermined, then all arguments would be moot. A proposition would be accepted or rejected mechanically and nothing could be claimed about its truth-value. Neither axioms nor the process of reasoning are fully predetermined.

It is entirely possible that the ideas of self and will are used pragmatically. Buddhism suggests neither really exists, but some ways of thinking about them lead us to realize how worthless they are. I am sympathetic, but in this sense I think of all reason as pragmatic. It's a game we play, but let us be conscious that *while playing the game* those are the rules we've agreed on. The game of reasoning has players whose choices change the outcome.

For the purposes of this book I will assume that you have will – that you can choose to change your axioms and that you can choose to reason well (or poorly). I have no doubt that all of us are burdened by thoughts we will have difficulty changing, but I am convinced that change does happen. I might even say that one of my axioms relates to the ability of humans to move toward better models of the universe. Otherwise, how could I have hope for science or faith?

Axioms need not be unquestioned or unchanging; they remain fundamental. They have no basis outside simple acceptance. Every system of reason requires at least one fundamental axiom: that the system works. In other words, every epistemology requires the axiom that that the epistemology is effective and that it may be carried out by someone. As you read through the various types of reasoning below, think about what other premises they might require.

LOGIC

"As simple as 1 + 1 = 2"

People use the word "logic" to mean a variety of things. They might use it to mean reason or the study of reasonable arguments. They might use it to indicate rigorous and unemotional thought processes. Overall, it carries some sense that a formal process has occurred – premises went into the machine and conclusions came out, regardless of the hopes and fears of the operator. If axioms tell us what type of raw material reasoning uses, logic tells us how to process that material, turning it into knowledge. In other words, logic applies to the way we use arguments to get from point A to point B. Above all we like to think that logic has the power to compel others. If I believe X and my neighbor does not, then by "force of logic" I can change her mind. I can make her see reason and come around to my way of thinking.

You may not have conceived of logic in quite this way before, but I hope you'll try it on for size. How many times have you heard someone say things like this? "She's impervious to logic." "He refuses to listen to logic" (implying that if he did listen, he could not help but change his mind). "You must see the logic in what I'm saying." It is the compulsive nature of logic that makes it so desirable. It forces us to question the consistency of our beliefs. It can be a tool to overcome emotions and see things more analytically.

In light of this metaphor, logic as force, we can see that there must be good logic and bad logic. Good logic will be inescapable. Philosophers have identified a large number of inescapable logical functions, the vast majority of which cannot be listed here. I will cover just a few, but any basic logic text will give you many more. One of the simplest is called *modus ponens*. For example, I might say something like this; it is raining outside; when it rains, I need an umbrella; therefore I need an umbrella. We start with a premise, "A," and a condition, "if A then B." These force the conclusion, "B". A slightly more complicated version, *modus tollens*, goes in reverse. When it rains, I need an umbrella; but, I do not need an umbrella; therefore it must not be raining. We start with a negation, "not B," and argue backwards through the condition "if A then B" to force a conclusion, "not A."

Modus ponens and *modus tollens* may seem too simple to be worthy of notice. The wonderful thing about logic, though, comes from an ability to stack logical statements together in patterns. We can use simple rules, like *modus ponens* and *modus tollens*, to construct more complicated rules. Material implication, for instance, follows directly from them: if we know "if A then B", then we also know that "either B or not A." When it rains, I need an umbrella; therefore I need an umbrella or it is not raining. This sort of stacking continues upward to form the foundations of mathematics, including statistics and set theory.

Conversely, logic can give us a very precise language for identifying why a given set of premises need not lead to a given conclusion. Logical fallacies point out errors in reasoning we might have missed. For example, the "complex question" asks a number of things at the same time, leaving you at a loss of which question to answer. "Have you stopped beating your wife yet?" asks both "Did you beat your wife?" and "Are you beating your wife?" in a way that makes it impossible to give a simple answer without saying yes to at least one. The "straw man" is an argument that sets up a caricature of the opposition so that it can be knocked down. The real person or issue was never addressed, but the stand-in took a thrashing. Politicians frequently oversimplify their opponents' views to make them less palatable. Finally, a "false dichotomy" presents you with a choice between two options, denying the existence of other possibilities. One commonly hears cases like this one: "Either you agree with me, or you don't really know what's going on." Each of these examples represents a diagnosis for a commonly used logical fallacy. Learning about the fallacies can help you construct strong logical arguments and deconstruct illogical ones.

I take the time to introduce these three specific logical fallacies because they are regularly committed in debates on science and religion. You might have heard that you must choose your faith over science or facts over religion – both false dichotomies. Or you could be told that, if you accept both your religious community and scientific knowledge, then you will need to do so on particular terms. Partisans of science might ask you if you've stopped relying on outdated superstition – a complex question – and partisans of religion might talk about how atheistic scientists get by without a foundation for their morality – straw man.[11] These are all fallacious arguments, arguments so common and compelling, and yet utterly illogical, that we have names for them. They encourage you to come to conclusions, but not in an unemotional or rigorous way. We need to be able to identify them when they come up.

The benefits of logic are immense. It gives us a systematic way to build upon our axioms (and observations, etc.) while identifying and labeling the processes we use. The only significant downside comes when we ask what constitutes logic. What one person says is irrefutable logic, another might claim is nothing more than rhetoric. How can we resolve this dispute? Several rules come to mind. Can I simplify my reasoning to a set of symbols (e.g., A→B)? Do the rules apply universally and not just in my argument? Can I think of a parallel argument? Is my logic capable of forcing me into a conclusion that I did not want to hold? Good logical reasoning should get a yes for every question.

For all of this consistency, logic does not rest on a logical foundation. There does not appear to be a way to force someone into your system of logic, no matter how hard you try, or how good you are at persuasion. Each person's logic must rest on his or her own set of axioms. Luckily, there are some very compelling sets of axioms

---

[11] Both are, incidentally, also cases of *argumentum ad hominem*, an argument against the person rather than the substance of the claim.

that are generally agreed upon by scholars. While different logical systems do exist, most share some important properties. Rules like *modus ponens* and *modus tollens* are accepted almost universally and fallacies like the false dichotomy are almost universally decried. When using logic, think about what sorts of rules you are using, why and when you think they apply.

☙ ✦ ❧

This chapter set the groundwork for talking about reasoning styles. As we approach the subject of reality and knowledge, we must be aware that not everyone links the two in the same way. Different avenues exist for coming to know the world. When people reason they begin with axioms, foundational premises about the way reasoning works. These premises do not have a logical foundation; they create the foundation for logic. Logic allows us to process the axioms and data we start with as well as reconcile multiple theories about the world. It represents an attempt to build up from the foundations in a clear and consistent manner. While not all people subscribe to exactly the same set of logical rules, many logical tools are so useful as to be practically universal. Logic can be a common ground for discussion – as long as we remain conscious of how we use it. We now turn to more complicated ways of processing information, including questions of how we get new data to add to our axioms.

CHAPTER 4
Reasonable Pursuits

Science and most religions engage in very complicated systems of reasoning. In the last chapter, we looked at axioms and logic, both of which are useful, but neither of which presents us with new information. Now we turn to ways of finding new knowledge. This chapter looks at ways of reasoning that produce raw data before engaging in any explicit epistemology, scientific or religious. They are deduction, induction, observation, and appeals to authority. Each has its strengths and weaknesses. Perhaps that explains why all of them continue to be popular. As we explore the details of science and religion in future chapters, we can come back and look at how they value the different methodologies, but I would be surprised to find that anyone did not engage in each kind of reasoning at some point in their lives.

DEDUCTION

"... and it must follow, as the night the day ..."

Two types of reasoning form a core for what we generally think of as reason. They take the names induction, or arguing up, and deduction, or arguing down. While induction is far more popular today, deduction was central to ancient and medieval philosophy, so we will start there.

Deduction means reasoning down or, more specifically, arguing from universal or general statements to particular or specific statements. All humans eat food; Bob is a human; therefore Bob eats food. When based on reliable general statements, deduction always produces the right answer. If we can be certain that all humans eat food and that Bob is truly human, then we are left with no doubts about Bob. He must eat food.

We use deduction so often that we rarely think about it. Take driving as an example. In the United States, rules of the road are set down to help drivers. The yellow line marks the center of the road, while a solid white line marks the edge. Broken white lines mark the boundary between lanes. Red lights tell you to stop; green lights tell you to go; yellow lights warn that the red light is coming. When we learn to drive, these rules and hundreds of others enter our consciousness so that every time we are on the road we know what to do. Every specific sign can be interpreted based on the general knowledge of traffic signals. Every time we enter a car, we know something about how it works, because of the common symbols. We deduce specific knowledge of cars and roads from the generic model we hold in our head.

The benefits of deduction come from its absolute reliability.[12] If our general premises hold true, then specific instances must as well. We know that the government sets traffic laws. Workers only place red, yellow, and green lights in intersections when they want them to mean stop, go, and caution. Many natural laws are equally reliable. Gravity, for instance, applies everywhere.[13]

The challenge of deduction comes from the reliability of the laws. Traffic signals and gravity can be depended upon, but what about other rules? What about the law of supply and demand or ethical imperatives? In a famous example, I could make the statement, "All ravens are black." The statement makes sense and is generally true. Ravens are indeed black. We can apply the rule using deduction. All ravens are black; Poe is a raven; therefore Poe is black.

Now, suppose Poe is an albino raven. A genetic mutation caused him to grow without creating any of the black pigment that darkens feathers and skin. Poe is not black. We could respond in a number of ways. We could say that Poe is not really a raven, because "all ravens are black." Partisans of deduction traditionally use this type of argument. The general law still applies and we have been

[12] In philosophy, "deduction" is sometimes used to refer to all fully reliable, logical arguments. This comes from an Enlightenment (*foundationalist*) way of thinking, which held there is only one set of logical rules for reason and we may discern it by reason alone. For the purposes of this book, I am using deduction in a narrower sense: arguments that move us from general principles to specific instances.

[13] Gravity may, in fact, apply differently in different places, depending on how you choose to describe it. Our desire for consistency directs what we look for and how we describe what we see. Chapters six and seven look at this more closely.

mistaken in calling Poe a raven. The ornithologists protest. Poe is the son of two ravens, a member of the family *Corvidae*, and genetically identical to a raven. What does color have to do with it? They counter that the assertion "all ravens are black" must be false. The vast majority of ravens are black, but rare exceptions do exist. This sort of response sounds much more reasonable, but it also opens a chink in the armor of deduction. Deduction always provides good results *so long as the general statements are true.* In the case of Poe, I suspect all of us would rather attack the generality than the particular bird.

How many general statements about the world we can be utterly certain of? We often call these generalities laws or universal statements. Where do they come from? Are ravens black because it is in their nature to be so or do humans simply call some birds ravens because they are black? There is a very fine line between things we recognize and things we assert. Philosophers who wish to challenge deduction need only argue that the universal laws invoked are asserted incorrectly. Human government enforces the meaning of traffic laws, but natural laws may not be so well policed. Even if we consider them to be thought out and enforced by a higher power, we have no guarantee that we know what the higher power was thinking.[14]

Plato and many other realists claim that we have access to universal laws by way of memory or meditation or dialectic reasoning. Remember that realists think universals are more real than particulars. They think we access the universal laws by way of our thought and reason.[15] Nominalists refused to buy it. They said that the universals, including laws like "All ravens are black," must be constructed from particulars. During the Enlightenment, similar arguments occurred between the *rationalists*, who said we could know by reason alone, and the *empiricists*, who said we have to make observations first. The realist/nominalist divide was ontological,

[14] That is, we have no deductive guarantee. One might claim such a decree by revelation, but then we have shifted to another type of reasoning, with another type of standard.

[15] In modern philosophy, this is called the question of "synthetic *a priori*" reasoning. Can new knowledge be generated purely from internal reflection and knowledge? Ancient and Medieval thinkers considered intellect to be a faculty for knowing universals just as senses are faculties for knowing particulars.

about the reality of universals; the rationalist/empiricist divide was epistemological, about how we come to know general laws. Both were about whether we could know things before using our physical senses. In both cases, deduction was called into question. If universal laws are to be more than axioms, where do they get their authority? Nominalists and empiricists claim that nothing new comes without one of the other forms of reasoning – induction, observation, or authority. Deduction, they say, is just another form of logic.

When appealing to deduction, ask where your general principle came from and how reliable it is. Does it provide new data or just rearrange the data you already have? If something new has been added, where did it come from? If you are using logic, are you using it properly? If it is logic, be sure your particular example falls into the category described by the general rule. Sometimes a category error (ontology) will lead you to think a general rule applies when it does not. For example, English roads often look the same as the roads in the United States, but cars drive on the opposite side. How universal are your laws? And do you know you are if you are in the right region to follow them?

INDUCTION

"As certain as the sun rising in the East."

Induction argues from specific instances to general principles or laws.[16] People think of it as arguing up, because it goes from the particular to the universal. As with deduction, we use induction so frequently that we may not be conscious of using it at all. One example comes from the sun. Yesterday, the sun rose in the East; the day before that, the sun rose in the East; and so on for as long as anyone can remember; therefore, the sun will rise in the East again tomorrow. Having seen something over and over again in a particular way, we count on it always occurring in that way.

Induction appears to be necessary in the prediction of any event. It will always require an axiom stating that the future will operate like the past. The sun will continue to rise, the Earth will

---

[16] Some modern philosophers limit this type of argument to "enumerative induction," stating that the modern definition of induction needs to be broader. The historical or enumerative definition suffices for my purposes here, but readers should be aware that this restricted definition is somewhat dated.

continue to spin, and gravity will continue to operate. We think that the next instant must be like all the instants that have gone before. It's a matter of consistency. Induction takes consistency and turns it into a law. All the ravens I have ever seen are black; therefore, all ravens are black. The sun has always risen in the East; therefore, it always will. Water has always boiled when I heat it up; therefore, it always will. Induction underlies our understanding of an orderly world and it requires consistency as an axiom.[17] General laws can be built up from individual experiences.

Induction suffers from an immediate and very serious problem. There is no logical reason to think that it should work. For all that the world has been consistent so far, we can never be certain that it will continue to be so. Perhaps we live in a piece of space that is different from every other piece. Perhaps we are nearing the end of a stagnant period of galactic history and things will suddenly change. History is full of examples of people encountering things for the first time. The atom was long thought to be the smallest possible chunk of matter, but observation proved this was wrong. Physicists showed that atoms were made of subatomic particles: electrons, protons, and neutrons. Then they discovered that these particles were made up of quarks. Even quarks might be made up of strings according to current theory. How do we know that we have seen enough of the universe to derive accurate laws?

At a more personal level, culture provides an amazing argument against induction. People growing up in small communities are often shocked to discover the incredible diversity of beliefs outside their own hometown. "I never knew people thought that way." "I thought all Christians believed the same things my parents do." Or, "I thought all Muslim women dressed like my mother and sisters." As we meet more and more people, we discover that they think in a wider variety of ways than we ever thought possible. They hold different axioms and reason differently, not only from us, but from one another.

Induction suffers from the problem of limited information. We simply do not have access to all the data. And we can never be sure that the data we do have accurately represents the whole. In science, we call this problem *sample bias*, the systematic error in your

[17] In chapter five, I give the formal name for one version of this axiom of consistency: symmetry.

predictions based on the limited size of your sample. We can minimize this error, or try to account for its effects, but until we have access to all the data – until we know everything – we will never eradicate sample bias.[18]

While the phrase "sample bias" neatly sums up the problem, it may present trouble for some readers. In common parlance, bias indicates prejudice, even ill intent. Sample bias does not convey this at all. A researcher might be prejudiced, limiting her observations intentionally so that a bias is introduced. This sort of thing can happen in science, but for the most part, biases are unintentional. All your test subjects come from one race, for example, because you live in a country where almost everyone belongs to that race. When the same experiment occurs in another country, they discover a whole new suite of genes that was not present in your test subjects. Limitations in the sample (using only Norwegians) produce limitations in the generalizations you make (dealing with only one type of gene) and bias your conclusions.

In spite of these challenges, induction proves to be one of the most useful types of reasoning. It allows us to go through the day without investigating every new person and object. We know from experience what people look like, how to use tools, and what to expect in basic social interactions. We work on the basis of information collected daily from the beginning of our lives and we construct rules about how people and things operate. Without induction, life would be a very scary place.

When appealing to induction, ask how large the sample size was and whether it was the right sample for the question you want to ask. If you want to make better inductions, figure out how to expand your sample in a representative, unbiased way.

Observation

"I'll believe it when I see it."

Observation has flourished since the scientific revolution. We might even think of this as a scientific age. The reality of observed things and our ability to make sense of them is rarely questioned. This was not always the case. Many ancient philosophers distrusted obser-

[18] I speak more fully on this topic in my book *Life in Space* (Harvard Press, 2009), specifically on pages 58-60 and more generally throughout the book.

vation. They feared that our earthly bodies corrupted our senses and gave us inaccurate information. Only by looking inward could we perceive truth. Philosophers gradually flipped on this question over the course of the Middle Ages so that now we are more inclined to look outward for answers.

Observation generates huge amounts of information for our lives and our understanding. Every day we learn new things by looking and listening to the world around us. What color is your dog's hair? What does an ambulance sound like? How long do you have to wait for the traffic light to change? We pick up this kind of knowledge by using our senses.

One cannot question that humans have always used observation to pick up information about the world around them. It is also clear that, at least in particular areas, our ability to observe improves with time. Our technology and methodology improve. The question becomes interesting, though, when we look at what kind of questions can currently be answered by observation and what expectations we have about answering them in the future. Does God exist? What makes humans human? What makes an argument valid? Each of these questions represents a complex discussion that will not be answered easily by observation. It does not seem to be well suited for them. I suspect that in every case we will need to import some other information in order to come to a conclusion. Our challenge will be to identify the source of that information.

Epistemologists over the centuries have spilled much ink on the question of how well observation works. Distrustful of the physical world, followers of Plato and Plotinus worried that anything known through the senses was corrupted by the changeableness of material things. Truth must be eternal and perfect. William of Ockham (C. 1287–1347), the chief proponent of nominalism, ushered in a whole new era for philosophy when he advocated looking at individual imperfect particulars instead of perfect eternal universals. Then things started to get messy. The careful cataloging of specimens – along with inherent doubts about whether you had collected the right ones – replaced the clean logic of deduction. Meanwhile, trust in things learned from observation went up dramatically.

Protestant thinkers like Martin Luther (1483–1546) and John Calvin (1509–1564) questioned the new optimism. They worried that original sin corrupted human reason. Truth can only be seen by divine revelation through scripture.[19] Enlightenment thinkers argued over the value of observation, though it gradually became more and more popular. Even its strongest proponents, however, have written about the intrinsic biases built into human observation. Not only are our senses limited (we cannot see in the infrared, for instance), but we have a disposition toward looking in the familiar places.[20]

Observation tends to be closely tied to induction and it shares many of the same strengths and weaknesses. It prompts us to look outside ourselves for answers, forces us to accept inconvenient conclusions (when they fit the data), and suggests definite activities for finding truth – notably experiments and field trips. It also requires some important assumptions about the differences between the observer and the observed as well as a trust in humans' ability to sense and to reason from sense experience.

When considering ap-peals to observation, ask yourself who observed and exactly what they observed. It can be easy to conflate the signal – perhaps a red cap – with other knowledge – our friend frequently wears a red cap – leading us to say we saw our friend, when all we really saw was the cap. Good observations should be reported as specifically as possible to avoid this type of confusion.

AUTHORITY

"I heard it straight from the horse's mouth."

Almost every system of reason relies heavily on appeals to authority, not just religion. The reasons are quite practical. As humans, we do not have enough time to learn everything for ourselves. As children, we learn the rules of speech and behavior from our parents. As teenagers, we struggle through the complex process of learning whom to trust. As adults, we surround ourselves with systems of meaning that rely on the knowledge of others.

---

[19] This topic cannot be covered in detail here. Calvin certainly valued knowledge gained by observation, but was skeptical about human reason. He felt revelation through scripture was far more reliable, but some of his writing suggests that he had a high view of scientific knowledge in particular areas.

[20] The cutting edge of epistemological doubts on observation can be found in cognitive neuroscience and behavioral economics, two fields that study the way we perceive the world. Enlightenment doubts are elegantly summed up in the works of Francis Bacon and David Hume.

Religious examples spring easily to mind. Christians rely on the authority of scriptures as divinely inspired and faithfully transmitted. Most Christians also place trust in some form of teaching authority, be it the Roman Catholic magisterium or the unique insights of John Calvin. They rely on the idea that someone has gotten it right, or at least mostly right. Different sects and different religions weight their knowledge differently. Islam, for instance, leans heavily on the perfectly revealed word of God in the Qur'an, but does not trust translators. The only Qur'an is the original Arabic version, and the Prophet was also the "Seal of the Prophets." He gave the final and authoritative word – though the application of that word has been richly debated by the legal scholars. Judaism, on the other hand, values scriptures differently. The original Hebrew texts are sacred, but revelation comes through the interaction of the texts with commentaries produced over the millennia. Rabbinic scholars draw upon the "font of Torah," which is continually revealing new insights. Both traditions discuss the basic, literal meaning of the text and numerous commentaries, but they have very different standards for when and how commentary is allowed. In every religion, there exist people who trust authoritative interpretation of scripture over their own ability to reason and others who believe that all thoughts must pass through the personal intellect.

Every religion recognizes the value of authority figures. Each remembers historical people who have somehow "known better." They might be called saints or bodhisattvas, but they always represent a better relationship to the world than most people enjoy. Their words then provide guidance to believers. More prosaically, religions require authority figures to preach, teach, and organize. As with scripture, variety exists. Their authority may rest on divine gifts, on knowledge, on birth, or on a specific skill set. Their authority may be limited to legal or scriptural interpretation or to the preservation of stories. Authority operates in a number of ways, but it always represents a human repository of knowledge and a source of reliable judgments.

Scientific appeals to authority are incredibly common as well. We generally do not think of science as using this type of reasoning, but careful inspection will show that it happens all the time. Individual people and references act as repositories of more reliable – though never unquestionable – knowledge. The vast volume of experimental data forces us to place trust in other people's reports of their experiments. Ideally, scientists might want to repeat every experiment themselves, but they cannot. As a result, modern scientists read about experiments done by other scientists and rely on data generated in other labs. We look carefully at how the data was generated. We ask whether the methods were sound and whether we trust the researchers. We trust other scientists, but we do not trust them blindly. We look for data produced by qualified people and published in refereed journals.

Individual sciences and religions construct epistemologies and set rules for who may be trusted, and in what circumstances. Skeptics often accuse religionists of resting their belief on irrational obedience. Without a doubt, that does arise, but surprisingly rarely. Charismatic leaders appear in politics as well as religion. They ask us to trust them without giving proof. And we follow for the sake of convenience or social pressure or some biological drive. Far more often, though, leaders derive their power from producing results or fitting into a system. The Pope, for example, passes through innumerable hoops in his rise to be the highest authority in the Roman Catholic system. He must subject himself to the authority of others, in study and in practice, for decades. He must prove himself as a priest, bishop, and cardinal. Personal charisma plays an important part, but so does evidence of sound character: justice, prudence, temperance, and fortitude; faith, hope, and charity. All popular religions require years of study for their leaders. Priests, muftis, yogis, and lamas all go through extensive training, learning scripture and tradition.

We must carefully distinguish between appeals to authority – any time we use personal testimony as input for the knowledge mill – and *proper* appeals to authority – when such a move is justified by the material and the authority in question. Life would be impossible without some appeals to authority. We trust our parents to teach us how to drive and we trust our teachers when they tell us about math. We even trust our friends in innumerable ways when it comes to places we have not been, events we have not seen, and people we have not met. The proper epistemological question is not whether to use authority, but how to use it well.

The particular value of scientific authority comes from our ability, at least in theory, to question and test it. In science, we presume that all judgments are open to reinterpretation in light of new knowledge. Scientists are judged on the quantity, quality, and relevance of the data they produce. Religious authorities are likewise judged on criteria such as lifestyle, obedience, competence, or consistency. Conversely, scientific authorities may achieve positions of power where they can suppress contrary opinions. Science gives us an important epistemology for questioning authority and reevaluating opinions, but it does not eliminate appeals to authority or the need to monitor how authorities exercise their power.

I have already talked about why appeals to authority are so important. It gives us a chance to deal with more data and more opinions that we could if we acted alone. I am even tempted to say that anyone doing science alone (or religion alone for that matter) must be doing it poorly. Authority broadens the scope of inquiry and limits sloppy and biased thinking.

Why might authority be dangerous? The answers are obvious. Bad authority leads to bad decisions. If a critical thinker listens to a duly constituted authority who happens to be wrong, then she will make bad decisions. We cannot call her irrational, however. At least, we cannot call her irrational simply because she uses an appeal to authority. We can only do so if she chose bad authority, or misused that authority's pronouncements. Here lies the crux of the problem. What constitutes a reliable authority? Who is qualified to speak on the topic at hand? And just how far do you trust them?

It would be irrational to trust an expert on basketball when we want an answer related to quantum mechanics, and vice versa.[21] A good authority has to have access to information we need for a given decision. Discussions of science and religion frequently fall prey to this kind of bad authority. Physicists rarely possess the expertise to comment authoritatively on evolution. They are scientific experts, but not in the relevant field. Theologians rarely possess the expertise to comment authoritatively on thermodynamics. We must do more than ask, "Is this person an expert?" We must ask, "Is this person an expert in the area about which they are speaking?" Without a doubt, use your own judgment, but give weight to the arguments of experts according to their degree of expertise in the relevant field.

[21] Unless, of course, they were an expert in both. The point here is that expertise in basketball can be legitimate expertise without being relevant to the question at hand.

☙ ✦ ❧

Deduction, induction, observation, and authority all represent rational thinking. Each one can be used to give us greater confidence that a given proposition is true. Likewise, each method opens us up to certain kinds of errors. Rationality comes from thinking clearly, transparently, systematically, and carefully. Axioms contribute to every system of thought, though some require more than others. Generally, humans value systems that require fewer axioms and that limit sets of axioms that contradict one another. Logic represents rigorous and rule-based thinking. What rules do we use and why do we use them? Deduction allows us to move from general rules to specific instances, but we need to judge the value of the general rules. Induction moves us from specifics to general rules, but we must watch out for biases in selecting specifics. Observation and authority provide valuable insight into the world around us, but both require discretion. We should be just as careful with the testimony of our eyes as we are with the testimony of our neighbor. In every case, clear thinking means taking a moment to consider what questions we need to ask in order to be confident in a new piece of knowledge.

As this book progresses, I delve into how we define science and religion. In each case, matters of epistemology will come to the fore. How do we think? In what do we trust? And how do we generate knowledge? Later, I will return to the matter of rationality and talk about "confidence," the extent to which we place our trust in the truth of a proposition. Comparing science and various religions, we will come to see that the relative weight placed on our six rational methods will produce different results in terms of human knowledge.

SCIENCE

CHAPTER 5
Science as Method

We turn now to science, the sorts of reasoning that go into scientific knowledge, and the philosophies that shape the scientific community. When I first went to college, I thought that science could be defined relatively easily. There seemed to be general agreement that scientists use the "scientific method" and come to understandings about the physical world. All my textbooks gave a simple list of rules for what that meant. Make a prediction, test it, and make a new prediction. While that simple understanding proved to be roughly correct, the more I worked with scientists, the more I came to understand that this simple overview covers a huge variety of ideas and methods related to scientific reasoning. What makes for a good prediction, and what counts as an acceptable test? Each scientist I met had a slightly different idea of how to apply the scientific method and how to understand the physical world.

Some of my friends have accused me of relativizing science – opening the door for creationists and others to critique the very solid work of thousands of thoughtful scientists. I have no such desire. The pursuit of science rests on a consistent bedrock of philosophy, reason, and experience. We shall see that some fundamental commitments to reality and ways of knowing are essential. At the same time, those fundamental commitments may not be what you thought they were. Ontology and epistemology rarely work well intuitively. Francis Bacon (1561–1626), one of the most important philosophers in the history of science, noted that our very humanness affects how we see the world.[22] It will be necessary to consciously check in on our own assumptions if we want to come to a true understanding of the world – and of ourselves.

Science can be divided into two pieces, the scientific method and the scientific community. The scientific method represents a

---

[22] His work *Novum Organum* contains a great introduction to the types of sample bias we are prone to and how to avoid them.

particular epistemology of observation, hypothesis, and comparison. It relies on certain important axioms about the way the world works and how we come to know. The scientific community is far more amorphous. Millions of people actively pursue the scientific method – usually living up to it as a philosophical ideal, but occasionally straying. Just like religious leaders, scientific leaders do not perfectly represent the concepts they follow and advocate. Beyond the leaders, billions of people work with scientific knowledge on a daily basis. We all make decisions based on the facts, theories, principles, and statistics provided by scientists.

One of the traps frequently encountered in the science/ religion discussion comes from a false comparison between scientists and believers. "Scientists," as we commonly use the word, refers to experts in the scientific method, people with five to ten years of college education who participate in a community with other experts. "Believers," on the other hand, refers to a ragtag group of individuals; it can encompass anyone who claims to have a relationship with the divine or other transcendent reality. A more accurate comparison would be between scientists and theologians. Theologians, like scientists, usually have an advanced education and work within an elite circle of thinkers. Alternatively, we can compare an average American using scientific knowledge and principles to an average American working with religious doctrine and practice. Of course in this latter case, we will be forced to admit that the two people are really one and the same. Most consumers of scientific knowledge have religious beliefs. Most faithful people manipulate scientific information daily. I will try to avoid comparing experts to non-experts. This is a false dichotomy.

In both science and religion, the experts fall into a number of camps. Those camps may have some knowledge of the epistemology in nearby camps. Most physicists, for example, will more easily grasp the rules of physical chemistry than those of sociology, just as most Roman Catholics will be closer in perspective to Anglicanism than to Zen Buddhism.[23] Science represents a much narrower range of ideas,

---

[23] As with basketball and quantum mechanics, one person may be an expert in both, but they don't come together. There are also areas where two perspectives have split precisely because of an epistemological divide. For example, Anglicans reject dogma, making them *in this respect* closer to Zen Buddhists than to Reformed Calvinists.

but it would be a mistake to assume that there is no diversity. All scientists share some common axioms, but each field has its own rules for deduction, induction, observation, and authority.

Axioms of Science

Scientists share a number of fundamental beliefs about the way the world operates. A coherent science requires them and benefits from their use. Scientists must assume that an external reality exists and that they are capable of knowing things about it. This philosophical position has been called *realism* or *objective realism* (not to be confused with universal realism discussed in chapter one).[24]

Scientists believe in a world that can be understood by talking about objects outside ourselves. They lean heavily on observation and induction. I cannot imagine science arising in a world of universal realism. Platonic realists thought that true knowledge could only be gained by looking inside oneself. Science requires the shift to nominalism and the belief that knowledge comes from looking at particular concrete entities in the outside world. William of Ockham's idea that true knowledge comes from particulars forms a cornerstone of scientific thinking.

Objective realism cannot be proved; the existence of the world must be taken as given. Likewise, nominalism and empiricism cannot be proved, but rather are held as axioms in modern science. The three fit together in a way that justifies our claims to know something about the world and allows us to judge the confidence we have in that knowledge. It suggests ways to test and refine our knowledge using observation. [25]

---

[24] A small number of scientists and philosophers of science are actually *instrumentalists.* They believe that you can think about the world in a way that empowers you to work within it without claiming to understand exactly why or how. They treat scientific claims as useful tools or instruments rather than "true" statements or facts. This way of looking at science is particularly useful in quantum mechanics and physical chemistry, where the world appears to be radically counter-intuitive and we need useful fictions to help us work. Think of a tightrope walker imagining being just a foot above the ground. It's not ignorance of the truth, but recognition that something a little untrue might be more useful for the time being. While this will probably be tremendously important for the future of science, it doesn't play a large role in the everyday thought of most scientists.

Building on this philosophical foundation, science lays down a particular method for acquiring knowledge. The manifestation of this *scientific method* varies from field to field, but four basic principles underlie good scientific reasoning: mutual observables, symmetry, hypotheses, and iteration. All four speak to the relationship between human knowledge and the world.

MUTUAL OBSERVABLES

Scientists believe that proper objects of study are real things, external to the observer and accessed by the senses. More than that, though, they believe that we all access them the same ways. We each have the ability to see, hear, touch, taste, and feel, and science is built on the idea that two people looking at the same thing are, in fact, seeing the same thing. Not only will I be able to hear the same sound every time the kettle boils, but you can hear exactly the same sound. Over the past two hundred years we have learned to expand and heighten our senses with instrumentation. We can measure mass and density, magnetic fields and electric charge. As complicated as our tools become, at some level we can still think of them as senses. And, we can still use them in the same way. If we both build Geiger counters (for measuring radiation levels) in the same way, we will both observe the same amount of radiation. All observers have equal access to the data. No matter who you are, you can see, hear, feel, smell, and taste the same objects of study and, when you do, you will have the same experience I do. It allows us to repeat experiments and test one another's work. Science depends on an assumption of consistency between observations.

Alas, it is not quite that simple. Some of us have more acute senses. Individuals can be blind, or color-blind, or simply have poor eyesight. How do we deal with things that different people see

---

[25] A fairly influential group of philosophers in the 19th century, called *pragmatists*, held that something can be considered true if it has practically useful consequences. For them, realism, nominalism, and empiricism can be defended on the grounds that they do work. Philosophically savvy defenders of scientific reasoning may use this to claim these are not, in fact, axioms. They are, rather, the result of an axiomatic preference for knowledge or power (neither of which is trivial conceptually) added to observation. Nonetheless, pragmatists still hold the three ideas to be true and necessary to science.

differently? First we have the question of whether we all, if in perfect health, would sense things the same way. That turns out to be very difficult, if not impossible, to answer.[26] There appears to be a consensus on ideas like "red" and "smooth," but not on things like "painful," "profitable," or even "green."[27] Even so, scientists prefer quantitative measurements, where a number can be clearly assigned to each outcome. If different scientists have different qualitative experiences, they can agree on numbers like pH (a measure of acidity) and temperature by constructing tests that always give the same numeric result in the same conditions. I emphasize *mutual* observables because it forces us to think about the rules we use for saying enough of us perceive "x" the same way.

Second, how do we understand secondhand observations using tools? Tools can make up for some of the differences in perception. They can also amplify our senses, making them more consistent and precise. Tools also create problems. Some researchers have access to tools that others do not. Is a faint star mutually observable when only one scientist has a telescope? What about really expensive tools like spacecraft and hadron colliders? Humans have developed tremendous technologies that expand our awareness, but often for only for a handful of people. Should we consider something mutually observable when it was observed with a single, truly expensive experiment? The results could be questioned by another group using the same equipment – at least in theory. In practice, the most technologically advanced tools rest in the hands of a very few respected scientists who take on the burden of using them carefully and constantly checking the accuracy of their own findings. These people often rotate and are required to publish their results.

The problem appears far more commonly in the guise of funding questions. Most science is too expensive to be done by everyone. Estimates from 2014 suggest that an average Ph.D. in Science costs $95,000-$574,000.[28] Even though much of the expense

---

[26] Philosophers refer to *qualia*, the internal experience of sensation.

[27] Research shows that different cultures label red and yellow in much the same way, but differentiate green and blue less commonly and possibly group shades differently. Likewise, relative intensity of pain appears consistent (X is twice as painful as Y) but absolute pain cannot be measured.

[28] These rough numbers are drawn from estimates of how much universities spent per student, not how much each student paid. "In 2011–12, total

in sciences is covered by a government or university, students still need to apply and be accepted. After this first step, this entry cost, research time, money, and equipment. Scientists regularly lobby for better and broader funding for precisely this reason. We want more people to have the resources necessary to produce data. We shouldn't fool ourselves into believing, though, that anyone could reproduce any data set if only they wanted to. Among other concerns, most funding agencies have no desire to pay for someone to repeat an experiment unless it was controversial for some reason.

The principles of the scientific method represent ideals rather than strict rules. We accept that individuals suffer small differences in perception. With the more complex technologies, we trust a limited number of scientists to run the most expensive experiments and report their results. Thus a large percentage of modern experiments rely on appeals to authority. So, while the principle does not apply universally, a number of mechanisms exist that help us operate as though it did. The key lies in repeatability and error checking, the concrete practice of replicating one another's work and challenging unusual observations. We appeal to authority, but always with the option and the ideal of direct personal observation.

We rely on the principle of mutual observables, admitting that it does not apply perfectly, but accepting that it is a tremendously useful axiom. When in doubt, have someone else do the experiment. Make another instrument or use it in a different way. Repeat the process over and over again to see if the same result always appears. The principle cannot guarantee the perfect result on the first trial, but it provides an important insight into how to get a better result next time. Look at the question from a different angle; get a different perspective. Important things, from a scientific standpoint, are things that everyone can see over and over again.

---

expenses per full-time-equivalent (FTE) student were much higher at private nonprofit postsecondary institutions ($49,036) than at public institutions ($28,371) and private for-profit institutions ($14,545)." U.S. Department of Education, National Center for Education Statistics. (2014). *The Condition of Education 2014*. The National Science Foundation reports that median years to doctorate (since entering graduate school) ranged from 6.5 in physical sciences to 11.7 in education. NSF/NIH/USED/USDA/NEH/NASA (2013), *Survey of Earned Doctorates 2013*. Numbers have been rounded to the nearest thousand.

Symmetry

Next we move from equality between observers to equality in time and space. The principle of equality says that things observed here and things observed there will be observed in the same way. Location, orientation (which way you face), and time do not affect the outcome of our tests. The overarching name for this is space-time symmetry. The universe appears to be symmetrical in a number of respects.[29]

The same experiment performed in the United States and Australia will produce the same results. We believe this is true of experiments done on the Moon or on Pluto, or in a distant galaxy. The same experiment performed today and year from today will produce the same results. We believe that the same rules applied a billion years ago and will apply a billion years into the future. All these claims, and many more types of symmetry, appear to be true, with one caveat. Scientists usually add, "all things being equal." Meteorologists know that rainfall measurements in Houston, Texas (49.8 inches per year[30]), and Coober Pedy, Australia (6.5 inches per year[31]), will provide radically different results. Economists might see huge diversity in spending patterns between a recession year and a year of surplus. In both cases, scientists are required to know what types of things can be expected to be constant and what types of things cannot. Important things, from a scientific perspective, are things that operate consistently over time and space. Interesting things, worthy of study, are the things that do not. The difference matters.

As with mutual observables, the ideal of symmetry is more a practical rule than an absolute reality. Cosmologists think that the universe has been pretty stable for the last thirteen billion years or so; but before that, it was different. We can't see anything farther out than about 13.8 billion years and theorize that before that time,

---

[29] For more details see chapter four of my book, *Life in Space*.

[30] 30 year average (1981-2010) as reported by the United States National Oceanic and Atmospheric Administration (NOAA) rounded to a tenth of an inch (http://www.srh.noaa.gov/hgx/?n=climate_iah_normals_summary).

[31] 30 year average (1981-1910) as reported by the Australian Bureau of Meteorology and converted to inches, rounded to a tenth of an inch (http://www.bom.gov.au/climate/averages/tables/cw_016007.shtml).

matter was in such a high-energy state that light could not pass through it. Similarly, we know that the laws of physics get a little messy within the event horizons of black holes. Does this mean local conditions in those cases are different? Observation cannot answer the question, but the assumption of symmetry simplifies our picture of the universe. We take as an axiom that, unless we find evidence to the contrary, the basic rules of time, space, matter, and energy operate in exactly the same way no matter where or when you find yourself. This axiom allows us to make significant claims about the universe, despite having only visited a miniscule fraction of it.

When thinking about symmetry, think about the range over which experiments have been done. How can we establish the best possible range of conditions: locations, times, temperatures, etc? More importantly, ask which variables would affect the outcome of your experiment if they were not symmetrical. The most robust experiment need not control all the variables, just those relevant to the information you want.

Hypotheses

Mutual observables and symmetry come together in hypotheses. Hypotheses are propositions about the world that either come from or predict observations. After seeing 150 black ravens, I might hypothesize that all ravens are black. Conversely, I could decide, before making any observations, that I would call every black bird a raven. The first represents induction while the second represents deduction. Both are hypotheses. Their hypothetical nature, however, does not come from how they were constructed; it comes from what we do with them. We compare hypotheses to what we observe.

The idea is simple but profound. We compare hypotheses with data. Much heat has been raised in science and religion circles about what constitutes a good hypothesis. Is the existence of God a valid scientific theory? Is life-after-death as reasonable (scientifically) as the Big Bang? I think these questions can be answered by looking at how the propositions relate to observations. Did observations go into the formation of the statement? Can we imagine experiments that test the statement's truth? Would some observation convince us that the statement is true or false? If we answer no to all three questions, then we cannot call the statement a scientific hypothesis.

Several philosophers have made more dramatic claims. Karl Popper (1902–1994), for instance, claimed that the only truly scientific propositions were those that were demonstrably falsifiable. His school of thought, called *falsificationism*, demanded that scientific theories come with at least one experiment that could prove them wrong. More recent philosophers of science have demonstrated that science does not always work on this model,[32] though many scientists still claim it as a touchstone. Others accept the existence of overarching theoretical frameworks, like evolution and chaos theory, that cannot be directly falsified. Instead, they represent ways of looking at a suite of observations. We accept them with a great deal of confidence because they establish a way of interpreting vast quantities of data and setting up smaller falsifiable claims. The framework may not be falsifiable, but it is composed of falsifiable pieces.

Science deals in theories that stem from and relate to the data in a meaningful way. Here we can see the difference between empiricism, which is only an axiom, and symmetry, which starts as an axiom but can also be seen as a hypothesis. Empiricism claims that knowledge comes from experience and observation. No quantity of evidence would dissuade us that this was the case. Even if we imagine a completely unpredictable universe, we would still be arguing that our experience – of random events – led to knowledge – that empiricism is wrong. Neither does evidence really improve our confidence that the world we observe is, at its very core, real. We have no way of getting an independent audit from an unbiased observer. We simply accept that empiricism works in order to reason about things.

Symmetry on the other hand is deeply intertwined with observation and experiment. Physicists regularly adjust definitions of symmetry based on experiments. For example, black holes pack matter so densely that we cannot understand it with the current state of quantum mechanics. Likewise, we believe that the universe started in an incomprehensibly dense state. We call space-time symmetry a hypothesis because we constantly update our understanding of the proposition by comparing it with the data. We rely on symmetry

---

[32] In particular, Kuhn introduced the idea of paradigm shifts – radical changes in the fundamental axioms (or at least overarching systematic framework) of a scientific field. His "paradigms" undermined Popper's notion of fully falsifiable theories, because the paradigms themselves were not falsifiable, only the models within them.

most of the time, but also keep careful tabs on times and places when it fails to apply.

When judging hypotheses, whether your own or someone else's, it is important to ask exactly how the theory interacts with observation. What data went into its creation? What experiments or observations does it suggest? What data would give you confidence it was correct and what data would convince you it was wrong?

ITERATION

This brings us to the last of the four principles, iteration. Science happens when we repeat the process over and over again. Each cycle of observations and hypotheses repeats itself, generating greater and greater confidence in how well the two go together. We get nothing from asking which came first. Like the chicken and the egg, one springs from the other. New observations provoke scientists to generate new hypotheses. New hypotheses suggest new observations. One step alone does not constitute science. Observation by itself can be done by anyone, and the smallest infant senses the world, as do most animals. Even plants and bacteria can be stimulated by their environment. Likewise, propositions are not scientific if they are not connected to experiments or observations. I would call the majority of religious doctrine reasonable. Propositions like the resurrection of Jesus Christ and the oneness of God represent complex and careful reasoning by theologians. I cannot, however, figure out how to relate them to an ongoing cycle of observation and amendment; therefore I don't consider them scientific hypotheses. Science appreciates the relationship between hypothesis and observation.

Questions of iteration should always be in your mind as you look at scientific data. I have seen countless examples of new and exciting scientific results that later proved to be unrepeatable. Sometimes the scientists made an error. Sometimes their sample was too small or they did the wrong tests. Sometimes they were simply unlucky and chance made improbable events appear probable. Scientific knowledge must constantly be assessed on the basis of how much data went into it. How many experiments were done? Were the experiments independent with regard to the important variables? (Or did they, for example, all use the same faulty equipment?) It is easy to find data that will support most any hypothesis. We want to know *how much* data supports the hypothesis, whether all the data support the hypothesis, and what kind of data we would have to gather to be even more confident than we already are.

I value science very highly because it provides a well-established link between the outside world and knowledge. The scientific method not only provides new insights into the way the world works, it gives us tools to question those insights and improve them. The sociologist Max Weber (1864–1920), writing on the subject of science, said this:

> "The first task of any competent teacher is to teach his students to acknowledge *inconvenient* facts, by which I mean facts that are inconvenient for his particular party viewpoint; and for every party viewpoint—even my own, for example—such extremely inconvenient facts exist."[33]

Good reasoning, like good teachers, brings us to places that we never expected to go. It works against our short-term self-interest in order to show us things about the world we inhabit. Science does this for the physical universe. It brings us into a better understanding of the world – even when we would rather it did not. This may be the greatest strength of science and the strongest argument for why we need it in our daily lives. Our four assumptions limit the confidence we have in certain claims about the world. They also and push us to explore new ideas. Scientists can react very strongly when others try to limit this sort of progress. I sympathize. I sympathize with fears that religious constrictions on scientific inquiry will rob us of the very inconvenience that makes science worthwhile.

Mutual observables, symmetry, hypotheses, and interaction all place specific and profound bounds on what we know through science, but not on what we know all together. Nothing inherent to the scientific method forces us to refute all other types of knowledge. Rather, the humility inherent in the scientific method encourages us to realize that some things will never be known by observation and

[33] Max Weber. "Science as Vocation." In John Dreijmanis. *Max Weber's Complete Writings on Academic and Political Vocations*. Trans. Gordon C. Wells (Algora Publishing, 2008). p. 43.

induction. At best it remains silent on the ability of other epistemologies to inform us about the world we inhabit. The scientific method provides one immensely valuable set of tools for coming to understand the universe.

CHAPTER 6
Science as Practice

Having introduced my concept of the scientific method in the last chapter, I want to turn to questions of how we apply that method. A number of important issues arise regarding exactly how we are to apply our four principles – mutual observables, symmetry, hypotheses, and iteration – in practice. Different scientific fields apply them differently. In this chapter, I look at how the principles are applied and how that affects our conclusions. Critics of particular fields – often evolutionary biology, cosmology, and climate science – may choose to critique their methodology, saying it is not properly scientific. I want to address some of those critiques asking where and whether they apply.

Science represents a culture as well as an epistemology. While that culture has spread around the globe, it has very firm roots in the Christian theologies and ideologies of Medieval and Enlightenment Europe. Those discussions, in turn, drew on the philosophies of Muslim al-Andalus (now Spain and Portugal) and the Middle East during the Golden Age of Islam. And before that, there was natural philosophy in Greece, Rome, India, and Persia. Reasoning always comes with a context, including both a thinker and a broader culture. That context tells us something about how the ideas are applied.

How does the culture of science relate to the epistemology? Are the two separable? Many critics of science have claimed that science is inherently atheistic (a belief proudly appropriated by some anti-religious pro-science partisans). A meaningful foundation for dialogue about science and religion will need to address what we consider to be the core of science and what we think of as optional extras. Our issues of epistemology fade into philosophical and sometimes ideological commitments about reality. As you read this chapter and the ones that follow, ask yourself where you draw the line between essential components of science and optional add-ons. The next few sections deal with four such philosophical grey areas.

HISTORICAL SCIENCE

What are we to do with history? Some skeptics of evolution and the big bang theory worry that science is not really science unless you can observe events in a controlled setting, like a laboratory. Is there a scientific way to approach events that happened only once? The rise and fall of the Roman Empire may not be a proper subject for scientific study, but a number of sciences do deal with historical events. Astronomers, for example, deal with events so far away that they happened years ago, sometimes millennia ago. Is not astronomy a science? Geologists try to understand the cycling of elements in Earth's surface and atmosphere throughout the ages. Biologists also study history. Paleontologists want to know about plants and animals that lived millions of years ago. Geneticists try to trace the history of genes through populations, from the short-term history of a viral outbreak to the deep history of photosynthesis.

Astronomy, geology, and biology are clearly sciences, but we need to think carefully about observations when we say so. We need to think about sample size and induction. Recall that induction suffers from biases because it generalizes from one part of a population (the sample) to make statements about a larger group. Historical sciences start with some small fraction of all observations of the past and try to generalize to what all observations of the past will show. Just because you cannot do experiments on past events does not mean you cannot make your observations over again, and in different ways. In order for history to be science, it has to make predictions about what will happen when you look again, and when you look in different ways. Our conclusions speak about the way things were (or are); our hypotheses always have to do with the way things *will be* perceived.

If you are doing history by assuming all the data has been collected and have no interest in continuing the search, if you genuinely don't care what future observers will find, then you are not doing science. That type of history can be tremendously rewarding. I am not saying it is not beneficial. I am only claiming that it becomes science when (and only when) the hypotheses are directly relatable to both past and future observations. Astronomy does more than model the lifetime of stars; it makes predictions about what we will and will not see in the sky tomorrow night. Paleontology does more than reconstruct the history of life on Earth; it makes predictions about what kind of fossils we will find. Biology goes even farther to make predictions about which traits of organisms will prove most useful in a given environment. History becomes science when it uses observations and hypotheses as part of an iterative process.

SCIENCE AND THEORY

I have been very careful to avoid differentiating between hypotheses, theories, and laws, mostly because philosophers have used this distinction in the science and religion field before. Some have argued that hypotheses become theories when supported by evidence and theories become laws when supported by overwhelming evidence. By and large, I don't think the distinction has served its purpose. Rather than clarifying what constitutes science, it has led to wrangling over who has the right to use what language.

Exactly how much evidence is needed? Clearly a single anecdote does not turn a particular proposition into a theory. We want something more. We want evidence of some sort of testing, some sort of iteration. The exact amount necessary will never be rigorously established, simply because there are so many different circumstances. I'm happy to call a single controlled experiment on a Mars rover science. Thought went into designing the experiment and thought went into analyzing the result. It was compared to other experiments. On the other hand, I'd be very skeptical if a scientist reported the same level of data for a phenomenon at sea level on Earth. There, it would be cheap and practical to do the experiment again, and it should be done again. Part of the expertise that goes into making a scientific authority – and part of the importance of peer review – comes from the practical knowledge of how much data you need to be convincing.

The same question applies when we look at the divide between theories and laws. When economists refer to the "Law of Supply and Demand" and physicists refer to the "Law of Gravity", they are speaking of very different standards of evidence. I am more interested in getting researchers in both fields to think clearly than I am in ruling which fields can and cannot be called science. I *can* say that a much lower level of confidence is required to use the word "law" in economics. The things economists study are far more complex, the experiments harder to replicate, and iteration occurs much more slowly. You may or may not decide that economics is a science on those grounds, but you should recognize the role epistemology plays in making the distinction.

Above all, we must ask, "Who has the authority to make these distinctions in a particular field?" In this book, I generally avoid using the word "law," use "theory" rather indiscriminately to describe explanations, and restrict "hypothesis" to propositions connected to observations. I want to emphasize the relationship between data, reasoning, and explanation.

Neither observation nor hypothesis alone can be judged scientific. Science involves a particular discipline of looking at the two in parallel. We start with the assumption that an objective reality exists. That reality can be accessed not only by me, but by everyone else as well. They see what I see; they hear what I hear; and so on. Furthermore, I can do the same thing over and over and get the same result – so long as I know exactly what it is I did. By doing it over and over and making subtly different observations each time, I come to an understanding of the physical world. I propose patterns of relationship between objects and then look to see if those patterns match up with the world as I perceive it. I compare my patterns with those of the people around me to see if they still hold up – asking more and more people and testing things over and over again. Together, we generate confidence in the hypotheses as observers and observations add up. Science grows.

Living with Uncertainty

This notion of growing knowledge has an important impact on how scientists address questions of truth and falsehood. While popular opinion looks at things as being known or unknown, scientists frequently deal with the best theory available. Our purpose will be to find better and better theories using a measurement called confidence, which I deal with in detail in chapter nineteen. Confidence has to do with how much of the observed data matches up with a given theory. For now, we simply note that scientists deal with theories that are not certain. Sometimes, they even hold fast to models for which they have very low confidence, simply because they are better than all of the other models that have been proposed.

As we look at theories like evolution and gravity, it can be easy to say that scientists are very confident. We may not have certain knowledge, but we do have incredible confidence based on millions of observations – all consistent with the theory. More problematic can be issues like string theory, dark energy, or emergence. Each of these deals with phenomena that have not been explained well enough to achieve consensus in their field. A number of theories have to account for data that just don't neatly line up, at least not yet. As the people that society educates, funds, and supports to pry into the physical world, scientists have an obligation to develop working theories. Often we need to make a best guess in light of what we know. Sometimes that's all that can be done.

Confusion arises when scientists try to be completely honest about the uncertainty inherent in the work. Scientific knowledge remains uncertain because we are always open to new data that will change our perspective, correct our biases, and generate better models of the universe. We are also open to new hypotheses that match the data better, give more accurate predictions, or simply appear more elegant. When scientists admit to uncertainty – we're always learning new things – the general public can misinterpret this as ignorance: scientists don't really know what they are talking about. Meteorology is a great example. Meteorologists predict the weather. While their predictions may not be as accurate as we would like, they do tell us important things about our environment. Without these imperfect reports, lives and property would be lost on a regular basis. The imperfect forecasts are tremendously useful, but the uncertainty leads to public doubt.

On the other hand, when scientists (and politicians) try to address public doubts they can promote false certainty. The public wants to be given clear answers; they want to be reassured that we are in control of the situation. Scientists, working against public skepticism, often represent good theories as incontrovertible facts. Thus, scientists face public pressure to be alternately more confident and more humble. The confidence necessary to convince us the research is worthwhile can be seen as a lack of humility, while the humility necessary to present data accurately is seen as incompetence. This cycle of over-confidence and under-confidence can only be stopped when the public understands scientific concepts of iteration and confidence. Knowledge is often more useful when we know how it was generated. Recipients of scientific knowledge should know three things: first, science does not provide perfect answers; second, science provides immensely powerful answers; and third, we can estimate just how much confidence the answers provide.

ELEGANCE

Scientists also make aesthetic choices. We judge hypotheses not only against the data, but against our standards of beauty and utility. This aesthetics of science is tremendously important. It is not enough to understand the world; we want to communicate our understanding. *Elegance* in science refers to constructing explanations that are both fruitful and compelling. That takes work. A successful scientist must share what she has discovered about the universe.

Philosophers have tried to pin down exactly what constitutes the scientific standard. There seems to be a consensus that scientists filter their theories on the basis of some measure of elegance, but the details can be hard to pinpoint. They may change with time. We consider "gravity" a great theory while "vital essences" are laughed at. We judge Darwin's "evolution by natural selection" as a triumph of science and are skeptical of "intelligent design." Experiments on the efficacy of prayer are ridiculed while cockroach mating habits are a respectable career choice. Most amazing of all, the "scientific community" – however we define it – manages to police itself well enough to make discoveries regularly and produce a coherent picture of the world. You would think there would be anarchy without consistent rules known to everyone. Despite lacking a single and clear rulebook, science works, and it works as a communal endeavor. We know it works because it continues to provide useful knowledge.

The primary concern has always been comparison with the data. If a hypothesis cannot explain old observations and predict new ones, it must be discarded. Some theories fall down on this criterion alone. After that, things get more complicated. A short list of scientific aesthetics commonly proposed would include:

1. SIMPLICITY – we favor theories that are less complicated, easier to remember, and easier to communicate. This more than anything else explains the importance of math in science. It allows unambiguous, concise communication of ideas.

2. UTILITY – we favor theories that are easy to use. Beyond simplicity, this requires that elements of the theory or terms in the equation can be readily grasped and related to familiar concepts. All scientific theories must make some accurate predictions. Useful theories will allow us to predict and control features of our environment using straightforward tools.

3. FRUITFULNESS – we favor theories that help us make and test other theories. The best theories make surprising predictions; they work in areas that we thought were totally unrelated to our initial question. For instance, quantum mechanics started with an attempt to understand how objects radiate heat and ended up revolutionizing the way we look at all matter.

4. COHERENCE AND CONSISTENCY – we favor theories that never contradict themselves or other useful theories. Scientists always dream of unified theories, very simple equations that explain everything. A theory in one area that matches theories in other areas will be preferred for the sake of simplicity, but also because it will automatically suggest related experiments and lead toward a greater universal knowledge.

Of course, these four principles only scratch the surface, but they give you some idea of the standards of beauty and productivity that inform the scientific community.

I have tried to address some of the most common areas of discomfort around how we apply the scientific method. Our simple sketch of principles in the last chapter presents a conceptual overview, beautiful in its simplicity and elegance. The day-to-day work of scientists involves far more chaos and complexity. Discovering truths about the world requires hard work and we must be aware of the practical challenges. History, theory, uncertainty, and elegance all reflect areas where the scientific method provides concrete tools for doing epistemology well. They also represent areas where we need to pay close attention to the standards we use. If we consider scientists to be authorities about the physical world, as I think we must, then we need to know exactly why and how their authority operates. We must challenge them to be consistent and transparent in their methods. At the same time, we must trust them to do the hard work of coming to knowledge when we do not have the time, the resources, or the expertise to do so on our own.

Over the past five centuries scientists, both as individuals and as communities, have fallen into a few other ways of thinking that we associate with science at large. Those philosophies include reductionism, physicalism, and progressivism. For the most part they represent axiomatic beliefs about what we observe rather than hypotheses, though the line can be blurry at times. They are tied together by pragmatism, a history of them working for us, and the conviction that what works must be right. In the next three chapters, I will explore the aesthetic, or perhaps ideological, additions to the scientific method that help us decide which hypotheses fit best with the scientific worldview. We will focus on three core concepts – simplicity (chapter seven), physicalism (chapter eight), and progress (chapter nine). Each one strikes me as immensely valuable when used in moderation. After looking at religion we will return to the question of priorities, and what exactly we mean when we say science "works" (chapter seventeen).

CHAPTER 7
The Simplicity of Science

Henry David Thoreau said, "Simplify, simplify." I love this quote, because it balances the desire to trim things back as far as possible and the rhetorical, even conceptual importance of repetition. We must simplify enough, but never too much.

If I were to give you directions to my house, I might say something like this:[34]

> "Drive up Lake City Way until you reach the grocery store. Turn right and drive up the hill. When you reach the top, turn left and stop at the second house on the right."

Alternatively, I could say:

> "Starting at your place, you should leave the driveway and turn right. Follow 5th Ave NE for five blocks until you reach 130th. Turn right again. Of course, 130th will veer south and be called Roosevelt for a couple blocks before turning into NE 125th. Don't worry; it's all the same street. When you reach Lake City Way, pull into the left hand turn lane and wait for the turn signal. When the light turns green, turn left. Head north nine blocks until you reach the Fred Meyers. Turn right and drive through the parking lot, driving east on NE 137th St. When you reach 39th Place NE, turn left. Be sure not to turn onto 39th Ave. That's a different street. Turn in at the horseshoe driveway on your right. Of course if, you're coming on Sunday, the Fred Meyer's parking lot will be closed, so you'll need to keep heading north…"

[34] Just in case you were wondering, I don't live there anymore.

That might get tiring, but I hope you read the whole thing. Not only did I include too much information, but I included too much information in a number of ways.

First, I included too much information about the beginning of the trip. If a friend needs to get to my house, they probably know how to exit their own driveway and get to the major road. Science communication, like any other type of communication, relies on readers being able to apply their own basic facts. Sometimes it comes from generic things learned in grade school. Sometimes it comes from specialized knowledge gained in graduate school. Sometimes it can be as simple as orientation to your local environment. A science paper will not tell you how to acquire ethyl alcohol, assuming anyone can find it. It may tell you how to find a rare strain of bacteria, however, or just the right kind of reagent to perform a chemical reaction. Background information turns out to be one of the most difficult questions in science. What can you assume readers already know?

Hopefully the last two chapters have convinced you that some of our most basic premises are also the most invisible. In practice, scientists from one field (e.g., microbial biology) write for others in the same field and general consensus exists, but when scientists start crossing disciplines, things don't always work so smoothly. A good theory, like a good article, is clear about how much background the user can rely on. Simplicity means allowing that work to be done in the background. The theory of gravity, for example, relies on some concept of mass.

Second, my driving directions included duplicate information. I named both a landmark for the turn and the name of the street. Were both necessary? That depends on who I am giving the directions to. Similarly, in science we can see different levels of explanation in theories. Evolution provides one of the best examples. It has been noted on numerous occasions that evolution will favor cooperation under special circumstances (biological altruism). Biologists agree that it happens, but have formalized the theory in a number of different ways (kin selection, reciprocal altruism, inter-deme competition). Currently the different formalisms emphasize different aspects of one real phenomenon and everyone seems to think they should be reducible to one common description. Nonetheless, different camps exist, each claiming that all the formalisms are best reduced to their own theory. An ideal theory has no duplication and no ambiguity. A good theory minimizes duplication and ambiguity without giving up the power to work in a variety of settings. You need to repeat yourself sometimes, expressing things in different ways to highlight different elements.

Third, my directions ended with a conditional statement. "If the parking lot is closed…" Generally we can assume that I know how to get to my house better than any of my friends. Not only do I know the shortest route, I know the quickest, and the easiest to explain. A full description of how to get to my house would include all of those, wouldn't it? Science is often in the habit of producing partial descriptions. One element of a theory or equation may be the one most important to a field of science. Particularly in physics and astronomy, it is common to see an equation simplified to make calculation more straightforward and still give the right answer, or to give the right answer most of the time. In physics, it is very common to replace a difficult integral with an easy one to calculate series of fractions. If you cannot come the shortest way, at least you can come an easy way. In a perfect world you will know both ways, just in case. So the best answer may be a combination of a simple version and a full ver-sion of the same thing (e.g., Newtonian and Relativistic mechanics).

I have generally heard scientists refer to the desire for simplicity as parsimony or Ockham's razor. Ockham said, "don't create more elements (in the explanation) than you need." Stick with the minimum number that gets the job done. Scientists will always favor the simplest explanation – as long as it accounts for all the data.

One can, of course, oversimplify. I could say to you:

"I'm just a few miles away at the top of the hill."

That would be too little information. Science deals with this frequently as well. I have no doubt you have seen models of the Solar System with all the planets in perfectly circular orbits around the Sun. Perhaps you have seen simplified electron diagrams with electrons displayed in perfect circular "orbits" around the nucleus. Both are inadequate models that poorly explain the things they describe. Both were popular among scientists at some point in the past. The latter (the Bohr atom) is still used when teaching grade school chemistry, despite now being considered utterly wrong. The electrons do not orbit the nucleus like planets around a star, even though we say they travel in "orbitals" for historical reasons. They exist as probability distributions in the vicinity of the nucleus.

You can oversimplify, either to make a point or simply because you are unaware of the complexities of the issue. When it comes to stellar systems and atoms, we have become fairly confident we know how to balance too much with not enough. We have simple, elegant, mathematical descriptions of the phenomena that nonetheless cover the full range of observations (elliptical orbits and Hamiltonian operators, respectively). When it comes to more general issues – like whether physical objects and forces are sufficient to explain everything we see and experience – no such common ground exists.

That will be our challenge, and an issue for regular debate. How simple can you make an explanation before it ceases to be satisfying? Make no mistake; there are wrong answers to this question. A model with the planets in perfectly circular orbits is too simple. A separate angel pushing every object in the heavens is too complex. One force, gravity, seems to do the work for all of the various planets, asteroids, and comets. As I said before, I think we have worked this one out for astronomy. When considering a simplification, ask first what things you need to account for in your explanation. Only then can you ask whether your theory is good enough.

In discussions of science and religion, we frequently find ourselves in conversations with other people who have different priorities. Do they want to explain what makes bodies move? Do they want to understand what makes people move? Do they want to understand what moves people? Those three similar questions represent radically different goals for explanation and different simplifications may be appropriate in each case. Be careful to avoid false dichotomies and straw men; they frequently occur when we attempt to solve other people's problems within our framework. When listening to others, we must identify the problem they are trying to solve before offering a solution. Our model may be sufficient to our cause, but not theirs.

REDUCTIONISM

We call it *reductionism* whenever we expect to find better answers by simplifying the types of explanations we can use. Generally this means either looking at things at a smaller scale or limiting ourselves to only one kind of theory. Reductions are beneficial when they provide a more coherent model or help to unify the way we look at different questions. In chemistry, we reduce matter to collections of elements, which come in roughly 100 naturally occurring types: hydrogen, helium, lithium, etc. That reduction helped chemists appreciate the regular (periodic) properties of atoms that lead to common properties. For example all noble gasses (e.g., helium) have a full set of electrons in their electron orbitals and thus are very stable. They rarely react with other atoms. A reduction can also be harmful. Aristotle tried to reduce all matter to four types of atoms: earth, air, fire, and water.

We can also think of astronomy. Aristotle and most medieval astronomers believed that planets only move in perfect circles. Over the centuries they inserted more and more circles into their explanations, rising into the hundreds, until Kepler proposed including ellipses instead. With an ellipse, you can explain a planet's motion with just one equation, instead of talking about circles within circles within circles. In one way, astronomy became more complex. Circles are simpler than ellipses; they have only one variable (the radius) while ellipses have two (the major and minor axes). In a more important way, astronomy became simpler. You only need one figure for each planet. The word reductionist can be used as either a compliment or an insult, depending on whether you think the simplification was beneficial or harmful.

The two major reductions that cause controversy involve scale and substance. *Scale reductionism* (generally just called reductionism) refers to the assumption that complicated objects and events can be completely understood by describing their components. An engine can be fully described by naming the individual parts (piston, spark plug, belt…) and how they fit together. *Reductionist physicalism* (or just physicalism) refers to the belief that only material things exist or are worth mentioning in an explanation. All the parts of an engine are physical parts and all of their interactions are physical interactions. For an engine, these sound like pretty good ideas.

Reductionism has been incredibly successful in helping us understand the world around us, but it is possible it can be taken too far. Should we consider a plant to be the sum of its tissues? How about an animal? How about a human? Most people are comfortable saying that a plant is nothing more than a collection of molecules with some special properties that allow it to reproduce. Many of these same people are not comfortable with the idea that humans are just collections of molecules – perhaps because people are human. Both the definition of life and the definition of person turn out to be difficult questions, scientifically. Organisms of all types respond to their environments in complicated ways. They maintain their complex structure by taking energy from their surroundings and they pass on that structure to the next generation. Organisms have many properties that currently cannot be reduced in a meaningful way (e.g., homeostasis, adaptation). They also appear to have functions proper to them. I say these things not to convince you that biology should give up on reductionism, but to show that biology in itself is currently less reduced than physics. Different scientists operate at different levels of scale and complexity. At the moment, it would be a mistake to reduce one to the other, even if we hope to do so in the future. Scientific elegance involves choosing just the right level of reduction for the task at hand.

Scale reductionism has been central to science for almost two centuries. It has proven immensely useful, particularly in physics and chemistry. We have discovered smaller and smaller particles throughout this period, each time finding that the properties of large things are really just aggregates or interactions among the smaller things of which they are composed.

Particles in Physics

Atomism, the idea that all matter is made up of tiny indivisible particles, has been popular since the time of the Greeks. The classical elements, however, were earth, air, fire, and water (and sometimes aether). The Greek elements do not correspond to the modern conception of elements, though; the idea of atomism was rebooted in the seventeenth century. Robert Boyle (1627–1691) thought that the physical world (but not the spiritual) must be composed of *minima naturalia*, the smallest primal bits of the material universe. As a proponent of the *mechanical philosophy*, he believed that the physical world was entirely composed of material particles and universal forces.[35] All physical properties could be reduced to those two factors. Over the next two centuries, this program became more and more successful, as modern elements came into the scientific consciousness. Metals such as iron and gold were already familiar as simple substances. Other elements were invoked as key to certain chemical processes: "oxygen" etymologically refers to acid formation while "nitrogen" refers to nitric acid formation.

By the nineteenth century, chemists started arranging lists of elements into groups (columns) and periods (rows) that corresponded to their properties. Groups I and VII, for instance came together to make salts. Sodium chloride is table salt. Listing the known elements by increasing weight, chemists discovered that the list would cycle through the periods – hence 'periodic' tables were formed. Coherence and consistency played a big role in choosing these models. By 1869, Dmitri Mendeleev (1834–1907) could construct a table very similar to the modern periodic table, in which atomic weight and period explained the properties of known elements and predicted

---

[35] The mechanical philosophy as a term in historical philosophy refers to a suite of ideas. They included the ontological reduction to particles and universal forces. They also included a shift in style from biological metaphors (e.g., the world is a giant organism with organs and breath...) to mechanical metaphors (e.g., the universe is like a giant clock which needs to be wound up, but proceeds automatically). Mechanists generally rejected concepts of extension and empty space, believing that every interaction resulted from particles in direct contact with other particles. Think of billiard balls. The mechanists thought sight required us to emit particles from our body that would interact with the external world before returning to our eyes with information.

Note that science has moved on in a number of respects. Our metaphors are now mathematical and field based (e.g., adaptation occurs in fitness space, space-time is like a rubber sheet). Vacuum and some action at a distance have been embraced, notably in the case of gravity. I maintain that we still adhere to the ontological commitment, however. Despite the fact that we characterize particles in terms of wave functions, the enumeration of fundamental particles and forces is still primary in all physics education. For the rest of the book, I will speak of the mechanical philosophy in the sense of the ontological reduction.

where unknown elements should be found. This aspect of prediction was key to making the periodic table a good scientific model.

The periodic table also set the stage for the discovery of even smaller pieces of reality. In the early twentieth century, physicists discovered that atomic weight could be explained by invoking protons and neutrons, *subatomic particles* that made up the nucleus of atoms. Other properties of atoms had to do with electrons – even tinier charged particles that exist in the region around the nucleus. Chemical reactivity could largely be predicted by how many of these electrons could be packed around the nucleus. The atom, literally "indivisible thing" in Greek, had been divided into smaller pieces. Those pieces were in turn explained in terms of even smaller particles called quarks. Today, chemists think of matter as composed of these quarks and other so-called *elementary particles.* Quarks were discovered in the nineteen sixties and seventies.

We have seen extensive scale reduction over the last 150 years, from visible matter to atoms. Atoms are measured in angstroms, or ten-billionths of a meter, and septillionths (that is one over 1,000,000,000,000,000,000,000,000) of a gram. Quarks are even smaller and much of the size and mass of subatomic particles appears to come from the strength of fields interacting between them. Nonetheless, most macroscopic physical properties, from mass to charge and spin can be fully explained in terms of properties and interactions of the elementary particles.

Genes in Biology

Scale reduction and atomism were similarly helpful in the development of modern biology. An Austrian monk by the name of Gregor Mendel (1822–1884) did experiments cross breeding plants to see if he could figure out the process of inheritance. Many others had proposed ideas of a smallest possible heritable trait, but Mendel was the first to demonstrate a clear mathematical rule for how particular characters were passed on. Many inherited traits, like skin color and height in humans, result from complex interactions of biochemistry and the environment. Mendel, however, studied pea plants, which have several very simple traits, each coded for by a single inherited factor. By cross-breeding plants with different heights, colors, and shapes, he found seven traits with clear and simple rules of inheritance. Comparing the ratios of traits in successive generations, he found regular patterns. Today we say that genes (units of inheritance) code for phenotypes (observable traits). Each individual in a sexually reproducing species has two copies of each gene, one copy (called an *allele*) from each parent. A simple mathematical model based on this premise led to very accurate predictions of what kind of traits the next generation would have. Not all traits are this simple, but research suggests that almost all inheritance happens through genes.

In the 20th century, the physical location of the genes was narrowed down until we knew that the information was located on long polymers called deoxyribonucleic acid or DNA. By 1970, molecular biologists had identified the way in which the information is encoded. A straightforward language – using only four letters grouped into three letter words – records the blueprint for making a new organism. Those "letters" turned out to be chemical side chains attached to long strings of sugars forming what we call *chromosomes*. The details may be complicated, but the take home message remains the same. The complexity of organisms could be summed up in chemical strands that behaved in very predictable ways. Just as in physics, biology was – to some extent – explained in terms of small physical things that followed simple mathematical rules.

At the beginning of the 21st century we can make sense of many biological questions by modeling the interactions of genes. The rules have become more sophisticated, but they are still mathematical and they still rest on the idea of individual units of inheritance. Reductionism works. Specifically, reductionism has worked exceptionally well for the past 150 years, a time in which biology, chemistry, and physics have made greater leaps than ever before.

Trouble

Unfortunately, reductionism is beginning to run into a few snags. In the case of physics, the reduction to fundamental particles produces an interesting dilemma. Can you get any smaller? Naïve scale reductionism says there should always be a fuller explanation at a lower level. It runs into "atomism" proper that suggests a smallest indivisible unit. Have we really hit bottom? Fundamental particles already have some fairly counter-intuitive properties. We think of them as probability distributions – in other words, fundamental particles exist over a range of possible states, rather than just sitting there like a billiard ball waiting to interact with another object. Alternatively, we think of fundamental particles as vibrations or fluctuations in a field, but we cannot say exactly what that field is. How can you have fluctuations in nothing? If they are fluctuations in something, what is that thing? If smaller pieces make up fundamental particles, will they have even more counter-intuitive properties? Worse yet, the math is getting more and more complicated the farther down we go. How far are we willing to go to get a comprehensive theory and who will be able to understand it?

In biology, we are beginning to recognize the importance of non-coding regions of DNA. Chromosomes contain vast stretches that do not form words (i.e., they do not code for proteins), but do shape the life and success of the organism. They affect how the coding genes are read. Should they be considered genes as well – even when they don't come in discrete segments? Worse yet, we have found that the "genes" themselves may be more abstract concepts. We often speak of one gene appearing in many different copies, each within a different organism. The most useful genetic math describes the behavior of these genes as types or patterns of information, rather than individual, physical units. Are we reducing life to information content? How does that reduction line up with physical reductions?

In all areas of natural science, we find that non-reduced explanations give the best answers to *some* of our problems. Particularly in terms of macroscopic mechanics and animal behavior, we find the simplified math of aggregates and large-scale systems far more helpful than the reductionist answer most of the time. And we find that the reductionist answers really help when the large-scale solution fails. Currently, biology and physics both give us great examples of wanting at least two versions of our theories – an easy everyday version and a comprehensive but highly complex reduced version.

EMERGENT PROPERTIES

What happens when reduction fails? What are we to do with things like consciousness, emotions, ideals, and abstract concepts? Concepts like love and duty have clear utility when we describe what we experience and how we interact. Currently, we have great difficulty expressing those things in a reductionist way. Something as simple as the concept of "I" shows no straightforward avenue of reduction to smaller pieces. The feeling of identity or self-awareness admits of no division. It seems to be a property of a whole being.

The word *emergence* expresses the idea of things that defy reduction, though scientists are divided on whether these are necessary failures or only temporary setbacks. The first camp says that emergent properties really do express something that cannot be explained at a lower level. The universe, they say, has rules that only appear when certain combinations of matter come together. They are emergent rules or emergent laws. The second camp says that those things we cannot currently reduce will someday yield to a reductionist understanding. We do not know how to do it now, but at some point we will. They point to phenomena like temperature, which has no meaning in the context of a single atom, only for a population of atoms such as a liquid or a gas. It can be explained, however, in terms of the average kinetic energy of the all the atoms in a system. So the reduction was not straightforward, but it was completely explanatory. We can fully account for temperature it in terms of the properties of atoms. Sometimes the two camps are called *strong emergence* and *weak emergence*. Both capture the idea of non-reductionism, but only the former really requires something new in terms of an explanation.

When evaluating scale reductionism, ask why you want to reduce this phenomenon to explanation at a lower level? What kind of power would it give you if you did? How would it simplify either understanding or action? Would any explanatory power be lost? Finally, we come to the most difficult question. What exactly, are we reducing things *to*? How do we decide which reduction to use, and when to stop looking for a lower level?

As Above, So Below

Scale reductionism, in some broad sense, has won the day in Western culture and in science. The only serious alternative of which I am aware is *holism*. In the early part of the 19th century, scientists believed in causal correspondences in place of causal actions.[36] They thought that, in some important way, parts of a system mirrored the whole and the whole mirrored the parts. Thus, if you were to change an organ within the body, you could change the body. You may be familiar with fictional accounts of voodoo, where a person's hair has been stolen and formed into a doll. What is done to the doll, to the hair, happens to the person. That is the only type of holistic causation, or *sympathetic magic*, that comes readily to mind. We think of it as silly today, but 200 years ago, it vied with reductionist explanations in science. Bearing this in mind, it becomes easier to understand a great deal of medieval and even early 19th century reasoning. Darwin, for instance, did not know about genes as DNA. He suggested a process called *pangenesis* that allowed all parts of a parent's body to inform the gametes (egg or sperm) as they were formed. Much more ancient forms of holism seriously considered the impact of celestial events on our daily lives. Astrology was thought to capture the influences of planetary motion on earthly events. As the whole system changed, individual events changed to match. As above, so below. The process might be thought to work in reverse as well, as we hear in Shakespeare's *Julius Caesar*: "The heavens themselves blaze forth the death of princes." One of the most significant distinctions (among many) between astronomy and astrology is that the former has rejected holism.

I introduce holism to show how much we really have accepted a reductionist view of the universe. The alternative sounds ridiculous to modern ears. We have changed. In large part we have changed due to science. And here we are treading on the delicate ground where observation meets axiom. I believe we started with scale reductionism in the 16th century as an axiom. There was a philosophical preference for simpler and more concrete explanations. That preference led us to ask questions in particular ways. The questions led to experiments and the experiments led to knowledge. The original preference was axiomatic, but our continued use can be justified by our observations. Non-reductionist causal explanations

---

[36] Correspondences were common in scientific explanations prior to 1600. They begin to disappear in the Enlightenment, particularly in physics and chemistry, but briefly return in a movement called *Romanticism*. Biologists clung to correspondences well into the 19th century, but finally rejected them in the "New Synthesis." For more on the shift away from correspondences, see Michel Foucault's book, *The Order of Things*.

have been tried. Influential scientists have proposed holistic theories and those theories have been tested. To my knowledge, none of them has outperformed reductionist alternatives. Thus observation has confirmed scale reductionism as useful.

Most modern claims of emergence and anti-reductionism do not deny scale reductionism *per se*. Rather, they wish to propose an alternate reductionist system. For example, some philosophers have critiqued attempts to reduce human choice to evolutionary and/or genetic causes. They claim that we cannot explain human behavior solely in terms of genes, but we can do so in terms of neurons, or social influences, or humors, or essence, or spirits... Some of these reductions could operate in parallel. Genes could shape how neurons function and neurons could shape behavior. Spirits could be another way of looking at social structures, which motivate human behavior. Other pairs of reductions compete. It is hard to imagine compatibility between genetic and spiritual reductions. In the next chapter, we will look at the ontological systems that form the basis of various substance reductions and whether or not they make sense.

When looking at reductionism, it will always be important to think critically about what you are reducing. Is it an event, an object, a person? What are you reducing it to? And does that explanation leave open the possibility of another reduction, or does it exclusively define what you are talking about?

☙ ✦ ❧

It can be difficult to distinguish between implicit biases, logical necessity, and observed fact. One of the greatest benefits of science arises from the clarity it can provide, the unflinching willingness to assess critically where our knowledge comes from and what might affect its reliability. The scientific method outlined in chapter five, including mutual observables, symmetry, hypotheses, and iteration, sets forth a basic framework through which we can understand the world. Those four pillars, however, are not enough to account for either the success or the specificity of modern science. We will also need to invoke some concept of elegance, the aesthetic criteria embraced by scientists as a community. Those criteria benefit from flexibility and change with time, but they too must be the subject of our critical analysis. This chapter focused in on simplicity and reduction. Both are immensely useful but they can be taken too far. The challenge lies in deciding exactly how far that is. In the next chapter, we ask just how confident we should be in our ability to find out.

CHAPTER 8
The Nature of Science

If you were asked to describe the world, what words would you use? This is a rather challenging question and one that becomes central to our discussion of how people change their minds. The words we use shape the thoughts we have. This chapter tackles questions of what we place at the very bottom of our explanations of the world. In science, good explanations are always simpler than the thing they explain; therefore, some sort of reduction will be necessary. If we are to be reductionist, what can we reduce the world to? Alternatively, if we are not reductionist, then what systems do we subscribe to for organizing things?

Describing the universe or "constructing a worldview" tells us something important about how we reason. It makes us spell out explicitly how we come to understand and know. In short, it reveals our axioms. Most people, unfortunately, are introduced to the problem backwards. We tell them all about our worldview and invite them to agree or disagree. They can then, if they are critical, identify our axioms and use them as a reason to disagree. I have atheist friends who find the theistic picture utterly confounding. They start with an empty universe and fill it with things; they wonder what possible evidence theists could have for putting God into the picture. For them, the preference for the fewest possible entities (Okham's razor) bottoms out at one. The process started somewhere – empty space – and they could not get over the hurdle to God.[37] I should note that this is only one of many possible thought processes leading to atheism, but I do think it is a popular and rational one.

On the other hand, I have theist friends, for whom the maxim "nothing comes from nothing" means that some entity must have started the whole process. They think the existence of anything necessitates the existence of a first thing. Aristotle called it the

[37] It must be noted that space – empty extension – is also an entity. Space represents one entity, not zero.

"unmoved mover" and reasoned it must be outside the normal realm of nature, precisely because it was unmoved. The things we normally encounter in the world all have causes. This must be something different. Notably, William of Ockham said there must be an unmoved mover. For him, the razor cuts out unnecessary entities and the unmoved mover is that which is necessary before all else. For believers in an unmoved mover, the process starts with God and no amount of reasoning can get them around that basic constraint.

Again, not all theists reason along these lines, nor is it obvious that "unmoved mover" corresponds to a theistic God. Nonetheless, I have presented two cases that show how our axioms constrain the way we make sense of the world. Even a small amount of skepticism will make it easy to trash other people's picture. The question is whether our own picture can face the same criticism. It would be unfair to place higher standards on other peoples' reasoning than we accept for our own.

WORDS FOR WORLD

At this point, I want to introduce an important distinction in the way that I use three words: cosmos, universe, and world. Both "cosmos" and "universe" convey a sense of the ordered totality of existence, the primary historical difference being that the first comes from Greek and the second from Latin. Curiously, the word "world" (from Proto-Germanic) was used with a similar meaning prior to our current understanding of planets. In order to tease out different meanings, I draw a line between the *universe*, which represents the set of all physical entities (possessed of measurable mass and/or energy), and the *cosmos*, the set of all things including the universe and those things traditionally called supernatural (God, angels, demons…) but also intangibles such as love, honor, and duty. You may believe that the cosmos is no bigger than the physical universe – a position called *physicalism* – or you may believe that something has to be added in order to complete the picture. In either case, it is useful to have words that allow you to express the relationship.

I use the word *world* when I want to refer to the set of all things experienced by one or more people. It emphasizes the way we sense, experience, and project the universe around us and highlights the place of consciousness in the process of worldview building.

Strictly speaking, I could differentiate between *physicalism, materialism,* and *naturalism.* The three words come with different metaphysical commitments. Physicalism refers to the ontological position that everything that exists is made up of matter, energy, or some combination of the two. The set of all things is identical to the set of things observable by physics. Materialism is usually used in the same way, though it reflects an older system of thought, one that distinguishes matter and form. Naturalism claims that nothing exists except the "natural" universe, presumably in contrast to the supernatural. In chapter eleven, we will look more closely at how natural and supernatural are defined, and why I think they hinder the discussion. For now, let me say that naturalism usually indicates a less distinct kind of physicalism. Thus, I will speak of physicalism when dealing with ontology; I believe it to be the clearest statement of this perspective. I will use materialism in a separate, ethical sense, later on.

WHAT LIES BENEATH

What shall we build with? Medieval philosophers used the word *substance* to ask this question. The word comes from the Latin for "to stand under." When you speak of something, what is it fundamentally? What are the pieces you use that cannot be reduced to smaller pieces? This is ontology proper – the study of what is and what is beneath everything else. It turns out to be indispensible when considering reduction.

There have been two main approaches to the problem. When looking at the world, Plato and others argued that we know we experience something, so experience must be fundamental. Substance has something to do with intelligence and world building. Plato saw thought as more important than the things we think about. Here we find the basis for his realism, which I introduced in chapter two. A second approach, often attributed to Aristotle, seeks to abstract the thinking process from the things we think about. Once you start thinking about thinking, you can speak of thinking about thinking about thinking, and so on to infinity. Aristotelians find this ridiculous. We should just start with the things in the world we are trying to describe. For Plato ideas were important, the things we touch and taste and see are only shadows of them. Ideas were underneath everything else. For Aristotle things we perceive were important. He thought we should build our model of the world out of particular observables.

I can imagine no experimental way to prove one approach is better than the other.[38] They rest on axiomatic assumptions about how we put the world together. In recent centuries, the debate has been slightly different, but follows similar lines. Some proponents of science argue that science relies on Aristotelian sensibilities. Particles and forces are mutually observable and therefore real. We should start there and build everything else on that foundation. Other proponents of science argue that this is fine and good so long as you have a thinking scientist to do the work. Without a mental arbiter to ask the questions, where are we? Thus, there is a desire to have a Platonic observer making sense of an Aristotelian external world.

Keeping that in mind, let us return to the idea of elemental particles introduced in the last chapter. Drawing on the mechanical philosophy, modern physicists choose models of the world with particles as substances. Elementary particles, the smallest unit so far discovered, constitute the building blocks of the physical universe. Quarks carry most of the mass, with three quarks going into the construction of every proton or neutron (and protons and neutrons making up the nuclei of atoms). They also make up a number of less familiar particles that flash in and out of existence so quickly that we do not register them on the macroscopic level.[39] Electrons orbit nuclei, allowing atoms to interact with one another, forming molecules, reflecting energy, and allowing countless other chemical reactions. Like the protons and neutrons, electrons have short-lived cousins, joined together in a group called leptons. Physicists see the entire universe as made up of this tiny cast of characters: six quarks, six leptons, and a few "force carriers" that help them interact. Photons, which make up light, get lumped into this last category,

---

[38] This statement is not strictly true. I can think of pragmatic arguments that favor one perspective over the other. For the past 150 years, I believe that the Aristotelian reduction to particulars has proven immensely successful in science while Platonic idealism has been ineffective. Alas, this judgment may not be so clear as we move into the 21st century. In physics, both relativity and the Copenhagen interpretation(s) of quantum mechanics suggest that the thing observed may not be separable from the observation.

[39] Charged pions and kaons, the most stable of these, have expected lifetimes measured in hundred-millionths of a second.

transmitting electromagnetic energy across space. By analogy, we feel there must be a particle, a graviton, that carries gravitational force in the same way the force carriers transmit the other forces, but we have never observed one. This model, called the *Standard Model* of fundamental particles and interactions, lays out a scientific ontology for the physical universe.[40]

NECESSARY FORCE

Now that we have objects in our universe – chess pieces on the board, if you will – we need to ask how they move. Note that this is not about why they move, the unmoved mover question again. That would be asking who moves the pieces. I will save that question for later. For the moment, we just want to know the rules of movement. In chess, for example, rooks move with the lines of the board while bishops move diagonally. What are rules for moving particles about within the universe? I am hoping most readers already have some familiarity with these concepts, but want to spell them out so we can ask just how much explanatory power they have. Will they be sufficient to explain everything we experience in the cosmos?

Along with the Standard Model come four fundamental forces, four basic ways in which particles interact and drive the chemistry of the universe. Gravity and electromagnetism apply in everyday life. We see that items fall to the ground because the immense mass of the Earth attracts the small mass of the items. Similarly the small mass of the items attracts the Earth, but the force is so small that we usually ignore it. Gravity holds us down because we have mass. We still cannot say exactly how particles communicate their mass to one another, in order to pull together, but we can model the results very well. We can see and predict the effects of gravity on any object once we know the mass.[41]

---

[40] For a much fuller, but still very accessible, treatment I can recommend *The Quantum World* by Kenneth Ward (Harvard University Press, 2005). The Higgs Boson, which received a great deal of press recently was popular largely because its absence threatened to break the model. Observations matched predictions and, as of 2014, physicists believe they have evidence of such a boson and confirmation for the Standard Model.

[41] Historically, some scientists and philosophers wondered whether this was simply a truism. Maybe mass was nothing more than the force of attraction

Electromagnetism refers to the force that draws together positive and negative charges as well as the north and south poles of a magnet. Under the current model, this can be understood as an exchange of photons between particles of different polarity or charge. Alternatively, the model describes this as the generation of a field in which particles interact. The details are less important for our discussion than the general idea that a small number of equations can account for all electromagnetic interactions and predict exactly how two charged (or magnetic) particles will interact.

The other two forces, the weak and strong interactions, have to do with how quarks behave and how they exchange the short-lived particles mentioned above. Because the particles have such short lives, the forces only work over very small distances. In another victory for simplicity and consistency, the weak and electromagnetic forces have been unified into a single model that describes the fields of the involved particles. Since the 1980s, physicists have thought they represent different manifestation of the same "electroweak force." Physicists dream of an even more elegant model, which would include gravity and the strong force as well, but currently such a theory is unavailable.

Filling Up the Cosmos

So far, we have a bare-bones ontology of the universe. It's true that we started with the mechanical philosophy as an axiom, but it has proven useful in allowing us to generate a comprehensive and elegant model. I have no doubt that it explains much of the physical universe beautifully. The hard question arises when we ask whether the model is sufficient to explain *everything* in the universe, much less everything in the cosmos. Starting with scientific simplicity, let us ask whether we have enough particles, whether we have enough forces, and whether we need anything else.

---

due to gravity. Technically, we call that gravitational mass. Another quantity, called inertial mass, reflects how much force is needed to accelerate an object. In the 20th century, the two were shown to be equivalent, demonstrating the simplicity, coherence, and consistency of our theories about mass. The discovery also established that gravity was a distinct force *acting on* mass.

Enough Particles?

The mechanical philosophy conditions scientists in a particular way. That is, it encourages us to think of the world in terms of particles and forces. Any scientist looking at questions of ontology will want to ask whether we have enough particles. Do the small number of particles we know about cover the whole gamut of things we experience? Do fermions (mass forming particles including quarks and leptons) and bosons (force carrying particles including photons and gluons) account for all the matter in the universe?

When phrased that way, the answer is no. Galaxies have far more mass than we can account for, something generally referred to as *dark matter*. We thought we knew how much matter there was in galaxies based on what we can see. Using the principle of symmetry, we assume that stellar fusion works the same throughout the universe. That means we can use the color of a star's light to estimate its mass. Planets turn out to have negligible mass compared to their stars (>99% of the mass in our Solar System is the Sun), so we do not need to worry about them. Unfortunately, if you add up the mass of all the stars and interstellar dust visible from Earth you only find about 15% of the mass needed to explain the rate of galactic rotation. There appears to be something else out there, something that generates mass but does not emit or reflect light. This observation is upheld by the fact that other galaxies bend light (because of gravity and mass) far more than we would expect based on their visible matter. We know that familiar matter makes up only a fraction of the universe. From this perspective, the Standard Model does not hold up.

Asking the question a different way, we get a different answer. Have we observed any kind of particles other than the familiar ones in the standard model of physics? Here the answer is also no. While we cannot explain most of the mass in the universe, neither do we have any better theories for specific bits of matter. Everything we can observe appears to be made up of fermions and bosons. Remember, scientists do not expect a perfect answer, only the best answer available. No one has proposed any new particles that give us better explanatory power than the ones we have. Scientists see no reason to invoke more particles. The theory we have is not sufficient to explain the universe, but it doesn't get better (so far) when we add things to it.

Enough Forces?

When it comes to forces, the story is quite simple. We believe that forces must act universally – all things being equal, the same amount of energy will always behave the same way. One aspect of this is that we don't think of forces having intentions. They do not choose between locations or outcomes. Rather, like water caught behind a dam, they rush forward when released and fill up the low spaces. That turns out to be nothing more than the force of gravity pulling water downward. With a dam in place, that force builds up behind the barrier forming potential energy. The water has potential to do work as it falls down and we often harness that energy by using it to turn turbines as it passes through the sluices. Neither the gravity nor the water has any intentions, only the drive to move downward, toward a lower energy state.

Within science, we see events as occurring based on different kinds of potential energy being stored and spent. Massive objects held apart result in gravitational potential energy. Charged particles held apart result in electromagnetic potential energy. Batteries, for example, work because electrons are stored up in one reservoir while the other reservoir has a positive charge. The force of electrons moving from one to the other does work. Similarly, animals run largely on carbohydrates or long chains of sugars. Plants use electromagnetic radiation (photons) to charge up electrons (so that they move in higher energy orbitals) and then use the charged electrons to push carbon molecules together in chains. Those chains have more energy than the carbon dioxide and water from which they are made, so they store chemical potential energy in the same way a dam holds gravitational potential energy. We break down the sugars, releasing energy. Animals work because chemical energy is stored up in sugars (and fats).

The question of forces in science has become one of looking for ways in which energy can be stored and released. The methods are incredibly complex in some cases, but they can be reduced to a very small number of basic forces providing the power for all reactions. So, let us ask, do our four forces – gravity, electromagnetic force, strong and weak interactions – account for all we see in the universe?

Again, if we ask the question this way, the answer must be no. We can explain stars and planets, electric and magnetic fields, even plants and animals. It turns out that even the particles with which we are now familiar make more sense when thought of as waves, oscillations within a field of some kind.[42] Two large questions remain, however.

First, where did the energy come from in the first place? If we are to follow our reasoning about work being done by potential energy, where did the energy come from originally? What fueled the Big Bang? The universe we observe started with a tremendous amount of heat, but we do not know where that heat came from. As far as we can tell, the amount of order in the universe is gradually decreasing as the universe expands and that heat spreads out over a bigger and bigger volume. Cosmologists think that the particles will eventually be so far apart that no gravitational or electromagnetic interactions will occur ("heat death"). As far as we know, no new energy is being applied to the system from the outside. So the first problem is this: What wound up the universe in the first place?

Second, why is the universe expanding? We know that objects with mass are drawn together by gravity. If all the mass in the universe started as a tiny speck, where did the energy come from to force it all apart? Why did it explode outward? If we only count the forces currently known, we have no way to explain that explosion. In more technical language, Einstein's equation describing the universe has a term called the cosmological constant (or the "energy density of vacuum") that describes the expansion of space. The universe is not only getting bigger, it is accelerating, meaning the cosmological constant must be greater than zero. Contrary to earlier assumptions, gravity is not winning this tug of war. We do not know what is winning, but it has been tentatively called *dark energy*. Things are happening in ways we cannot attribute to the known forces.

On the other hand, gravitation and electromagnetism do account for all the processes we see occurring below the universal

[42] The heat of a substance may be reduced to a composite of the kinetic energy of particles within the substance. This kinetic energy, or velocity, can be described as a property of the wave that describes the particle and, therefore, counts as a derivative of electromagnetic energy.

scale. The philosophical question of *causal closure* asks whether the universe is causally closed. Do all events occur within the universe because of internal causes? Or do some of them happen because of forces from outside the universe? As with particles, we find that the standard model, while not complete, is better than any variant we've considered. There has never been an experiment that demonstrated (as a mutual observable) work being done by a force other than gravity, electromagnetism, the weak and strong forces, and derivative forces. Looking at a system, if we measure the potential energy going in and coming out in terms of known forces, the output is always the same as or less than the input. This is the second law of thermodynamics and it has held up very well after billions if not trillions of observations.

If there were some other force out there and we were not measuring it, we would expect it to do work at some point in a way that we could measure. We would expect it to be converted to another form just as humans use chemical energy to build dams and store up gravitational energy – just as plants use solar power to build molecules and store up chemical energy. To date, this type of event has not been shown to happen.

For the record, I have heard numerous anecdotal claims about one-time events. One case involves rumors of an experiment that showed bodies lose weight upon death. If that were true, we would have evidence that the force of life within the body somehow has mass. The loss of life would result in a loss of mass and a new force and/or particle would need to be invoked. To the best of my knowledge, these experiments – once we correct for the air, which is no longer held within the lungs – do not demonstrate a measurable loss of mass. As far as we can tell (as scientists) the universe is causally closed. No forces have been proposed that add to the predictive power of the four forces.

☙ ✦ ❧

Our very quick sketch of particles and forces demonstrated the importance of how we ask the questions. Science (in this case the Standard Model) does not explain everything in the physical universe. Science does explain everything in a way that outperforms every other available model. And in science that is exactly what you hope for – the best theory available. We seem to have a pretty good grasp on matter and energy. Our model quite wonderfully explains all the mutual observables, but does it explain everything?

The concept of physicalism can be divided into two possible perspectives that will be important as we go forward. *Ontological physicalism* claims that our scientific ontology of particles and forces is enough to explain everything in the cosmos: all substance, all action, and anything we care to talk about including ideas like life, personhood, duty, and compassion. On the other hand *methodological physicalism* will make the much weaker claim that our scientific ontology is sufficient to explain mutual observables.[43] We have set it up as one of the rules that dictates how we play the game of science, but are not committed to the larger metaphysical claim about all of reality. From my perspective, methodological physicalism is right and good and necessary to science. The stronger claim of ontological physicalism goes beyond the areas where induction and observation are informative – it attempts to rule out all non-scientific episteme-ologies.[44]

Any rational rejection of ontological physicalism must come from a demonstration that the world, at least the physical universe, is not enough. In chapter ten, we turn to possible areas where the cosmos may transcend the rules of the scientific game. First, though, I want to ask what we can expect of science in the future. We may not be there yet, but will we get there?

---

43 Careful readers might also be interested in a similar distinction between natural substances and natural causes. When we put up the net for science, are we introducing a restriction on what we can explain or on how we explain it? Each limitation has been called naturalism. My suspicion is that attempts to use one without the other are really attempts to smuggle in non-mutual observables, while retaining the name "science." I am unsympathetic.

44 Ian Hutchinson explores this idea in his book, *Monopolizing Knowledge* (Fias Publishing, 2011). If you are interested in the history of philosophy of science, I also highly recommend Margaret Osler's book, *Divine Will and the Mechanical Philosophy* (Cambridge University Press, 1994). She shows the divide between methodological and ontological physicalism goes all the way back to the first mechanists, Descartes and Gassendi.

CHAPTER 9
The Hope of Science

Scientists have relentless optimism when it comes to knowledge. A better theory can always be found. This means we exist in a constant state of flux. Today's theory is better than yesterday's; tomorrow's theory will be even better. This strange middle space, between complete ignorance and absolute certainty, provokes scientists to continually press forward in the search for knowledge, but it requires a careful balance of optimism and skepticism. The optimism tells us we *can* know things about the universe, while the skepticism cautions us from being too confident about what we do know. No hard and fast rules tell us where the line lies, but the scientific community acts to maintain common standards. Thus we cannot count either optimism or skepticism as essential to the scientific method on their own, but we can appeal to a balance between them in the ethos and aesthetics of science.

ONWARD AND UPWARD

Does human understanding improve over time? Science after the Enlightenment – indeed, most culture in the period known as Modernity – has been deeply committed to the idea of progress. Things get better with time. Our knowledge improves and our understanding exceeds that of any previous age. Recall the idea that science works iteratively. The more experiments we do, the better hypotheses we can make. We learn to make better observations and gradually move toward our ultimate goal – full knowledge.

At first glance, this appears inseparable from the scientific method. Iteration presumes an idea that has come to be known as the asymptotic approach to knowledge. In math, asymptotic lines form curves that start by rapidly approaching a line and then gradually veer off as they come close, getting nearer and nearer, but never quite touching. Throughout the nineteenth century, physicists became more and more confident that science would explain all phenomena and engineering would yield all power. This trend became so intense, that by the end of the 1800s, William Thomson (Lord Kelvin, 1824–1907) could say, "There is nothing new to be discovered in physics now; all that remains is more and more precise measurement." Thomson's comment reflects the extreme optimism of scientists. He thought that physics had gotten very close to the truth and need only make tiny refinements as things got better and better.

It was a common belief in the late nineteenth century with regard to physics and medicine, and culture in general. Science and engineering, given sufficient time, would provide all the answers. Mostly, this was a good thing. Nations invested heavily in science and turned toward authority figures in science and academia for answers to social problems. In political philosophy there was a gradual rise in optimism about the ability of law to regulate human behavior and produce a just society as demonstrated by the progressive movement.[45] In medicine the germ theory, supported largely by the work of Louis Pasteur (1822–1895) and Robert Koch (1843–1910), gave doctors hope of someday eliminating disease altogether. But there was also a sinister side. The rising ideology of Marxism promised a better life for everyone if we would just turn over all wealth to the expert managers. Likewise, the eugenics movement promised to breed better humans through the application of biological and agricultural knowledge.

This belief in the gradual upward movement of humanity, whether over the long haul or over a shorter period of time, has been referred to as the "myth of progress." Here 'myth' suggests not falsity, but the idea that the proposition is axiomatic, popular, and explanatory of the world. The myth of progress states that things are getting better. Within the modern context it usually carries the connotation that things are getting better because we know more (through science), people participate more (through nationalism and democracy), and societies are more flexible and efficient in allocating resources (through capitalism). Many may not even separate the three

[45] While the progressive movement of the early-twentieth century shares some features with contemporary progressivism – such as belief in communal action and strategic social planning – it also differed radically in a number of areas, particularly those related to which social and economic outcomes we desire.

concepts, feeling that the first suggested the latter two, while they made the first possible.

Progress is not the only myth. Two alternatives come to mind. Rather than progress, we might believe in a myth of stasis – things stay the same – or the myth of the golden age – things were much better at some point in the past and have been going downhill ever since. Both ideas appear commonly in religious communities, which may explain some of the more strident and fearful arguments around science. The myth of stasis can be seen quite clearly among Christians in the line "What has been is what will be, and what has been done is what will be done; there is nothing new under the sun" (Ecclesiastes 1:9, New Revised Standard Version). Many religions emphasize the circularity of nature or the inability of humans to significantly change their station in life. The myth of a golden age is even more prevalent. Renaissance Europeans looked back at Antiquity as the height of culture while many Romans and Greeks believed that things were better even farther in the past. Many Muslims recall times when a single caliph ruled all of Islam from Morocco to India and Baghdad had the greatest universities in the world.

It can be hard to say whether things are getting better or worse over the long term, because we do not all share the same priorities or concept of "better." Conflicts can arise as this uncertainty mixes with the three myths. Believers in progress may feel that believers in the other myths are getting in the way. Meanwhile believers in the other two myths may worry that progressives are pushing an agenda that at best will maintain the status quo and at worst will drive them farther from the perfection of the past. My short descriptions are, perhaps, over-simplistic. They are not meant to be logical arguments against any of the three myths (they would be straw men); they are meant to capture a very real emotional tension between three different camps.

Progress in Science versus Progress of Science

At this point, we must be careful to differentiate two very different notions of progress as it relates to science. On the one hand, there are many thinkers for whom science demonstrates progress in the world. Both scientists and philosophers have attempted to claim scientific evidence for progress in the world. I would call this progress in science or progress as a scientific theory. While the idea was tremendously popular in the 19th and early 20th centuries, subsequent judgment has been ardently against it. Largely this rests on a question of mutual observables. Any claim of progress, in the sense I'm talking about here, requires us to claim movement from worse to better. What constitutes better? Currently no common standards exist for measuring better, so science categorically cannot make statements about progress. Mind you, once you've stated exactly what you value (for example, intelligence or purchasing power or horse power) then science is very good at measuring progress toward that specified goal. Thus fields like education, economics, and engineering can use science to chart progress. Just remember, they had to start by importing their value structure from somewhere else. Science can neither create nor critique goals; it can only judge whether your actions achieve them.[46]

On the other hand, the practice of science today depends critically on our belief that scientists will come to know more and more about the world. We rely on scientists to value knowledge and to keep producing new and better knowledge. The very notion of iteration emphasizes the power of collecting greater and greater stores of data against which to compare our hypotheses. Thus, as a scientist I can – indeed must – conclude that science progresses, that there is progress of science. The conclusion that the world progresses, however, requires additional knowledge about values, something that a scientist (as scientist) can not have.

Historical Progress

The myth of progress has not always been central to science. During the Middle Ages and Renaissance, European scholars frequently thought of themselves as rediscovering the lost arts of the ancients. They and their colleagues in the Abbasid Caliphate revered the wisdom of Aristotle, Galen, and other Hellenistic thinkers. For the most part, science turned to the myth of progress only with the Enlightenment. Francis Bacon, in particular, saw science as our process of regaining dominion over the world, which we had lost in

[46] I will talk more about the question of values – and why I don't think science can produce them in chapter ten.

the Fall.[47] From the 17th to the 20th century, progress was all the rage in educated circles. Sometime between the 1880s and 1940s, our confidence that things were getting better began to change. The brutalities of World War II and the holocaust convinced people around the world that societies were not uniformly getting better. Germany, which before World War I had been considered the height of modern culture, proved that industrial technology could be turned to evil purposes. Nations began to see the horrible moral cost of Marxism and eugenics and the failure of international law.

A number of scientific discoveries weakened the pre-war optimism as well. Physics, so confident at the end of the nineteenth century, ran into trouble in the form of quantum mechanics. Max Planck (1858–1947), Niels Bohr (1885–1962) and Werner Heisenberg (1901–1976), among others, demonstrated that some things simply cannot be known. Other things will only be known in a probabilistic manner. In the 1950s, medical research uncovered antibiotic-resistant bacteria showing that disease-causing organisms could fight back.

Whereas earlier philosophy of science had emphasized positive and definite growth of scientific knowledge, new theories suggested that the truth may be a moving target. Thomas Kuhn (1922–1996) in his book *The Structure of Scientific Revolutions* proposed that science occasionally undergoes paradigm shifts in which the whole framework of scientific reasoning, explanation, and hypotheses changes. Such a change had occurred in the shift from Newtonian to Einsteinian mechanics and in the shift to Darwinian theories of evolution. These shifts meant that, while we do make progress, it is not always in the same direction. We find ourselves at the start of a new era, one in which scientists are confident that they can improve the world, but also confident that some things simply cannot be known in the ways we want to know them. Further, we have come to recognize the social and ethical aspects of science that can make it a force for ill as well as a force for good.

As a scientist, I like the idea of progress. I agree with the arguments that say we are better off with indoor plumbing and modern medicine. Science provides these benefits and they convince

---

[47] The book of Genesis in the Bible, specifically chapters 2 and 3 tell a tale of early times when humans had a perfect relationship with God and the world, but lost it due to pride.

us to invest in modern science. I think it may be necessary to draw the line, however, at moral progress. The scientific method seems unable to grab hold of questions of value, as value is not mutually observable. As a theologian I do not see how science can unilaterally improve our morals, our epistemology, or our self-understanding. These have to do with how we apply science. In some ways these have improved, but in others I fear they have gotten worse. Any concept of improvement must ask the question, "progress toward what?" What constitutes better or worse? And who decides?

Science starts with hope for the future, hope that we will find knowledge and make good use of it. Though that optimism has been tempered by the increasing strangeness of science and a history of abuses, we still see science as a way forward. We think that science will continue to provide real, useful answers. We must be careful to recognize, though, that this progressivism is a fundamental axiom of science – a hope we bring to the process – rather than a product of science – something we can defend with data. We are not perfect observers and we are not perfect in our application of the power science gives us. Worse yet, some aspects of the world – like the properties of fundamental particles – might prove beyond our grasp. This is never an excuse to stop trying, but it is a reason to be suspicious of any claim that science will continue to advance knowledge forever and in all areas. Personally, I favor a cautious optimism. More observation and more discussion can only lead to better models. Knowledge is progressive (as long as we keep good records), but we never know just what the next discovery will unleash or overturn. Scientific knowledge can be progressive precisely because we are willing to challenge it on a regular basis. We must always be willing to question our axioms, and make new observations. We must compare the new data to old ideas and let the observations win.

Learning Doubt

The flip side of scientific optimism is scientific skepticism, the rules we have for challenging our beliefs and the refusal to be complacent. The term skepticism in popular parlance means incredulity or disbelief. It conveys a lack of trust, but generally opens up an avenue for that trust to be mended. I might be skeptical about the claim that a parrot can have a vocabulary with over 500 words, but if I met such a parrot, I would probably change my mind. Philosophical skepticism has a weightier meaning. In this sense, skepticism means that I will never accept a certain type of argument or statement. Plato was skeptical of knowledge gained through the senses. He thought that the changeable character of physical things meant we could never learn anything definite by studying the world in this way. Francis Bacon, on the other hand, was skeptical about knowledge gained without observation. He asserted that that was the only way to learn. Clearly science has adopted a view much closer to Bacon's, but modern scientists do rely on deduction as well. Other than a few extreme skeptics, everyone thinks we can have some knowledge (or at least some confidence, see chapter nineteen) and that reflection and observation will both be useful. What matters is what we count as reliable justification, how careful we are in using it, and whether we are willing to question it later.

Science provides courage to begin the learning process. Because we trust in our ability to know, we feel empowered to investigate. Because we know the best possible knowledge will only be temporary, we have no fear of starting with a very poor hypothesis. The trick will be allowing it to improve.

An Open Mind

Skepticism always entails a negative claim: "such ways of reasoning cannot provide knowledge." Empiricism was originally a blanket claim that nothing could be known that was not known by observation. Most people found that unappealing, however, as it seems to rule out things like math and logic. Immanuel Kant (1724–1804) attempted to reconcile the empiricism of Bacon – emphasizing observation and induction – with the work of Descartes – emphasizing logic and deduction. Kant thought some things could be known *a priori* (prior to observation), while other things could only be asserted *a posteriori* (after observation). Modern scientists embrace both types of reasoning, but often place severe limits on the former.

A clear example in science and religion involves the origin of the universe. Some thinkers suppose that nothing comes from nothing. This statement appears, for them, to be an *a priori* truth. (I challenge readers to defend that claim on the basis of another claim.

It seems simply to be intuitively obvious.) Let us call this camp the *eternalists* because they think the universe must stretch back forever, cause after cause, so that there is never a time when something "miraculously" appears. Everything in the world that we understand was caused by something else.

Other thinkers find this ridiculous. They think that an infinite chain of causes stretching off past the horizon (an "infinite regress") is *a priori* unreasonable. Often an appeal is made to parsimony, which we discussed earlier. What could be less simple than an infinite number of causes? We will call this camp *initialists* because they think the universe must have started somewhere and somewhen. Any other hypothesis would simply be sweeping the question of beginnings under the carpet, as it were. (Again, I challenge initialists to defend their claim on the basis of another claim. Remember that parsimony is an aesthetic commitment to simple answers, not a claim about the universe.)

Here is where the story gets interesting. The idea that the universe started as an incredibly hot, incredibly dense point exploding into reality was first proposed by Georges Lemaître (1894–1966), a Roman Catholic priest and astronomer. The astrophysicist Fred Hoyle (1915–2001) lampooned the idea, calling it the "Big Bang" theory. He meant it as an insult. Hoyle was an atheist and an eternalist. He worried that the Big Bang supported the Christian creationist position. The name stuck, but Hoyle's analysis worked against his preferences; it helped prove that an expanding universe was, in fact, the best theory. Score one for science providing inconvenient facts.

In recent decades, the debate has flipped. Eternalists claim that the Big Bang must have been preceded by another physical universe in which prior events took place. Those events led up to the Big Bang. It is the only way, they believe, to rationally speak about the universe, based on their *a priori* claim that nothing comes from nothing. Meanwhile, initialists like Stephen Hawking (born 1942) claim that time actually curves with space in the first moments after the initial event, and the Big Bang explains why "previous" doesn't really make sense. Time acts as a closed bubble contemporaneous with the current physical universe. For Hawking, this means that God is not necessary; the universe is fully self-contained.

The important thing to note is that *a priori* claims about the eternity of the physical universe appear impervious to science. Observations of cosmic expansion and the Big Bang can be aligned with either position, and both sides have tried to use it as ammunition. It is unclear whether, or even if, these *a priori* beliefs can be updated or shown to be false by the data. Nonetheless, axioms about eternity do influence the hypotheses scientists propose and thoughts about eternity played a role in the history of Big Bang theories.[48] Scientists work with *a priori* assertions on a regular basis, though debate continues about how they should.

As another example, consider the notion of species in biology. From the time of Aristotle (384–322 BCE) until the time of Darwin (1809–1882 CE), species were often considered to be immutable chunks of reality. Just as nothing comes from nothing, so dogs come from dogs and cats from cats. This was an *a priori* statement about the way the world works. Biological classification meant identifying essential traits of each kind so that they could be properly understood. Species might go extinct, but new ones could not be formed. Darwin's notion of speciation – when one species splits into two – allowed for a radical change. Species became part of a continuous string of populations stretching from past to future, with intermediate kinds everywhere. The *a priori* assertion that species are permanent gave way to the observation that species change and divide.

Similarly, we can think of matter and energy. Kant followed the example of countless generations of physicists who saw physical matter as the fundamental stuff of reality. It can neither be created nor destroyed – a type of eternalism, again. He used the permanence of matter as the type example of *a priori* reasoning, when he introduced it in his *Critique of Pure Reason*. We know now that matter can be converted to energy and vice versa. Einstein's famous equation, $E = mc^2$, expressed exactly how much energy matter is worth and reflects the possibility of converting one to the other, as in nuclear reactions.[49] Does that mean Kant was wrong in his *a priori*

---

[48] Phil Dowe, *Galileo, Darwin, and Hawking* (Eerdmans, 2005). pp. 142-154. Robert Russell also deals extensively with this topic in *Cosmology, Evolution, and Resurrection Hope* (Pandora Press, 2006).

[49] The full equation is actually $E^2 = (m_0c^2)^2 + (pc)^2$. It only simplifies to $E = mc^2$ for an object at rest – a lovely example of simple versus complete explanation.

reasoning? Or does it simply mean that our definition of "matter" differs from Einstein's? Philosophers and physicists continue to debate that question (which follows roughly the same lines as our problem with Poe in chapter four). When we talk about matter, what are we doing? We could be talking about an *a priori* ontological category, from whose definition we deduce the permanence of matter. Alternately, we could be talking about an *a posteriori* distinction we make about things we perceive, from which we induce rules that describe the universe. Both avenues are reasonable, but they represent very different kinds of reasoning.

At some level we must admit that *a priori* axioms are necessary for us to interpret observations. We need categories that allow us to frame our experience and talk meaningfully about it. We need words and theories and models, through which we can interpret and communicate our observations. Bacon considered these to be undesirable, but necessary, limitations in our ability to understand the universe.[50] Kuhn considered them just a normal part of science although he thought they began to feel too tight after a while. His notion of paradigm shifts was, in many ways, optimistic. Data that do not fit well with the present paradigm eventually cause so much discomfort that scientists are forced to come up with a new one. The new model will account for more data (progressive), but will also force us to radically shift our ideas about reality (skeptical).

Science has given me a profound distrust for *a priori* claims, but philosophy has convinced me that we cannot live without them. Modern science relies heavily on (objective) realism, symmetry and parsimony, none of which is necessarily "true." The idea of reason itself has little empirical precedent. Rather, it rests on an *a priori* belief that the universe can be understood, that I can understand it (at least partially), and that we can understand it better together than alone. Science needs *a priori* beliefs to operate at all. It can, however, seek to identify them clearly and challenge them whenever possible.

---

[50] In *Novum Organon*, he called them Idols of the Marketplace (biases inherent in communication) and Idols of the Theater (biases inherent in any systematic worldview).

A Critical Approach

Good science requires skepticism at every level. Scientists are trained, at least from graduate school on, to question every aspect of scientific experiments. Are the assumptions valid? Were the right things observed? Was the data analyzed properly? And so on. Sometimes this can look like antagonism, but in principle scientists are equally critical of their own work. The point is to find every possible flaw in a theory and then check to see if you can eliminate it. Scientific critique, including peer review, means that the most informed people are always the most critical of results.

The general public can find this frustrating. Why can't they give us a straight answer? Why do they need so many caveats? Scientists speak carefully because they think carefully. We ask them to be as critical as they possibly can about their results. I worry more when a scientist speaks uncritically.

Alas, scientific criticism has a down side as well. Because we are trained to be so very critical of our results at every level, we can find it difficult to try on the perspectives of other people. Many philosophies and most religions ask for an initial suspension of disbelief. It is not a matter of closing off questions, but of coming along for the ride, experiencing things that cannot be understood or even felt until we are immersed in an environment. Scientists, myself included, often want to know beforehand. We want to intellectually grasp the nature of an event before looking at the details. We want to have controlled environments and parallel experience so that we can critically assess what is happening. I understand that. I feel it deeply. And I know as a religious person that sometimes it just doesn't work. Indeed, I know as a teacher that some ideas are so foreign that they can only be entered into on their own terms.

I have very clear memories of learning Japanese. I chose it partially because it differs so radically from English. There are *phonemes* (symbols for sounds) just like English letters, but there are also *ideograms* (symbols for concepts). Japanese also has tonal variation and a very strong sense of hierarchical formalisms (peculiarities when speaking to people of higher and lower social status). I loved the shift in perspective, but I also found it difficult to think in a new way. How do you think of ideas that have no English equivalent? I wanted to express myself precisely, but the only way forward was to use the best words available and see how they actually came out. At one level, this is nothing more than experimentation. At another it requires letting go and muddling through in a way that offends scientific skepticism. How can you know anything unless you know how you know it – in detail? Scientists can have difficulty with different languages – be they literal languages or just the thought structures of other academic fields – because we want to analyze at every level possible. Sometimes you simply have to experience a new way of thinking.

Scientific skepticism may be responsible for the distrust that many scientists and engineers have regarding metaphysics. (And the same applies to analytic philosophers.) The desire for transparent consistency can make exploring alternate perspectives seem frustrating and counter-productive. One philosopher has called philosophical theology "intellectual tennis without a net."[51] Apparently, he is offended that theologians fail to play by the same rules he does, because that *must* be the only possible set of rules. Perhaps the central point of this book is that different people are actually playing different games. Just because you don't know the rules doesn't mean there aren't any. You may not want to play their game, but it is irrational to assume they are simply playing your game badly. Metaphysics requires stepping out of your personal game for the moment – whether that be science, faith, philosophy, or simply having fun – to appreciate the games other people are playing.

The cost is not negligible. You may actually lose a turn. It would be bad to leave at a critical juncture. A tennis player who forgets about the net in the middle of the French Open will regret it. Similarly, an evolutionary biologist will genuinely lose out if she begins inserting ideas of biological progress into a paper on paleontology. It's good to have rules. It's also good to know that you can choose whether or not to play.

☙ ✦ ❧

I like to think of this strange middle space, embracing both optimism and skepticism, under the heading of "method over doctrine." In a very important way, the rules of the scientific method outweigh any

[51] Daniel Dennett in *Darwin's Dangerous Idea* (Simon and Schuster, 1995); he is quoting Renaldo de Souza.

particular result they produce. Meanwhile, even the rules must bend before both pragmatism and observation. What works? What do you see? Method over doctrine means you are more committed to learning than you are to learning any particular thing. It means you see your premises as part of the process rather than necessary foundations. The myth of progress works for us. It gives us something to reach for and an incentive to remember. It makes science part of a grand endeavor. At the same time, good science asks us to think of it as a provisional axiom for our work. There is no guarantee of progress. Only by constantly questioning ourselves can we hope to move forward. Only by recognizing the insufficiency of today's truth can we find tomorrow's better theory. We believe in progress – and I really think "believe" is the right word here (see chapter twelve) – because it works, not because it is true. The same can be said of parsimony and even symmetry.

All of the axioms of science are open to question. That does not mean we can simply throw them out. They have so much weight behind them, the added value of so many observations (often billions or trillions) that they will not be shaken easily. We are part of a process that involves millions of people and hundreds of years and that means social pressures will affect what we can and cannot take for granted. Still, we never know when the world will change. We have to live with provisional knowledge, because it is precisely this "good but maybe not good enough" attitude that forces science forward.

CHAPTER 10
Beyond the Universe

Many of the things we reason about can be difficult to fit into the scientific model of the universe. As we build our pictures of the world, we must figure out where we want to put them. To use the language I introduced in chapter eight, we ask about things that are clearly part of the cosmos, but less clearly part of the universe. A strict scientific reductionist would be tempted to say they do not exist, or that they exist only in our imaginations. That, however, turns out to be a difficult question in and of itself. Where exactly are our imaginations? If we have not observed something, how do we know what rules it will follow? We feel confident distinguishing between things that might exist but do not (*e.g.*, genetically engineered unicorns) and things that could not exist at all (*e.g.*, a square circle or a perpetual motion machine).[52] At least intuitively, we think we can "know" something about these imaginary objects and that begs the question of how. It clearly cannot be scientific or empirical; they are not mutually observable.

A less strict scientific reductionist might say that they are not physical, but they can be reduced to interactions between physical, scientifically observable things. Philosophers call such entities *epiphenomenal*, "secondary things" that can be fully explained in terms of other substances.[53] I suspect this is a very popular opinion. It rests

---

[52] A school of thought called *actualism* holds that it is meaningless to speak of possible entities. We can only make rational claims about things that actually happen. I find this line of reasoning very compelling from a physicalist standpoint, but also recognize that it differs radically from the way we talk about the universe, both within and without science.

[53] Strictly speaking, for something to be epiphenomenal, it is not only reducible, but causally negligible. People who speak of consciousness as an epiphenomenon of the brain mean that all decisions are made in the brain and conscious choices have no impact on events. Rather, they reflect a byproduct of the decision making process.

on *a priori* axioms about progress: science will explain them using the current rules of reason. We need new experiments, but not substantially new theories. From my perspective, I am willing to hope that science will explain them one day, but I do not expect it will happen within the next two hundred years. Further, if science does come to that point, I think it will be so radically different from the science we now know that it would not make sense to call it science in the modern sense. Two hundred years ago reputable scientists found holistic arguments compelling. Five hundred years ago reputable scientists thought objects in the heavens moved through the action of crystalline spheres. Who knows what scientists will consider rational and irrational two centuries from now?

To be clear, I am not making the argument from ignorance. Many religious apologists have claimed that, since we do not currently understand something scientifically, we never will. I feel this to be an overconfident induction. We have not known in the past, therefore we will not know in the future. We have countless examples of scientists understanding things for the first time, from Hippocrates' medicine in the 4th century BCE to Einstein's physics in the last century. More than this, there are classes of unsolved problems that look very similar to problems that have already been solved. We continue to discover new objects on the periphery of our Solar System – Kuiper Belt Objects or KBOs. One of the largest KBOs, now named Eris, even convinced astronomers to redefine "planet."[54] Pluto apparently travels around the Sun with many other very large objects in the same region of space. Nonetheless, we know how to calculate orbits and are confident that, as we discover new KBOs, we will be able to predict their orbits very accurately. We have confidence that the picture will slowly be filled in using current methods.

We also have many examples of questions for which no clear scientific framework exists; we may not even be asking the right type of question. Scientific definitions of life, consciousness, and will, as well as reconciliations of quantum mechanics, relativity, and gravity represent areas of genuine confusion. To claim that science has

[54] Eris was not the only cause of the change; it was, however, the most dramatic piece of data in an increasingly complex model of the Solar System. It was named after the Greek goddess of discord because of the strife it caused in the astronomical community.

solved problems in the past, therefore science will solve all problems in the future also strikes me as an overconfident induction. Science is ever hopeful – we must continue to try for scientific solutions – but science is also skeptical – we should not always bet on finding them in the near future. In the meantime, we will need other methods, other ontologies and epistemologies, to deal with these questions.

NUMBERS

Some readers will be familiar with our first case – the question of math. Philosophers have long debated whether math is discovered (the way we discover new planets) or created (the way we make new words). Our mathematical systems are based on axioms. They may be the foundational claims of science – like symmetry – or the conventions of language – like the alphabet – but they are profoundly shaped by their philosophical pedigree. One example would be the *Peano axioms* that define how we understand arithmetic. They establish definitions for equality, addition, and multiplication as well as spelling out ideas like (mathematical) symmetry (if $a = b$ then $b = a$), transitivity (if $a = b$ and $b = c$ then $a = c$), associativity ($[a + b] + c = a + [b + c]$), and distribution ($a \times [b + c] = [a \times b] + [a \times c]$).

Some philosophers argue that math, like science, involves discovery. In some way, the numbers and relationships between them exist within the cosmos independent of and prior to our thinking about them. Surely several mathematicians can discover the same "truths" independently of one another. If math is discovery, then it proceeds from observation, but numbers are not perceived by the senses. That means math as discovery requires some other faculty for observation. It is difficult to say where numbers and relationships reside before they are discovered and how we encounter them. Plato thought they existed in the realm of ideas, but science has no such realm. After William of Ockham and Francis Bacon, we are hard pressed to say where exactly we would find numbers such as pi or mathematical relationships such as Fermat's Last Theorem.

Other philosophers claim that math is more like language. We use it to describe the universe in the same way we use words. In this case, math proceeds from axioms and logic without introducing new information. Then we cannot really say that mathematical claims are true. Rather, we have to limit ourselves to saying that they communicate effectively. No one would claim that the word "ontological" was discovered, even though we think it communicates something significant about the way we think. Why should the Pythagorean Theorem be any different?

I subscribe to the second idea – math as language – but I also recognize some very important truths that seem only expressible in math. The irrational number we call pi shows up again and again in our discoveries about the universe, from the relationship between a circle and its diameter to the normal distribution to the wave functions that describe elementary particles. It feels insufficient to say we simply like using this number. Some people argue that it is somehow built into the laws of the universe, and therefore exists in its own right. Starting with the relationship between a circle and its diameter, anyone can calculate pi and everyone calculates it the same way.

If you think numbers are real, rather than just useful, ask yourself what sense you have for perceiving them. Where do they exist within your scheme of the cosmos such that you have access to them? What does it mean to discover a number or an equation and who decides whether it is real or not? Don't forget that people can, and do, lie with mathematical symbols ($2 + 2 = 5$). How can you test it against reality? Are there ways of discovering inconvenient truths through math? Alternatively, if math is a convention, a set of rules we agree upon for communicating, how do you decide which parts of it to accept? Which authorities set the rules for the math "game"?

Choice and Possibility

A second open question for the scientific universe has to do with motion. In chapter eight, I mentioned the unmoved mover. Where does all the energy in the universe come from? The problem arises at a smaller scale as well. When I decide to do something, does that represent some addition of energy or order into the universe that was not there before? My understanding of physics suggests that the universe is causally closed; there is no new contribution from "me." Whatever "I" am is simply the product of physical forces that are already around. On the other hand, my daily activities and a surprising amount of my mental (and chemical) energy are devoted to the "choices" I feel I am making. I believe I have an impact on the world. I believe that my intentions cause things to occur.

It is entirely rational to believe that our choices are made for us by our genetics or neurology or some other mechanism within our bodies. And yet, if I think those mechanisms are all there is to me, I must also admit that they have conditioned some sense of self-consciousness. The idea that we make choices appears to be useful to us biologically – adaptive in the language of evolutionary biology. If we have mechanisms for will (making choices) that feel conscious, shouldn't we take advantage of them? Thus even the most physically reductionist theories counsel us to think of ourselves as conscious actors, whose choices make a difference in the world around us. Any theory of the cosmos will need to take account of those choices in a meaningful way.

How do your ideas of choice fit into your picture of the world? Do you see yourself as part of the picture? Do you have an impact on the universe, and if so how? Do you have complete control over your choices ("free will"), partial control, or none at all?

Along with questions of consciousness come questions of personhood. Do you see yourself as the sole actor in the cosmos, or one among many? Do you influence choices made by other people? Do you have ways of influencing your own behavior in the future?

A related question has to do with possible futures. Much like numbers, possible futures take part in our processes of reasoning. When I choose between A and B, I think of both as real options, futures that may occur. Where do we place those possible futures? Can we discover things about them? What types of induction will we need to make in order to be confident about their properties? What happens to them when they become no-longer-possible? If they are discerned through observation, by what faculty are they observed? Are they mutual observables or just subjective projections (or something in between)? If they are not discerned through observation, how do we generate confidence about them.

Many simplistic answers to these questions work on a theoretical level but present practical difficulties. The challenge is not just to come up with a logically sound picture of the world, but one that accounts for all the observations available and acts as a guide in the future. Possibilities may be abstract, but they are not inconsequential. We reason about possibilities when deciding to bring an umbrella to work, when investing in futures and derivatives, and in strategic planning and risk assessment. The recent world recession was caused by inaccurate assessment of financial possibilities by banks and investment firms. We care deeply about this type of reasoning; it impacts our lives.

VALUE

This brings us to the most difficult, but perhaps most important area where science may not provide a good enough picture of the cosmos. When we set up a model for the universe, how do we orient ourselves with regard to the future? How do we decide which choices to make and which outcomes to prefer? Neuroscience, evolutionary psychology, and behavioral economics are just starting to make predictions about the choices we will make. They cannot, however, tell us whether they are good or bad. There is an important distinction between *explanation* – the reasons a thing came about – and *justification* – the reason for a thing being preferable. Science does the former very well, but in modern times completely avoids the latter, chiefly because ideas of correctness are not mutually observable. If you and I have different ideas about how an event should turn out – perhaps an election or a war – we cannot turn to modern science to resolve the dispute. Our senses do not detect morality; at the very least, they do not detect it consistently across all times, places, and observers.

We are left with the same questions we had for numbers and possibilities. If values are discovered, where do they reside before they are discovered and how do we encounter them? If they are conventions, how do we choose which convention to adopt?

Where do morals and values fit in your picture of the cosmos? As with numbers, we can think of them as real and external to ourselves. Perhaps they exist in some abstract realm of thought, accessible only to our intellect. Plato thought so, as did Augustine of Hippo. On the other hand, maybe morals are just necessary consequences of the physical world. Maybe biology really does determine – or at least demonstrate what is right and wrong. Thomas Aquinas (1225–1274), surprisingly, agrees with many modern atheists on this issue. They think we can reason logically from the state of the physical universe to the truth of moral propositions. *Moral realists* –

who think morals are real, external entities – still have to explain where their real morals fit within the scheme of the cosmos and how we discern them.

Most modern thinkers follow the dichotomy presented by David Hume (1711–1776). He proposed an "is/ought" divide. For Hume, arguments based on the senses were very good at giving us confidence about the state of the universe. Science can tell us what is true. He also thought we needed to reason about what ought to be true. That type of reasoning relied heavily on deduction, logic, and revelation. We rarely question the need to use observation when reasoning about ethics but, following Hume, we think that you need to add something. Ethical premises are necessary for ethically meaningful conclusions. In other words, observation alone can never lead to moral truth. Ethics must go in to our reasoning for ethics to come out.

When thinking about preference – whether framed as morals, ethics, utility, or simply favoring one option over another – ask yourself where the preferences are coming from. The proposition that truth is better than falsehood seems self-evident. An accurate model of the world is better than an inaccurate model. I think almost everyone would agree with this in theory; it appears to be fundamental in science and in general reasoning. And yet, the proposition is not a scientific hypothesis. Nor is it amenable to confirmation (or refutation) through observing the world. How do we justify moral claims?

Trivially, let us assume that all value comes from biological adaptation (traits leading to longer survival and more offspring). Such a contention seems popular among many anti-theists. In this case it is demonstrable that intelligence and knowledge are not uniformly related to success and should not always be valued. Evolutionary arguments suggest that we could have faculties for the truth *most* of the time, but not always. They would have to be faculties for survival, which is *commonly* related to the truth. In a few cases (*e.g.*, confirmation bias, avoiding cognitive dissonance) we would expect ignorance of the truth to be more adaptive.

Do you value human life? If so, why? What warrants that conviction? If we are honest with ourselves we will need to put a flag on assertions like this and find out why we agree with them. In the abstract, it sounds simple. Everyone values human life, don't they? In the concrete, it can be immensely complicated. What constitutes a human life? When does it begin? When does it end? Is it as valuable as other abstract concepts like justice, duty, and compassion?

Several modern authors have suggested that the killing of humans is obviously immoral, but history and sociology do not bear this out. The sixth commandment is often incorrectly translated as "thou shalt not kill." A better translation would be "You shall not murder."[55] The original Hebrew refers to taking human life unjustly, but transparently admits of killing justly in cases of war and capital punishment. Already by the time of the New Testament, we have controversy over what constitutes justice in this case. In Matthew 5:21-26, Jesus not only limits the cases of killing justly, but extends the rule to prohibit any action taken in anger. Even in the most conservative read on Christian scriptural ethics, we can see debate on what constitutes murder. War, capital punishment, and euthanasia all provide difficult visceral, contemporary, questions about how we orient ourselves with regard to value. We need to reason about these issues and we need rules for reason that allow us to do so transparently. As it turns out, very few people believe killing is always immoral, regardless of the context.

Answers to this type of question will rely on understanding what is meant by "value," "human," and "life." Understanding why you disagree with others will rely on even deeper understanding, specifically knowing how you and others construct your picture of the cosmos and the place of humans in it.

Questions of value tend to be the most challenging matters in epistemology precisely because they impact our actions. Our values matter. And yet, we disagree about what makes for good ethical reasoning. Religions can provide communities where the guidelines for moral arguments are clear, allowing the group can reach common conclusions. Religion *per se* is not necessary for morality, but some form of moral reasoning is: one that deals with non-mutual-observables. Constructing frameworks for moral reasoning is one of the core functions of religion – frameworks for creating, maintaining, and changing our value structures.

---

[55] They are both Exodus 20:13. The first is from the King James Version of the Bible; the second is from the New Revised Standard Version.

ଓ ✦ ଓ

Each of us has a model of the cosmos inside our heads. That model contains ideas about substance and causation as well as ideas about mathematics, choices, and values. Some models will be more consistent than others, some more beautiful, some more accurate. They need not be comprehensive or even useful. They will, however, affect the way we behave. No doubt there will be numerous bits of trivia included as well, things we remember but have no particular use for. Those bits can be interesting too, but I have found that we change those pieces relatively easily. It can be hard to get a song out of your head, but it is infinitely harder to get an ontology out of your head, at least while you are using it to navigate the world. We lean on our intuitions about the way the world works. We depend upon our basic assumptions about what is and is not worth thinking about, talking about, doing something about. We use our metaphysics every day in sorting out our relationships and planning our activities. If you tell me you don't have a metaphysics, I won't believe you. You must. Even the act of believing or disbelieving what you are reading right now – that requires having some thoughts about what is right and wrong about your notion of the universe.

I don't want to lay down one particular view of the world and say, "you must have this view." I want to give you the tools you need to see the view you have already. Then I hope to show you that you have options. Science teaches us to acknowledge inconvenient facts about the universe. What do you use to find inconvenient facts about thought, choice, and preference? What tools encourage us to be rational about the cosmos? What criteria can we use to decide whether the scientific picture of the universe captures everything, or even just everything we need to deal with?

In this chapter, I have covered just three things that are very difficult to fit in a scientific picture. Mathematical ideas, choices, and values all present serious problems when we try to reduce them to particles and forces or learn about them through mutual observables. Throwing away the scientific picture of the universe seems like a lousy option; science does too much for us. Therefore, we will have to think carefully about how the scientific picture of the universe relates to the bigger picture we make, our concept of the cosmos. How do we go about deciding what can and cannot be included –

what should and should not be included – in a given picture? Conversely, we will want to ask how much we are willing to allow *a priori* assertions and individual (non-mutual) observables to inform our bigger picture. Religion can help with that process.

RELIGION

CHAPTER 11
What is Religion?

Ideas, choices, and values present us with a definite problem. How do we incorporate them into our picture of the universe? How do we frame our understanding, create new models, and test those models, when science does not provide guidance? I want to be very clear on this. Science works so well precisely because it has rules for what we can and cannot do with it. Science works because it has a transparent, effective epistemology. That epistemology – at least for the present – means that it cannot give us guidance on issues unless we can relate them to mutual observables, hypotheses, and iteration. What, then, are we to do about other issues when making decisions in daily life?

Any claim that we are reasonable in our thoughts and behaviors will require a critical assessment of how we deal with these issues. Mutual observables may not be available when thinking about ideas, actors, and values, but other tools of reasoning are. We must use them to the best of our ability, applying the same hope and skepticism applied in science. How do we know what we know? How confident are we, and how confident can we become? Every day I make choices about how I interact with the world. I assess good and bad outcomes and try to bring them about. Such assessment requires me to ask about the values I currently have, but also what values I want to have. It requires making predictions about other people, their values, and how I impact them. It requires critical thinking about the role my own thoughts play in shaping the lives and thoughts of others. Chief among these thoughts will be the axioms with which we started the discussion. Once again, these things may be reducible in principle; they are not reducible in practice. Thoughts and values may simply be a product of our physical, biological selves, but we have yet to understand exactly how. In the meantime, we must reason about them and, if we are rational, must use means other than science. Religions have traditionally been workshops for this type of reason.

Coming to Terms with Religion

As complicated and diverse as science is – in method and practice and associated philosophies – religion can be even harder to pin down. We face a diverse array of complex systems, related to politics, practices, and philosophies as old as history itself. No matter what part of the world you find yourself in, your image of the world will be partially shaped by the thoughts, actions, and communities of people who use this label. No matter what you believe, you will be acting for or reacting against ideas that arose in religious settings. That makes the matter of definitions hard; we all have something at stake.

First and foremost, it will be important to deal with concrete examples of "religion" in the world. I start with the four labels that identify the vast majority of humans. I list them in the order of popularity worldwide according to 2010 estimates: Christianity (33.4%), Islam (22.7%), Hinduism (13.8%), and Buddhism (6.8%). No other category of "religion" can claim more than half a percentage of the world population, though 2% are identified as atheist and 9.7% as non-religious.[56] Even looking at this short list, we find that some common assumptions about "religion" as a category do not apply to all members of the group.

Americans will be most familiar with three religions that can be called Western elective monotheisms. Judaism (0.22%), Christianity, and Islam all invoke a single "theistic" god who has a personality – relating to and interested in creation. This God has elected a particular people as chosen representatives on Earth. Belief in this God includes claims about reality but also about our relationships: to God, the chosen community, and the world. More than half the people alive today consider themselves part of one of these traditions. Two more religions, Hinduism and Buddhism, account for an additional fifth of the world. These "traditions" do not advocate for a particular deity, but by and large hold a picture of the cosmos in which individual gods exist, but may or may not be important to believers. They often focus on practices as their core element rather than particular beliefs or relationships. Looking through the lens of elective monotheism, Westerners may be tempted

[56] Percentages come from the CIA World Factbook. Data collection is from a number of sources and "non-religious" appears to incorporate both agnostic and unaffiliated individuals.

to shoehorn Eastern religion into boxes based on their own experiences, expecting their concepts of faith, community, authority, and even truth to align with more familiar models. This risks dramatically misinterpreting them. Hindu and Buddhist concepts of gods do not align with the personal Creator of the Bible, the unmoved mover of Aristotle, or even the spirits of the Renaissance. Their communities rarely consider themselves elect or exclusively correct. Their intellectual tradition has been shaped by metaphysical questions different from the ones that drove European theology and its (post-) Enlightenment heirs.

The need to account for real world religions rules out some popular definitions. One – religion as belief in God or gods – fails when applied to traditions like Buddhism and Taoism. Even Shinto and Animism will require us to stretch our concept of gods beyond the point where it communicates meaningfully. Another popular definition invokes the supernatural, saying that religion deals with things beyond nature. I think this falls down on a number of levels, but primarily I dislike it because it presumes an ontological distinction between nature and non-nature, a distinction that Buddhists (and some Christians) do not make. We cannot neglect one or more of the top four examples and hope to come to any common understanding.

Communication about religion requires us to be sensitive to how people use the terms they use. It is not enough to assume that my definition of religion is the same as yours. We may have radically different definitions of religion, Christianity or any other of the categories I have listed above.[57] You may decide to use the words differently, but I hope to be clear so that you will understand me when I use them.

The closest I have come to a working definition comes from William James (1842-1910): "Religion is the belief that there is an unseen order, and that our supreme good lies in harmoniously adjusting ourselves thereto."[58] This definition conveys some concept of cosmos – an unseen and comprehensive order – as well as value formation – how we determine what to desire. It even includes some

[57] For example, some claim that Mormons are Christians because they believe in Jesus Christ. Others claim that they are not, because they have additional scriptures and do not have the same concept of the Trinity.

[58] William James, *The Varieties of Religious Experience* (Kessinger, 2004), p. 39

sense of action – we adjust ourselves to conform to the order. In the West, that word "belief" may get us into some trouble, as it still sounds as though religion were something we did solely with our brains. James may have intended this heavy mindedness, but I would vote for his definition with a broader view of belief. As we will see in a few chapters, my concept of belief involves action. But I'm getting ahead of myself. For now, let us say that religion has to do with propositions about order and value, how we generate them, and how we react and respond to them. Ontology and epistemology fall out of religion, almost by necessity. This is not to say that one cannot have those two without religion, just that to have a religion is to have those two. Religion brings metaphysics with it, and not just metaphysics, but metaphysics applied to life.

CREATING COSMOS

Religions make worldviews – models of the cosmos. That is one of their primary activities. These models help us navigate in the world. They set up expectations about where we stand in relation to people and ideas. They also tell us how our choices will change those relationships. As with science, the models can be useful without being perfectly accurate. Sometimes they can help us get what we want even when we are blind to or confused about how and why they work. Some work better than others. The hard question of how to judge success comes wrapped up in the process. Is our primary goal being correct, getting what we want, communicating, or something else entirely? Every religion has a worldview, but not every worldview is inherently religious.

The structure of the cosmos presented by each model places individuals in relation to other real things. At a more fundamental level, worldviews always contain an ontology that delineates real things from unreal things. Some branches of Christianity, for example, set up humans as more real than other things in a fundamental sense. According to Aquinas, humans participate in the spiritual creation while other animals do not. According to some Reform theologians, all of nature was corrupted in the Fall and only humans have the opportunity to return to a state of grace. In both systems our primary obligations will be to God and other humans. In the end times, all other physical things will pass away and our obligations to them only apply when they serve our relationship with God and humans. Alternatively, one could look at Mahayana Buddhism, which calls into question the reality of all things, but creates a scale of sentience from plants to gods. Humans may be more aware, but we have obligations to all sentient beings.

Starting with ontology, our model of the world details relationships. In Christianity and Islam, humans have a primary obligation to God as created to Creator. This fundamental dichotomy sets up expectations for how we should behave – generally with worship, love, and obedience. Buddhism and Hinduism also propose fundamental relationships, though they generally have more to do with the illusory nature of independent existence, choice, and persistence. Some philosophers have claimed that without religion there can be no morality. It might be more reasonable in our context to say that without ontology and worldview there can be no morality. Morality rests on some connection between actions and consequences, be they physical, mental, spiritual, or other. It depends on a model of the world in which such interactions take place. The evaluative quality of our moral judgments rests on premises about the players involved and their correct relationship to one another. Even before we ask questions of value, we need some idea of who has preferences, who can act on those preferences, and how much freedom they have to do so.

Multiple Perspectives?

It is possible, indeed common, to hold more than one worldview. For example, you may think you have no control over your environment and, simultaneously, fear that you have made the wrong choice. Such a situation demonstrates an emotional model of the cosmos with agency – the ability to act or choose – and a conscious model of the cosmos without it.

Even with well-understood physical forces, we can find ourselves divided between two worldviews. I love tackling a high ropes course, moving around obstacles forty feet off the ground supported by a harness and rope. I know I cannot fall; I fear that I will; and the fear can shape my actions. Some thinkers will only credit the conscious, intellectual model as a worldview, because it can be rational and systematic. The emotional model of the world is something less, something to be avoided. Setting aside the value judgment in that line of thought, I simply want to assert that both models exist. I will call both "worldviews" for the sake of highlighting that both are informed by our experience and both affect our behavior.

Some people have multiple rational, systematic worldviews. Some doctors have studied both traditional "Chinese medicine" – focusing on the effects of energy flowing through the body – and modern "Western medicine" – focusing on chemistry, tissues, and physical systems. It is irrelevant to my point whether one is more correct than the other. The same person can recognize and attempt to heal through both systems. And, of course, one person may have different irrational models of the universe as well. They may feel fully empowered in making choices at home, but literally powerless at work – without ever reflecting on either situation.

Science and Worldview

In practice, the scientific method generates a provisional worldview, one in which only the proper objects of science exist. I say "provisional" because I have found that many people place science within a broader context. For them, it comes as part of a larger picture, which incorporates values, etc.

Scientists practice *methodological* physicalism. They agree, in certain contexts, to only talk about models of the world reducible to matter and energy. This presents us with three interesting questions. First, does the scientific worldview exclude all other perspectives? Clearly it does not. Many people do science well while holding on to religious belief or some other additional picture of the world. Some of the most influential scientists have been committed to beliefs beyond the range of their science – Copernicus, Galileo, and Newton were all ardent in their Christianity, as were Boyle and Mendel.

Second, does a scientific worldview necessarily trump any other worldview, in practice or even in theory? That question causes more difficulty. Of course you can have two pictures of the world, but one of them has to be really real, doesn't it? One of them has to be your primary worldview. The ideal of forming a single, perfectly consistent, perfectly accurate model of the universe appeals to me, but I recognize that it may not be possible. Evolutionary, genetic, and social constraints mean that I may not be able to achieve full consistency. Practical concerns mean that success in different areas will call for different ways of modeling my actions in them. And, of course, others do not share my preference for consistency or my definition of success. It would be a mistake to identify any one person, much less any one religion with exactly one optimal model. It may be an ideal, but we do not know how close it will be approached in each case without a great deal more information. Many people operate with several worldviews. The extent to which they are integrated, or even interact, will rest on how much the individual values coherence and consistency. I value integration; so I work to find it. Even so, I have not succeeded…fully…yet. Nor can I think of anyone, except a few religious ascetics, who has. We have to deal with too many complex situations.

Finally, how well does the scientific worldview fit with other worldviews, particularly those provided by the major religions? At the very least, science provides both understanding of our environment and power to act. For Christians and Muslims, science provides insights into the world and, therefore, into the God who created it. For Hindus and Buddhists, it helps identify the consequences of our actions. The scientific worldview gives us a counterpoint to other worldviews; it allows us to challenge our ontological axioms, to see if they fit with our core values. Do our ideas about reality help us accomplish the tasks that matter? Do our choices produce the outcomes we expect and hope for?

Reason should allow us to differentiate between a personal worldview, and those given to us by our religious community, or by the broader society. All of us come with a built in worldview (at least one). Our physical and social circumstances give us a general picture of who we are and how we fit into the grand scheme of things. Our worldview tells us what we can and cannot do, what we should and should not do, and what we will and will not do. We must reflect on how our default picture matches up with the pictures presented to us by others.

Modern science gave humanity a great gift by challenging some of the dominant religiously generated worldviews. It helped us see that Earth was not the center of the universe, that humans were related to other animals, and that we don't always behave in accord with our conscious model of the world. Each of these was a wonderful discovery and, in my opinion, terribly important morally. Science gave us these benefits primarily because it provided a good contrast, not because it is inherently right. Don't get me wrong; any perspective has to be mostly right to make the contrast worthwhile. Still, we need multiple clear perspectives if we want to make a three dimensional image. One perspective will never give us all the information we need. Until such a time as we have perfect knowledge – something science and the major religions place in the distant future – we will benefit from having multiple worldviews, as long as each of them provides useful insights.

Eliminating all of our religious worldviews would not provide us with the clearest picture of reality yet. It would virtually blind us. The scientific worldview fails to give us even the most basic models of human interaction, value formation, and abstract reasoning. When taken dogmatically (without question) and exclusively (without peer), it becomes just as tyrannical as the religious doctrines it has helped to displace – e.g., the belief that the Sun travels around the Earth. Only with multiple avenues of knowledge can we hope to continue learning. It's not just about truth. It's about a fundamental willingness to accept you might be wrong. Some pictures are better than others, but no one picture is perfect.

Natural and Supernatural

While on the topic of creating worldviews, I would like to say a word about the concept of "naturalism." Most people I interact with are interested in the specific concept of physicalism, which I have spelled out above. Hopefully chapters eight and ten have convinced you that this philosophy can be very useful methodologically in the context of science, but fails as a complete ontology. This divide has inspired some philosophers to propose naturalism in a broader way, which is not limited to the physical but nonetheless rules out all "supernatural entities" including ghosts and gods.[59]

It is unclear to me exactly what the term natural, in this sense, is intended to convey. Unfortunately there is a great deal of rhetoric about the natural and supernatural in religion and science discussions. To say religion deals with the supernatural almost always presupposes

[59] Noteably, Thomas Nagel in *Mind and Cosmos* (Oxford; 2012).

physicalism – in which case to say "religion" is to say "fiction" – or presupposes some notion of transcendent reality – in which case we have already subscribed to a particular Western ontology. In either case, we find that the definition has short-circuited the very discussion we wanted to have: what is religion and how does it affect our views about the world? Using the concept of naturalism outside the context of physicalism muddies the waters and stops communication. If the idea is important to you, it is worth thinking carefully about what work it is doing in an argument and whether speakers and listeners share a common definition.

ORIENTATION

The word "orientation" has a wonderful history. It comes from the tradition of building churches so that the altar is on the side closest to Jerusalem. Christians are rarely so careful in the 21st century, though we still refer to the wall closest to the altar as the "East" side of the church. And we still refer to direction-finding as orientation.[60]

Value orientation refers to the process of establishing preferential directions within your picture of the cosmos. Those directions can be physical (as in the case of "toward Jerusalem"), categorical (as in choosing life over death), or more abstract (as in preferring accurate models of the universe). Any time you prefer one state over another or one outcome over another, you have made a value judgment.

Some people believe that values exist independent of valuers. They treat values, like physical laws, as external, objective, mutual observables. If this is the case, we will need to consider carefully how we come to have knowledge of values. Other people believe that values are subjective and contextual. Each individual has preferences, which arise from their own conditions and choices.

However you think about preferences, everyone agrees that we have them, that societies influence them, and that they shape our

[60] For most of Christian history, most believers were in Europe and North Africa; Jerusalem was to the East. Chinese churches would, confusingly "orient" to the West. Muslims and Jews have similar customs. Mosques and other Muslim worship spaces clearly mark the *qibla*, the direction of Mecca. Jewish synagogues are built so that the congregation is facing Jerusalem when they face the Torah Ark, the cabinet in which scriptures are kept.

behavior. Thus at any time in your life you will find that you have default values, the preferences you use in making choices unless and until you work to change them. Most of us have some dissatisfaction with the choices we make and, thus, are invested in having different preferences than we do. We want to reorient ourselves with regard to values, often trying to align our implicit emotional model with our explicit rational model.

As with reasoning and knowledge, we will find that we have axiomatic preferences as well as preferences which have been derived with appeals to logic, induction, deduction, observation, and authority. In some cases, there will also be an appeal to revelation. We may be rational or irrational in our approach, but we must remember two key points. First, preferences for rationality, consistency, and truth are, in themselves, values. No appeal can be made to reason without at the same time asking that reason itself be preferred over some alternative. Second, the preference component, the "ought" is not a mutual observable and cannot be derived through observation and logic alone. Value conclusions require value premises. The major religions provide conscious, conscientious means for generating premises – for orienting and reorienting ourselves. Whether you subscribe to a particular religion or not, I believe it is useful to identify what your value premises are and where they come from.

Boundary Formation

Model formation need not be a communal process. We can conceive of a person growing up on a desert island and coming to conclusions about the world. Still, in daily life, social influences are both expected and desired. How can we not be influenced by the categories our parents used in explaining the world? How can we not react to the models we are presented? Whether we accept or reject them, it can be very hard to shake their hold on us. Science benefits from multiple observers, and so do most forms of worldview construction. They do not benefit because more people are automatically more correct, but because more people can explore a greater variety of options. The final result, the rational result, will only be better if multiple critical thinkers can assess and evaluate all of these options.

Only communal reasoning can produce mutually understood models, which is both a blessing and a curse. The narrowing of thought allows for clarity and precision – as with rigorous definitions and peer-reviewed conclusions – but it also allows for common blind spots – a situation we have come to call *groupthink*. Groupthink occurs when groups of people try to reach a common conclusion; forces (social and individual, conscious and unconscious) stop us from considering options outside common norms. The constraints of common thought can be mild an unintentional. For example, a false dichotomy can be set by language, as with the distinction between matter and energy that stopped physicists from even considering them as the same thing for centuries. Common constraints can also be serious and intentional. Under party rule in the Soviet Union, biology research was suppressed unless it matched the orthodoxy of one party biologist (Lysenko), who resisted Darwinian theories of evolution.

Usually, science makes the best of communal reasoning. It involves asking and answering questions with the brainpower of millions of people across hundreds of years. It attempts to use diverse thought and experience to give us as many options as possible. It attempts to use peer review and skepticism to critique the most cherished of theories. The epistemological benefits come not from immunity to challenge, but from continual questioning.

In science and other forms of communal reasoning, we require common boundaries to be set. Authorities establish which words can be used in which ways. Rules and policies set up common ontologies, epistemologies, values, and communication styles that regulate the group endeavor. And this creates a problem: what do we do with those who do not follow the authorities and regulations? Do we say that they are wrong – that they cannot achieve truth outside the boundaries? Do we say that communication between them and the in-crowd is impossible? All communities must negotiate those questions carefully, keeping the process open but also keeping the process rigorous. Communities form when everyone plays the same game. That requires rules and, often, people to make and enforce the rules.

As rational individuals each of us has to negotiate our relationship with the rational community. To what extent do we allow the boundaries of our group to be personal boundaries? Living in multiple rational communities, I often question myself about which of my methods I share with which of my colleagues. When is a scientific argument valid for a theological audience? When is a theological argument valid for a scientific audience? How do the models I share with each group relate to my overall model of the cosmos?

One of the benefits of fundamentalisms, if benefit is the right word, is that they simplify this process. They eliminate the need to negotiate between different worldviews and different communities by making one of them all-important. They dictate one community and one standard as authoritative. The answers are clear and often compelling. They do not, however, promote communication with those outside the community, making it hard to get internal truth out or external truth in.

On the other end of the spectrum, relativisms also simplify the process. By making all perspectives valid, they encourage openness. By denying absolute boundaries and norms, they allow flexibility in how you answer the boundary questions. Unfortunately, they also stop us from being accountable to one another. They rob us of the ability to meaningfully critique one another's reasoning, because we lack common definitions and standards.

We all seek a middle ground, where some things are standard and other things are left open to individual preference (or individual conscience). The challenge comes from figuring out together which is which. Different communities will have different boundaries, both for membership and for reason.

What communities do you belong to? Do you know the costs and rewards of membership? Do you know the rules for belonging and reasoning within the community?

Open Space

Known and unknown exist in balance. Different worldviews call for more or less know-ability in the world; different epistemologies make the world more and less comprehensible; and different value systems set different goals for how much should be known. Chapters eight and nine explored those commitments within science. Where do religions fall on these questions? Different religions believe differently. Just as science balances progressivism and skepticism, so the major religions each set their own agendas for the known and unknown. They make assertions about what can be said, but they also address how we deal with the unsaid and, perhaps, the unsayable.

Scientists feel extreme discomfort about unknown things. They want them to become known. I share that desire and recognize the power it has to inspire me to question and learn. I also recognize that the limits of my time, resources, and intelligence – not to mention the peculiarity of the universe – establish real boundaries to my knowledge. There are things I do not, will not, and even cannot know. The future is chief among them, as are the internal thoughts and experiences of the people around me. How am I to deal with this uncertainty? The major religions all provide tools for dealing with the unknown. They create spaces in which we can practice coming to grips with it. They intentionally place us in situations where decisions must be made without intellectual preparation. Thus, they train us to deal with conversion and trauma by first practicing on smaller ambiguities and more comfortable shocks.

Religions offer us open spaces where the central model breaks. They teach us about boundaries, how they are formed and what is on the other side. Some will be presented as fearful, dangers to be avoided. Every group has incentives to stay inside. Movement in is easier than movement out and conversion toward will seem more appealing than conversion away. Not all change is bad, though. Christianity presents repentance (*metanoia* – changing your mindset) as a central act and practical goal. Buddhism casts all of existence in the light of letting go unhealthy attachments (and aversions). All the major religions have rituals and philosophies constructed to open up mental space. They also have ways of opening space for change in our practices and communities. It is impossible to set boundaries without some understanding of how you make them, how you cross them, and even how you move them.

Think about the open spaces within your communities. Where is skepticism encouraged and when is progress sought? What tools are provided for navigating at the edge? What tools have you been given for dealing with major changes? With whom can you talk about these issues and who provides the definitive answers?

☙ ✦ ❧

This chapter set forth some of the common attributes of religions – at least major religions. They are active in the process of worldview construction, not just as an intellectual or theoretical exercise, but as a group of people dynamically working in the world. That worldview is communally set, understood, and (for good and ill) changed by the thoughts, actions, and policies of people living and working together. The process involves making models of the cosmos, orienting people with regard to value, establishing boundaries, and creating open spaces for change.

I have addressed all of these areas in a very abstract way, mostly to present you with my best attempt to summarize the commonalities of religion without committing to any one of them. Religion turns out to be a somewhat slippery concept. Nonetheless, I think all religions have this common function – coming to a common understanding of the world we find ourselves in, one that attempts to be both functional and comprehensive. Such a perspective, including issues of thought, value, and agency cannot fail to move us to act, aligning our deeds with our preferences in light of our model.

We have returned to James' definition: "the belief that there is an unseen order, and that our supreme good lies in harmoniously adjusting ourselves thereto." This time, however, we have a more explicit understanding of the constraints of communication, reason, and history that must color the endeavor. In the next few chapters, we turn to the particular models of thought, value, and agency that I use based on my background as a Christian in the Anglican tradition – with a little help from friends in many other traditions.

CHAPTER 12
What It Means to Believe

Science represents one specific philosophy. Modern science represents a particular methodology and an associated worldview roughly 200 years old. That worldview comes from the work and worldviews of thousands of people over thousands of years; it does not stand alone. And so, if I am to compare the way people reason in science to the way people reason in religion, I must be equally specific. My perspective comes from modern Anglican Christianity. Just as science rests on a firm foundation of observations dating back to Aristotle and beyond, just as modern science draws on nominalism and empiricism and reductionism, so too, modern Anglicanism draws on hundreds of years of reflection, reason, and action in the Christian tradition, the insights and experiences of Christians and Jews going back three to four thousand years. Science and Christianity both update their understanding of those basic insights in light of new knowledge, though they often do so in different ways.

I know this idea will face some criticism, both from Christian readers and from anti-Christian readers. Is not religion about timeless truths, or at least unquestionable doctrines? I believe that question presents us with a false dichotomy between absolute certainty and uninformed opinion. Most epistemology, in Christianity as well as science, lives in the realm between, where we are less than certain, but more than clueless. How do we deal with intermediate levels of confidence and conviction, when we have evidence but not certainty? How do we deal with basic principles, like symmetry, which are both necessary to begin the discussion and reinforced by our experience?

DOGMA

Dogma is a technical term. It refers to propositions held true without question, generally in the context of an authority that will punish you if you do. Many institutions, past and present, hold to dogma. It has something to do with the nature of community and authority that groups will try to enforce certain worldviews. We can see it clearly in the late Medieval Inquisition, when the Pope and Christian monarchs attempted to quash dissent through torture, execution, and fear. We can see the exact same phenomenon in the Communist purges of Stalin and Mao. The consequences need not be so stark, of course. Modern communities often suppress questions in subtler ways, including taboos and emotional manipulation.

Sometimes it can be hard to see the lines between asserting unassailable truth (e.g., the sky is blue), setting social norms (e.g., the word dogma means…), and punishing dissent (e.g., refusing to hire someone who uses the word "dogma" in the wrong way). That is a job for critical thought and an aspiration of reason. I suspect you will agree with me that burning heretics is unacceptable. It remains unclear to me, though, whether we can assert this as objectively true, or only as an important social norm. I know how I think about it, but I don't know about you, and I have many friends who see it both ways. Both objective and subjective concepts of morality present problems. Questions of truth, norms, and social punishment all fall squarely within the realm of value – one of the biggest challenges for thinking about reasoning.

I use the word dogma, following common usage and the Oxford dictionaries, to mean something believed without question. Dogma has been popular in Christian communities, indeed in religious communities in general. It creates a common vocabulary and constrains the worldviews of members in a way that reinforces the conviction they hold in their beliefs. Nonetheless, religion as I have described it does not require dogma. Academics in any religious group will usually admit that the dogmatic core of their faith is quite small. Many beliefs will be held strongly, but very few will be held without any commentary or question. Less academic believers and local leaders may suggest, or even claim contrary to authority, a broader role for dogma.

Anglican Christianity and Tibetan Buddhism both (at least in principle) reject any type of dogma. All beliefs should be open to question and reassessment. Most practitioners would say there comes a point when explicitly denying something (for example the divinity of Jesus or the possibility of Enlightenment) represents so great a step as to put you outside of the tradition. This does not, however, mean that you cannot ask the question, that you cannot come to the conclusion without believing a falsehood, or that you will be required to leave the community in either case. Scientists would probably be comfortable making the same kind of statement. If you no longer believe that the universe is comprehensible through observation and experiment, chances are good that science is not the right career for you. A belief is only dogmatic when it represents unquestioned and unquestionable commitment to a particular proposition. No type of reasoning could ever convince you that the dogma was incorrect, because dogma is epistemologically sealed away.

Scientists have been understandably allergic to dogma; it gets in the way of comparing observations to hypotheses. Any agreement of science and a particular religious tradition will need to account for this. If you do hold dogmas, it will be important to ask why and how. It will be important to ask just what you believe dogmatically and what you simply hold with great conviction. Is science or anything else capable of changing the way you think? If you do not (consciously) hold dogmas, it's worth taking a close look at your axioms. Regardless of whether they are theoretically questionable, have you ever seriously questioned them? Sometimes the most dangerous beliefs are never questioned because they are invisible.

Knowledge and Belief

In recent years, I have been particularly impressed by the variety of uses to which we put the word "belief." It seems to be both a rallying cry for the pro-religious and a vicious insult for the anti-religious in our society. When I looked it up, I discovered two radically different senses, both of which have some stamp of authority. The *Compact Oxford English Dictionary* tells us that belief is "a feeling that something exists or is true, especially one without proof," while Merriam-Webster claims it is a "conviction of the truth of some statement or the reality of some being or phenomenon especially when based on examination of the evidence." I have pretty high respect for both of these dictionaries and find myself baffled that belief can simultaneously be thought "without proof" and "based on evidence." The ambivalence about belief appears to be pervasive.

With an eye on clearing up some of the troubles between scientific and religious worldviews, I would like to propose a new sense for belief and knowledge, one that I think remains true to the common definitions while providing insight into the problem. Let us say that a statement reflects some proposition about reality. A thing exists, or does not. A claim is true, or is not. We want to cover a wide variety of claims without requiring them to be verbalized. Propositions – correct and incorrect, factual and fictional, rational and irrational – all apply. Any thing you can think qualifies as a statement. I want to separate the process of what goes into the statement (making it and defending it) from what proceeds from the statement, notably action. In this sense, knowledge reflects not just a statement, but a statement for which I have some evidence. Some line of reasoning leads me to suppose the statement accurately reflects the state of the world. Belief, on the other hand, reflects a statement that changes behavior, what I like to call conviction with consequences. Beliefs change the way we interact with the world.

Using knowledge and belief in this sense, it should be clear that a single statement can represent both knowledge and belief. For instance I *know* that gravity operates because I learned about it in school and can give you equations for how it works. I also know that gravity operates on the basis of daily experience; when I let go of the book, it drops. I also *believe* that gravity operates. This can be demonstrated by my caution around the edge of the cliff and my casual dropping of keys on the hall table. Knowledge represents input, belief output; the statement in the middle stays the same.

We can also see that sometimes knowledge and belief don't go together. I know, for instance, that the Earth rotates on its axis and revolves around the sun. On the basis of authority, I know the statement to be true. I have observed the procession of very large pendulums, so I can say I know it on the basis of observation as well. On a day-to-day basis, I believe that the Earth stays in place. I say (and probably think unconsciously) that the Sun rises over the eastern horizon and sets in the West. My knowledge and belief don't match up and, as long as I'm not launching a spacecraft, this disconnect works for me. As another example, I could say that I believe in the efficacy of healing prayer. While I have almost no evidence to suppose that it works, nonetheless, I pray for healing on a regular basis. The belief affects my behavior.

Savvy readers will point out that both these cases include elements of knowledge and belief. In the first case, I really do believe that the Earth travels around the Sun. It shapes the way that I think about the universe and the trust I put in astronomers and physicists. In the second case, I have reasons to know that healing prayer works; I take it on the authority of people I know, both religious authorities and personal friends. So we haven't really separated out the two things. Precisely. What we have done is identified two elements of the same phenomena, the reasoning that goes into statements and the consequences that proceed from them. The value of this approach comes from what it allows us to do.

Frequently, scientists arguing for evolution will load us up with the facts about natural selection and the origin of species. They give examples from nature and show elegant mathematical models. Meanwhile, creationists arguing against evolution (with the exception of creation scientists) point out that evolution makes people think they are no different from animals. They complain that evolution leads to excessive competition and immorality. Regardless of how I feel about all of these statements, I know that the first argument deals with knowledge, while the second deals with belief. No matter how well the scientists argue, no amount of knowledge will assuage fears about human morality based on a belief in evolution. No matter how well the creationists argue, no amount of ethical worry will affect the scientific model that explains the diversity of life on Earth. These charges take place on completely different battlegrounds, but nobody recognizes it because everyone uses the same words and deals with the same statement. I'm perfectly willing to argue the knowledge question (the evolutionists have a slam-dunk argument here) or the moral question (somewhat murkier), but I've tried to stop using one question to battle the other. That engagement cannot be won.

Lest you mistake me, I am not claiming that knowledge is a thing of science and belief a creature of religion. Consider climate change. Purely secular arguments can be made both for the weight of evidence and for the consequences of disbelief. Purely secular decision makers might know the evidence but find that their own actions are wholly motivated by other factors, such as short term economic or employment concerns. No religion need be involved for knowledge and belief to diverge. On the other hand, most Christians can claim strong evidence for the importance and efficacy of forgiveness, from scripture, tradition, and authority. And yet few of us are able to live up to the standard we confess ideal. Religious beliefs need not conform to religious evidence.

One of my central goals for this book is to explore religious rationality. Here I simply wish to emphasize the distinction between the evidence for thinking things true and the consequences of thinking them true. How you relate the two is important, whatever brand of religion or irreligion you subscribe to. The question of how scientific and religious models of nature agree or disagree relies heavily on matters of knowledge and belief. The generation of knowledge rests close to the heart of scientific epistemology. The scientific method provides excellent, useful, and often irrefutable knowledge. As a scientist and as a Christian I will not give that up. The metaphysical aspect of religion means that religious people have an important stake in how knowledge is formed. The argument needs to take place on the battleground of epistemology between those who believe that science is one of the most important ways of learning (and here the author raises his hand), and those who believe that scientific knowledge should be subordinated to knowledge obtained through the interpretation of scripture.

If that epistemological question were the only one on the table, this might be a much easier discussion. Once we had determined the better epistemology, we could rationally follow it to the end. The truth would fall out of our reasoning like sausage out of a grinder. Alas, this is not the case. Creationists have a strong moral case. Evolution, within a suite of modern ideologies associated with science, has produced some ugly worldviews and dangerous moralities. It seriously challenges our ability to think of humans as uniquely created in the image and likeness of God. It interferes with centuries of theology and, as a pragmatic theologian, that concerns me. Evolution can be a belief as well as knowledge. For me this second question also needs to be addressed.

I'm not proposing that we get rid of evolution. For one thing, the inputs are entirely too strong. After 150 years of popular opposition, evolution by natural selection stands on epistemological bedrock. Not only does it make wonderful sense of the world we observe, without it we would be at a total loss to understand huge swaths of nature. We would lose power over disease and agriculture that serves us well. I do think that theology, along with the moral and social facets of religion, asks us to do some serious thinking about the belief systems related to evolution. Natural selection may be unassailable, but ideologies of materialism, dominion, and progress, are not so solid. These ideologies exist in scientific culture, but are also prevalent in Christian culture. The worst abuses seem to arise when people use evolution as a prop for previously held beliefs about morality. How can the cultures of religion and science change in a way that they deal with the very real insecurity people feel around equating humans with other animals? How are we to understand ourselves if we do not stand, as Aquinas suggested, at the pinnacle of physical creation?

We will never be able to completely separate belief from knowledge, nor would we want to. We can look at the different processes and try to ensure that when we argue, we know what ground we're on. We can also ask some very pointed questions about the strength of our beliefs and whether they have the effects we think they do. Our behavior reveals many unconscious beliefs at odds with our knowledge and at odds with the beliefs we claim to have. What tools do you have for discovering what you really believe?

As we continue in the discussion of religion, it is worth pausing occasionally to ask how a particular proposition (e.g., God or souls) operates with respect to knowledge and belief. On what grounds is it based and what consequences does it have for you and for others? Where do knowledge and belief diverge? How do beliefs shape the way you produce knowledge as an individual and in groups? What does your knowledge tell you about the beliefs other people claim to have?

These questions will be key when we want to judge between competing truth claims, whether from science, religion, or both. Contrary to popular conception, when Galileo came before the Inquisition on charges of heresy, the question at hand was not simply science versus scripture. Two different debates were underway, one over how scriptures should be interpreted and one over how best to interpret the astronomical data.

The Tale of Galileo

Popular legend reports that Galileo, a man of profound scientific convictions, was moved by what he saw through his telescope.

Observations of the Jovian moons proved beyond a doubt that it was possible for something other than Earth to have satellites. He advocated for a solar system with the Sun in the middle and all the planets traveling around it. His trust in science and empiricism led him to confront the religious establishment who, based on Biblical authority, insisted that the sun travels around the Earth. According to the myth, Galileo was arrested, tried, and confined on the basis of this conflict.

The real story has a few more twists and turns. Ptolemy (c. 100–c. 170) – an Egyptian astronomer using Platonic realist axioms – supported the idea of a geocentric universe, with the Earth at the center and all the celestial objects revolving around it on spheres. The sphere, according to Aristotle, was the ideal shape and celestial objects, being perfect, must travel on paths defined by spheres. Is that a scientific proposition or a religious one? A little bit of both, actually. For now, let us say that it was a philosophical axiom of the time. That axiom would find its way into both religion and science, much as the concepts of power and progress have become central to modern science and religion. Scientists thought that heavenly things should come in perfect spheres, and so created hypotheses based on that idea. The astronomical models depended upon these spheres (and eventually smaller circles called epicycles) to explain the apparent motion of stars and planets in the night sky. The geocentric (earth-centered) model warrants the name scientific hypothesis because it was intimately related to the data. For about two thousand years, astronomers refined the model by adjusting the proposed size of the spheres and epicycles. By the seventeenth century, the Ptolemaic model had become cluttered with numerous additional elements and a few exceptions, but it still explained the data rather well.

Two European scientists challenged the Ptolemaic model in the sixteenth century. Nicolaus Copernicus (1473–1543) proposed a heliocentric model of the universe, with each of the (then) seven planets traveling around the Sun and moons traveling around planets. Copernicus still had some idea that these planets traveled in circles and in some ways his model did not explain the data as well as Ptolemy's; after all, astronomers had refined the geocentric model for hundreds of years. It should come as no surprise then, that the astronomers of the day did not immediately embrace the new model.

Why mess with something that worked so well? Why displace earth as the center? (Incidentally, this was another realist deduction supported by Aristotle and countless others.) From the religious perspective science moves at light speed, but from inside science, it can feel very slow. Paul Samuelson, a twentieth century economist, once remarked, "Funeral by funeral, theory advances." So we need to start with the knowledge that many sixteenth and seventeenth century scientists resisted the heliocentric model, some of them quite dismissively. Their interpretation of scripture may have had something to do with it, but mostly, it just didn't fit the data that well...or their axioms.

The issue came to a head in the trial of Galileo Galilei (1564–1642) who, with church sponsorship, investigated the heavens. Using his own observations, he defended the new model, much to the consternation of scientific and religious traditionalists. In retrospect the heliocentric model won the day, because more data made for a better model. Johannes Kepler (1571–1630) introduced the idea that planets travel in ellipses rather than circles. Elliptical orbits proved that the geocentric model could be not only simpler than the Ptolemaic model, but more accurate as well. With Copernican and Keplerian hypotheses, the model had a beautiful elegance and simplicity that eventually converted the majority of scientists. Modern scientists respect Galileo because he stood up for a theory that turns out to be right and revolutionary. He stood up for it at a time when the scientific establishment would not.

While astronomers were fighting over how to follow the stars, theologians were fighting over how to follow scripture, an argument that had already been going on for at least a thousand years. Modern popular movements in Christianity and Islam have obscured the extent to which science-religion dialogue was occurring in Christendom in the period known as the Middle Ages (in Islam during the Golden Age). As early as Clement of Alexandria (c. 150–c. 215) we can see discussion about how Christians should use secular knowledge when interpreting scripture. Augustine of Hippo (354-430) in his work *The Literal Interpretation of Genesis* speaks about the difference between Biblical passages that should be interpreted plainly and those that need to be interpreted metaphorically. Clearly, for Augustine, the simplest reading of Genesis regarding celestial phenomena only opens up Christians to ridicule.[61] Scripture trumps all other forms of knowledge but other knowledge often makes us reevaluate what scripture truly means. The Muslim philosopher, Al-Ghazzâlî (c. 1056–1111), speaking about the natural sciences, put it even more pointedly.

> "If you tell a man, who has studied these things—so that he has sifted all the data relating to them, and is, therefore, in a position to forecast when a lunar or solar eclipse will take place; whether it will be total or partial; and how long it will last—that these things are contrary to religion, your assertion will shake his faith in religion, not in these things."[62]

There have always been people on the other side of this debate – people for whom the Bible and Qur'an can only be read one, literal way, but for the most part, authorities in Christianity and Islam have both held to the idea that some passages cannot be read in a strictly literal fashion. The question becomes: which passages?

Then, as now, theology and science were related by a commitment to reason and understanding the world. We differentiate them based on modern categories, but from the 13th through 18th centuries, math and astronomy were considered prerequisites for studying philosophy or theology. Likewise, theology was considered foundational for concepts of an intelligible universe. Theology and astronomy were two conversations being held by many of the same people.

In the time of Galileo, two things were at stake for the theologians. First, should the passages in the Bible referring to the creation of the celestial lights (Genesis 1:14-16) and the Sun stopping

---

[61] "Usually, even a non-Christian knows something about the earth, the heavens, and the other elements of this world... If they find a Christian mistaken in a field which they themselves know well and hear him maintaining his foolish opinions about our books, how are they going to believe those books in matters concerning the resurrection of the dead, the hope of eternal life, and the kingdom of heaven, when they think their pages are full of falsehoods on facts which they themselves have learnt from experience and the light of reason?" *The Literal Meaning of Genesis* [I.19]. trans. John Hammond Taylor, S.J. (Paulist Press, 1982). pp. 42-43.

[62] Al-Ghazzâlî. *Tahafut al-Falasifah*. trans. Sabih Ahmad Kamali. (Philosophical Congress, 1958). p. 6.

for Joshua (Joshua 10:12-13) be interpreted to support the geocentric model of the universe? Second, do scientific and theological models of the universe correspond to reality or are they simply tools for the exercise of power over the world? Andreas Osiander (1498–1552), in an unauthorized preface to Copernicus' book on the heliocentric model, claims that hypotheses work when they provide good predictions, regardless of whether or not they are true. For him, science was useful, but did not provide objective knowledge. Likewise, Calvin argued that Genesis gives us infallible knowledge about salvation, but has not the intention of teaching astronomy.[63] Remember that the interpretation of scripture was a matter of life and death for these people. Regardless of their belief in non-physical realities, Europe was settling into a protracted and bloody struggle between Roman Catholic and Protestant worldviews. Where you fell on the authority of scripture could have a profound impact on your life.

We can see that models of reality and nature vary within both science and religion to a significant degree. I suspect that Galileo genuinely believed in the reality of the heliocentric universe and the reality of science in general. He also believed in scripture but thought, along with Augustine, that it needed to be interpreted in light of astronomical knowledge.[64] Belief, as I have described it, will always require us to commit to some particular worldview, even when the data is incomplete or contradictory. We need to make choices, preferably with some awareness of how good our knowledge is. Galileo lived at a time when both scriptural and astronomical standards were under debate and he suffered because his choices alienated traditionalists on both issues.

The questions being asked by theologians and scientists at the time of Galileo influenced the way that society operated and the way people thought about themselves. Contemporary debates have the same effect. The struggle over science and religion cannot be viewed simply as a conflict of two cultures. It represents the battleground on which many contests have been fought – including ontology, epistemology, and value orientation. Understanding the underlying

63 See *Commentary on Genesis* 1:5, 16

64 See Phil Dowe, *Galileo, Darwin, and Hawking* (Eerdmans, 2005), pp. 29-31

issues will be one of the toughest challenges we face. What questions drive the conflict? Who is invested and what is at stake?

I have attempted to separate out issues of knowledge and belief in a way that makes matters clearer. By looking at our own structures of thought and reason, we can see that two important elements appear. First, we have the knowledge process: how do we move from data (unprocessed input) to propositions about the world? Second we have the belief process: how do we move from statements about the world to action? In the case of evolution, experimental evidence has to do with knowledge, while concerns about what it means to be human have more to do with belief. In the case of heliocentrism, the same division applied. Knowledge questions include which models best describe the data and whether models reflect reality or simply make predictions. Belief questions include how we interpret scripture, how we model the world, and who has the authority to decide on behalf of the community.

In the first chapters of the book I suggested that, while many types of reasoning exist, they are not all equal. Each must be judged by its own standards. When we look at statements about nature, we should ask where those statements come from (knowledge), what effects they have (belief), and how carefully we've moved through whichever process we've decided to use. Modern science has tried to separate the questions, focusing only on knowledge. Religious tradetions also provide ways of knowing, but usually consider them inextricably bound up in ways of believing. Your epistemology may not be separable from your actions and the communities of which you are a part.

It matters whether the beliefs of your community support curiosity about the universe. And it matters what sorts of beliefs arise as a result of your knowledge. In the next chapter, I turn to the role of particular Christian axioms in reasoning. I want to look at how they relate to the epistemology of science, but also how they interact with beliefs about community and morality.

CHAPTER 13
Creation and Understanding

Scientists move from axioms about knowing to pictures of the universe. Christian theologians often move in the opposite direction. They start with the axiom that God created the world, all things seen and unseen. From this axiomatic belief flow more complicated rational beliefs about the nature of reason, why it works and why we should be reasonable. Note that the Christian (and Jewish and Muslim) perspective attempts to be comprehensive; not only does the idea of creation ground an epistemology – with empiricism and revelation – it also orients a value system – relating preference and morality to God's will. Additionally, it explains human agents as being in the image and likeness of God. Thus it constitutes a *belief system*; it covers a wide range of convictions with consequences. That system of beliefs includes explicit propositions about the history of the universe and what lies beyond or beneath physical reality. It also includes propositions about how humans gain knowledge and belief in light of our relationship to God and creation.

Christian theologians are unapologetic (objective) realists. We believe that something exists independent of our observing it. As you consider where theologically and scientifically produced worldviews overlap, ask yourself what standard you might use to judge one against another. If an independent reality exists, what are your criteria for deciding whether science or theology provide accurate pictures of it?

TRADITIONAL CREATIONISM

Christians take God, not as an object within the universe, but as the cause of the universe. Aristotle pointed out that all natural objects have causes – explanations for why they are what they are. Those causes, he said, were other natural things. In order to avoid an infinite chain of causes, one unnatural cause must start the process, an unmoved mover as we discussed in chapter eight. Note that Aristotle was an eternalist. He thought that the universe extended forever into the past and future. His unmoved mover was not the first event in the chain of history. Rather, it was a cause for other causes, an epistemological and ontological starting point. Medieval Christians adopted this position for their cosmology, finding it consistent with the idea of God as creator in the Bible. *Creationism*, in the traditional sense, is neither more nor less than the idea that God created the heavens and the earth, in other words, the world.

Some confusion arises over the relationship between this God, the unmoved mover and eternal source, and the God of Israel. The first does metaphysical work as an axiom for ontological and epistemological reasoning about the universe. The second does narrative work as a person in the history of the community. One need not identify the two, though Christians traditionally have. Usually the "Creator" is invoked as an ontological claim about the way the world was and is organized. It did not happen by necessity or without intent; it proceeded in an orderly fashion through the action of something outside of the normal limits we perceive in reality.

The notion of a Creator is a boundary condition and not an argument from ignorance. It is a positive assertion that there are principles of explanation for every physical thing; and therefore, there must be a principle for the explanation of the entire physical universe. And yet the universe does not explain itself, so we must look for explanation somewhere else. We bound the exercise of explaining the observable world by noting that we cannot explain everything. At some remove in the chain of causes, we will reach a cause that is radically unfamiliar. This notion of an unusual, eternal Creator appears in Exodus 3:14 – "God said to Moses, 'I am that I am'"[65] – and in the Gospel of John's references to Jesus as the eternal word (Greek: *logos* or organizing principle). God the Creator represents an axiom of order in the cosmos associated with an agent that gave the order.

Order proves terribly important for theology as well as science. It would not be rational to make models if the thing we modeled were unstable. The process of rationality itself rests on some belief in order and our ability to perceive it. I'm not just talking about a structured universe; I'm talking about our ability to structure a

[65] Jewish Publication Society translation

response. The rules of logic and the laws of nature both require some concept of fundamental order in the world as we encounter it.

By positing an all-good, all-powerful Creator, Christians set the groundwork for empiricism. The Creator who made all things good (Genesis 1) gives us reason to pursue understanding of them and hope that they are understandable. The Creator who made us gives us reason to believe that we (being made like the Creator) can comprehend the world. The order that proceeds from God can abide in us. Genesis sets the groundwork for belief in science in a way that would be hard to duplicate. Mere opportunism, Epicureanism, or a desire for power would suggest we only study useful subjects. Belief that some things were made without good intent (or without the ability to actualize good intentions) would suggest that some things might be harmful to learn. Genesis sets a foundation for unbridled inquiry about the cosmos.

When thinking about your worldview, ask how consistent you believe the universe to be? Is the cosmos comprehensible? If the cosmos is comprehensible, why do you think so? If the cosmos is not comprehensible, how do you connect reason to knowledge in a meaningful way? These are questions of ontology and epistemology, which Christians answer with a concept of God as Creator.

20th Century Creationism

Recent use of the term "creationism" goes beyond the belief that God created the heavens and the earth. It generally refers to some form of opposition to ideas about evolution by natural selection. Specific brands make specific claims. *Special creationists* hold that God created species or kinds of organisms in their current forms instantaneously at the beginning of time; large-scale evolutionary change does not occur. *Young earth creationists* hold that God created humans and other species from four to ten thousand years ago; there has not been enough time for evolution by natural selection to result in the huge diversity of life we see today. Whether you agree or disagree with this modern creationism, it represents something in addition to the traditional doctrine. Personally, I find that modern creationism works against traditional creationism, because it discourages open inquiry about how and what God created. Thus I am not a modern creationist for profoundly theological reasons.

Reason

Traditional creationism sets the stage for reasoning based on observation and revelation. It does not guarantee that they will always work, or that we will always use them appropriately, but it does give us hope for real knowledge of the external world. Francis Bacon along with Gassendi, Galileo, and Newton set the foundations of modern science based on their confidence that God had given us the ability to reason about the world.[66] They further thought that God expected us to use our abilities to observe and model the universe. As I mentioned before, this particular philosophical foundation is not necessary for a belief that science works; however, some such philosophical foundation is. A minimal set of axioms might assert that the universe is (sufficiently) ordered, (sufficiently) intelligible, and (sufficiently) good along with a belief in a (sufficient) human ability to reason. Christianity achieves this elegantly with the doctrine of creation.

The founders of modern science gave us the language we use today, speaking of physical objects 'obeying' and being 'governed' by natural laws. Newton (1642–1727) and others explicitly mentioned God as the 'law maker' and 'governor' in this framework. They drew their confidence in order and intelligibility from a theology that says Christians have a particular responsibility to learn about the natural world. Aquinas in Christianity and al-Ghazzâlî in Islam set forth theological justifications for the use of natural philosophy to know things about the physical world and the God who made it. I mention al-Ghazzâlî because we can trace the intellectual opinions of Aquinas, through the Jewish theologian Maimonides, and the Muslim scholars Ibn Rushd, al-Ghazzâlî, Ibn Sina, and al-Farabi all the way back to Aristotle. The intellectual history of the West is interwoven through many cultures. The theology of Newton does not mean science is Christian, but it does mean that theistic beliefs have significantly contributed to shaping science.

Scientific beliefs have also shaped Christianity. Theologians, from Clement of Alexandria to Origin to Augustine, Albert, and Aquinas have all drawn heavily on pre-Christian understandings of

---

[66] Descartes also invokes Creationism to justify *a priori* reasoning.

the physical world. Just to name three classical examples, they cite Aristotle's physics, Ptolemy's cosmology, and Galen's medicine.

Revelation

Christianity also admits of revelation – knowledge gained directly from the divine or some other cosmic source, without reference to logic, induction, deduction, or observation. For Christians, this appeal comes from our belief that God wants to communicate. The reliability of revelation is often defended in terms of God's being all-knowing, all-powerful, and all-good; thus, God perfectly communicates perfect knowledge. Note, however, that the possibility of revelation is necessary but not sufficient to establish actual revelation. As with any other type of argument, there must be standards.

Revelation appeals to a very specific kind of non-human authority that provides premises directly into human understanding. Those premises are not the product of our reasoning, but their provenance and profitability can be reasoned about. For me, it is exactly parallel to observation. Observation is not the product of reasoning, even though we carefully assess its credentials. So appeals to revelation can be reasonable, reasoned, and thoughtful. Throughout this book, I speak of reason as including systematic and careful ways of thinking, and so I will include revelation, thoughtfully applied, in that category. Like observation, it can be a source of premises and also a way of testing hypotheses. Like observation, it is also prone to mistakes when we attempt it alone (anecdote) or trust someone uncritically when they report it (hearsay).

While most religions include appeals to revelation, they do so in cautious ways. They subject claims of revelation to different standards depending on whether they are claimed as private revelation or public. Private revelation will always be balanced by the experience of the community. If you say you have had a vision, I will not simply "take it on faith." That would have to be faith in you, rather than faith in God. Instead, I will judge whether your vision matches up with my experience of God and the tradition.

In stark contrast to the picture of credulity presented by many modern anti-religionists, Christianity and Judaism both have an intense ambivalence about private revelation. We remember saints and prophets almost exclusively in the context of persecution. We remember them because they said something unexpected, which no one at the time believed. Their truth was recognized only in retrospect. They are remembered for the strength of their conviction in the face of official and popular resistance. In general, organized religions suppress claims of private revelation when they regard anything of significance to the community. For good and ill, coherence and consistency are too important to be disrupted on the claims of one individual – and individuals speak up all the time. It is not about waiting patiently for the rare claim of revelation, but constantly sorting through the many claims to find one true case.

Public revelation means claims accepted by the community. Communities authenticate revelation with appeals to authority – someone special recognizes its provenance – and appeals to popular acclaim. Both of these are strong rhetorical devices, provided you use them properly. Specific religious epistemologies must be consulted when deciding what constitutes proper use.

When appealing to revelation, ask to whom the revelation was made, what purpose it serves, and how the community received it. In the simplest case, you are claiming personal revelation, which can shape your actions profoundly, but need not impress anyone else. In order for a doctrine to be public revelation, it needs a pedigree. That pedigree differs for different communities, but usually involves coherence with other statements of faith and some notion of how it was revealed. Christians assume that God is benevolent; therefore, communication from God should be in the context of some benefit. For example, the Revelation of the Law at Mount Sinai was to form a covenant between God and Israel. When considering a claim for new revelation, we must ask whether this revelation serves a good end.

The claim "this is revelation" has no more weight than "this is logic." The proof is in the details. Individuals disagree about standards, but every community has them. Indeed, we disagree on induction and deduction on a regular basis. The challenge will be to identify why someone considers a particular instance of revelation to be reliable, why it counts as evidence.

Working with Revelation

Revelation can be a touchy subject in conversations about science and religion. The principle of mutual observables, while malleable with respect to heightened (or diminished) senses, revolts at the first sign of revelation. Revealed information generally appears to a single person and comes without independent verification. The angel Gibril said recite, and the Prophet recited. The angel said to Mary, "You will conceive and bear a son." In both cases we only have their word for it. I don't say that to be disrespectful. I say it to point out the very real and very important difference between revelation and authority. When God speaks to me (should God do so) I may call it revelation, but when God speaks to you, I need to rely on your word. For me to be reasonable, I must call it an appeal to authority and not an appeal to revelation. People inside and outside faith communities frequently blur the line by attributing things to revelation when they, as individuals, have no reason to do so. In my view, revelation happens often, but is almost never transferable.

Revelation represents direct knowledge of some subject without either an appeal to sensory data or internal mental processes. It also usually suggests divine intervention, but this seems to me an unnecessary addition. The broader definition allows us to include non-theistic transcendent experience as well. Even non-theistic religions claim that this kind of experience occurs and can be encouraged, if not explicitly brought about by ritual action. One can imagine a religion without this element, but the belief in an unseen order really benefits from some contact with that unseen order. Prayer and meditation usually serve this purpose. Most popular religions state that they will not produce knowledge magically or automatically – prayer does not guarantee revelation – but they can make interaction with the unseen more likely.

Revelation can run the gamut from highly social, as in the speaking of tongues in church, to the highly private, as in angelic visits. It can occur in formal settings with public recognition, as in the Oracle at Delphi, or outside all expected boundaries, as with Moses and the burning bush. The common feature has to do with the transmission of information by uncommon channels. In theory, this ability to bypass human senses and human reason makes it less likely to be corrupted by human experience. Many Christians, citing the Fall, have harbored a profound distrust of human reason. Our history has so corrupted our ability to understand that no amount of personal inquiry (*a priori* or empirical) could bring us to the truth. Revelation through Scripture was the only uncompromised method of knowing. For Augustine (following Plato) revelation provides a way for imperfect humans to comprehend a perfect God. For Martin Luther, revelation provides a way for sinful humans to comprehend a righteous God. For many Christians, revelation will be the preferred option, one that corrects the biases inherent in the human condition.

Thomas Aquinas and Richard Hooker (1554–1600) had a much more positive view of our condition and our ability to come to know the world. For both of them reason (with observation) and revelation led to the same end, true understanding. While revelation, they said, was less prone to error, it was extremely rare; reason is available to everyone. Therefore most of us must find our way according to reason. In this, I am very sympathetic to Hooker, in particular. He thought that, for the vast majority, no amount of meditation, prayer, and reflection could short circuit the tendency of the fallible mind to get involved. He agreed with Francis Bacon: people who think they have approached the world without using their reason are fooling themselves. He differs from Bacon in the assertion that some people have a legitimate experience of revelation – just very, very few.[67]

If you have had an experience you would like to attribute to revelation, these are the questions that need to be asked. Was the experience private or public? Was it witnessed and affirmed by others? What did they experience? Does the statement attributed to revelation align with your personal knowledge of God or nature? If not, do you understand the reason for the difference? Does the experience resemble revelatory experiences reported by others in your tradition? Who do you have in your faith community who can affirm or challenge your experience?

The last question may be the most important. Several comedians (and not a few theologians) have asked, "Why is it that when you talk to God they call it prayer, but when God talks back, they call it schizophrenia?" Undoubtedly, our society at large can be quite skeptical of revelation, but faith communities can be helpful in this regard. Any reasonable appeal to revelation must occur within a social framework that has rules and practices for dealing with such

[67] Thomas Aquinas is probably the most influential theologian in the history of Roman Catholic epistemology. Similarly, Richard Hooker provided the foundations for Anglican epistemology. Contrast the skeptical epistemology of John Calvin within Reformed Christian traditions.

things. In general, they affect belief profoundly, but knowledge only weakly. On rare occasions, when working with appeals to authority or other types of reason, they can be game changers.

It will be necessary as we foster dialogue around issues of science and religion to set the ground rules before entertaining appeals to revelation. Conversations within a single faith community will use that community's standards for weighing claims of revelation. Conversations between faith communities must establish shared beliefs in a way that creates space for some revelations, but not for others. Christians and Muslims, for instance, might agree on the account of creation in Genesis, but disagree about revelations to the Prophet. Secular conversations, especially those including atheists, will probably bracket all issues of revelation, leaving them unresolved, but looking for other areas of agreement.

THE GOSPEL TRUTH

The primary means of revelation in Christianity (and Islam and Judaism) comes through scripture, the Bible. That book has been the source of extended controversy over the centuries, because of the influence it has and its relationship to authority and revelation. Christians agree that scripture qualifies as an important authority because it represents revealed truths about the world. Debates arise when we try to specify to whom it was revealed, in what fashion, and how faithfully it was recorded, preserved, translated, and interpreted.

Those who believe in the *inerrancy* of scripture fall at one end of a spectrum. For them, scripture was revealed to prophets verbatim; they wrote it down or dictated it to faithful scribes. The words were recorded perfectly in the order that God intended them and God intended them to be clear, explicit, and literally true in every sense. God intervened in history to ensure that the current canon (collection of books in the Bible) represents all and only the writings so perfectly revealed. This comes very close to the dominant Islamic position on the Qur'an. Christians who lean in this direction generally also favor divine inspiration safeguarding the perfect transmission and translation of the Bible into English (often the Authorized or King James Version).

Christians who follow the "new criticism" fall near the other end of the spectrum. While they think that the Bible was divinely inspired, they also think the process was less precise. God spoke to people in a manner consistent with their time and place. Those people recorded their experiences, aided by God but not in a verbatim fashion. The records incorporate not only God's Divine Word, but also human confusion, prejudice, and whimsy. Scriptural authority can be further obscured by imperfect canonization – as humans decided which books to assemble and call scripture – imperfect transmission – as humans passed the stories down over hundreds of years – and imperfect translation – as humans shifted from one language to another. Even in English, there are significant differences between translations, for example the King James Version and the New Revised Standard Version.

Most Christians fall somewhere between the two extremes, but individuals and communities vary greatly in their thoughts on each of the five issues (perfection of words, recording, canonization, transmission, and translation). For example, someone might think that Moses wrote the first five books of the Bible in his own hand, but doubt everything thereafter. Christians have a particularly rich and diverse set of scripture and therefore may be willing to accept some books before others. Charles Simeon (1759–1836), a famously evangelical Anglican, probably fell very close to the inerrant end of the spectrum, but even he said, "There is not a decided Calvinist or Arminian in the world who equally approves of the whole of Scripture...who, if he had been in the company of St. Paul whilst he was writing his Epistles, would not have recom-mended him to alter one or other of his expressions."[68] Even perfect scripture must be approached by imperfect humans; Even rigorous inerrantists recognize some people will misinterpret scripture. Who interprets correctly and how do we know? The challenge for reason and conversation will be to find out exactly where differences in interpretation arise.

Concepts of scripture cross philosophical, moral, and social realms of religion – but primarily the first and last. An appeal to scripture will always be an appeal to authority and the construction of that authority is deeply social. This does not necessarily mean it is inseparably human, fallible, or corrupt. That depends on your

[68] from Charles Simeon, *Horae Homeleticae*, found in H. C. G. Moule, *English Leaders of Religion: Charles Simeon* (Methuen and Co., 1892). p. 99. Calvinists and Arminians both defend a very literal interpretation of scripture.

personal position on the transcendent character of the community. One might assert that the Holy Spirit dwells within and among a specific faith community and that, therefore, that community faithfully and truly preserves the form and meaning of scriptures. There is no logical problem with such an argument, but it will have limited value outside said community. What is reasonable can depend on the people with whom you are trying to reason.

Galileo Galilei fell afoul of differing standards of Biblical interpretation, specifically the role of the church in moderating the interpretation of scripture. The Christian community in Europe was struggling with a serious identity crisis as different authority structures fought for control of the faith. Epistemology could not be separated from social identity.

Christians appealing to scripture must ask several questions. Who sets the standards of canon and interpretation for your community? How much interpretation is open for individuals and how much must be done in accordance with group norms? Is the interpretation of scripture considered revelation, or only logical reasoning on the basis of a revealed foundation? Where do you draw the line?

These questions have resulted in a deep divide between Christians in the twenty-first century, all of whom believe the texts are revealed. A highly vocal minority believe that their personal interpretation is infallible, usually due to some appeal to private revelation, authority, or consensus. The majority, including Roman Catholics, Anglicans, and Orthodox insist that scripture is revelation primarily in the context of a worshiping community and that common scholarship, vigilance, and discussion are required to understand it properly. The future of the faith depends critically on whether and how those differences in belief are resolved.

Christian understandings of the world and how we interpret it draw heavily on beliefs about the Creator of the world. Those beliefs may be axiomatic, but they form the foundation for a complex system of reasoning based on a belief that the world is ordered and understandable. As with symmetry in science, the traditional doctrine of creation starts as an axiom, but finds reinforcement in personal experience, reason, and practical results.

By invoking an abstract unmoved mover, Christians ground the order of the universe in transcendent reality. By invoking a personal, loving God who wants to communicate, they ground our ability to reason about the world in a meaningful way. By tying the two together, they present a very ordered and hopeful model of the cosmos. For many within and without the Christian community, this view of the cosmos appears simpler, more beautiful, and more functional than the alternatives. For a few, historically significant, thinkers, they provided the foundation for modern science – applying skepticism, induction, and observation consistently to reason about the world.

The doctrine of creation also opens the door to the possibility of revelation, though there will always be debate around how much and to whom? Private claims of revelation will continue to shape the beliefs of individuals on a daily basis, but public claims of revelation occur only infrequently. When they are accepted, they can radically shift a community's view of the world, from metaphysics to ethics and politics. In the coming chapters, we will explore how these views shape individual and communal reason.

CHAPTER 14
Does God Cheat?

If God set the laws of the world, does God ever break them? In common English, do miracles occur? Remember that Christians did not invoke God as a supersized agent within the universe, but as something utterly different upon which the universe rests. We must then ask whether that difference ever breaks in and changes things.

This turns out to be a fairly modern question. God's intervention has been pondered for millennia, but the idea that God might break the rules is new. It rests upon two recent inventions – "laws of nature" from science and "the rule of law" from politics. I spoke in the last chapter of early modern scientists proposing an Almighty lawgiver, who put the rules in place and enforced them. The presence of such laws (and our similarity to the lawgiver) allows us to figure out how things work. From that perspective, the question of miracles is really one of consistency. Does God ever deviate from the rules set in place at the foundation of the world? Deism, a branch of Christianity popular when these ideas were being worked out, holds that God made the universe but no longer intervenes. After establishing the laws, no more was necessary. The perfect craftsman had made the perfect clock, wound it up, and let it run. Such a perspective is highly conducive to science because it insures the unaltered regularity of the universe. While this mechanical formulation only became popular in the last few hundred years, the idea is much older. It builds upon the Neoplatonic notion of God from late Antiquity and emphasizes the Creator God over the personal God in theological models.

Another idea, long in coming, crystallized around the time of the Enlightenment. We take it for granted in the United States that all citizens are equal under the (civil) law. For much of human history, law was a matter of the strong providing rules for the weak. The courts were nothing more than the ruler exercising his (or her) power to decide the outcome in particular cases. No one could bring the ruler before a court. More often than we remember, the people rose up to put rulers in their place – riots, insurrections, stonewalling… These events, however, were never considered "law." They were just the will of the people or, occasionally the will of some cosmic King whose whim trumped even the whims of the local king. Law was a tool of the people in power – the more power you have, the more control you have over the system.

This might makes right attitude slowly changed in Western Europe over the course of the Middle Ages, partly as a role of the Christian church in moderating (and competing with) military leaders. By the 13th century, people were starting to talk about God's laws trumping human laws. No one imagined the law applying equally to everyone – the rulers still had more rights than anyone else – but there were laws, "natural laws" that even rulers could not break. Over the next eight hundred years, these natural laws came to play a bigger and bigger part in our understanding of society, so that today, the idea that "all men are created equal" and "endowed by their creator with certain inalienable rights" seems "self-evident." Such a doctrine means that everyone in the United States, from a homeless addict to the President in the White House, has the same basic rights and freedoms. It forms the foundation for a legal system in which they are treated equally.

We forget that these two uses of natural law arose side by side and reflect the same unifying impulse. They fostered a desire for the organizing principles of government and morality to be universal and without exception. Thus the philosopher David Hume (1711-1776) and many of the new scientists wanted no privileged place for God in the physical world. Everything must always obey the laws. Thus Thomas Jefferson (1743–1826) and many of the social elite wanted no privileged place for the aristocracy in the political world. Everyone must obey the same laws. And thus, Immanuel Kant (1724-1804) and many of the philosophers wanted an abstract, rational morality that applied indiscriminately. We can be said to live in the age of universal law. I think it is mostly a good thing, but we must not forget that this has only been a common social axiom for about three centuries.

Christians, while historically champions for the rule of law under God have never bought into the rule of law over God. We started with the premise that God was an unusual entity; the doctrine of creation loses power when we insist that God is, in any way, just another actor. God cannot cheat, because God is not playing the game.

When I introduced religion, I noted that it involves both construction of an ordered worldview and regulation of boundaries. Our attempt to understand the world as an ordered whole always runs into difficulties. Logic, induction, and observation cannot logically prove their own premises. Instead we are attempting to make a model of the universe that accounts for apparent irregularities in the rules. Our observations are not neat and consistent – changes occur, we learn things. The physical world defies expectation on rare occasions, and the interpersonal world defies expectation all the time. We must, then, look for the least irrational position, knowing that a fully consistent, provable position is not within our grasp. The introduction of an unmoved mover came when we realized our system could not be complete as structured. We cannot return then, and complain that the unmoved mover does not fit within the system. That was the whole point. It must be understood as a reference to something at the boundary of the known.

CAN MIRACLES OCCUR?

Christians have long argued over the question of miracles. Before setting out to explain what I see as the dominant doctrine of Antiquity and the Middle Ages, I should mention a few of the more modern responses that have been popular recently. They all share the central premise that God is not playing the same game we are, but they differ on how they rationalize that concept.

Some theologians, wishing to preserve the regularity of the universe, are willing to jettison any idea of personal interaction with God by making God absent (in some types of Gnosticism), indifferent (in Deism), or utterly impersonal (in Neoplatonism). By removing the personal aspect, they hope to preserve the doctrine of Creation. It seems questionable whether revelation must also be avoided in this approach. Perhaps the Bible or other means of special divine communication were set up before God departed. It becomes awkward in terms of the traditional narrative of Christianity, making it less appealing to the general public and occasionally quite alien to faith as presented in the New Testament. Nonetheless, some modern thinkers (e.g., Francisco Ayala) attempt to resolve problems in worldview construction with a non-interventionist God: all Creator God, no personal God.

Other theologians, attempting to preserve God's ability to act in our lives, to reveal truth, and be consistently good, have suggested that God is not fully in charge. They are willing to lose the consistency gained by a Supreme Governor and place God as one actor among many in the universe. It remains unclear how they would answer the creation question. They usually emphasize the power of humans to effect change (free will), but occasionally appeal to some higher standard of order, by which God makes choices (and can be judged). Curiously, C.S. Lewis (1898–1963) flirts with this solution in *The Lion, the Witch, and the Wardrobe*, when he presents God as beholden to the "deep magic." The non-omnipotent God also appeals to Harold Kushner, John Polkinghorne, and many other modern theologians as a way out of the problem of theodicy (why bad things happen to good, or at least innocent, people). This school of thought leads to a strong personal God, but a weak Creator.

Some even suggest it is improper to think of God as a discrete entity. Instead, they say, we should see relationships as real, with God and self being two sides of one process, rather than two things that exist independently. Process theology, drawing on insights in physics, takes this tack.

Two more attempts to solve the problem turn it back upon the human questioner. The first presupposes that the underlying order remains orderly; we simply do not understand it yet. When our science and religion are complete we will understand why miracles were not only orderly, but necessary under God's law. This is the position C.S. Lewis takes in most of his works. It solves the consistency problem, but leaves me somewhat cold. It sidesteps the issue of whether God takes a personal interest in the world. It also breaks down our trust in the connection between our knowledge of natural law and the law itself, removing some of our justification for being able to do science.

The second approach, sadly one of the most common, states that God does not wish us to understand. Some young earth creationists have claimed that God placed fossils in the ground as a way of testing our faith. We should put our trust in the Bible and not in the evidence of our senses. Alternatively, the bones were placed there by Satan and God, for some unknown reason, has not corrected this. Again, we have logically solved the problem. God's actions with the bones and with miracles are not inconsistent or illogical, only obscure. In this scheme, science becomes even less tenable, as it must always be beholden to our understanding of scripture. Worse yet, it makes God a perfectly logical tyrant, who is willing to actively deceive us. Ontology and logic have been saved at the expense of axiology, not to mention our ability to relate to God. The perfectly orderly lawgiver has given way to a personal God, whose personality is both unkind and unpredictable.

It should be clear that none of these approaches appeal to me, though I can see why they are popular. They solve the consistency problem and make miracles fully reasonable. Still I am not willing to pay the cost. Nor, do I have to; there is a much better solution, suggested by Christian and Muslim theologians nearly one thousand years ago.

THE SUBNATURAL

The central problem arises from an ontological category error. We have a tendency to view God as an added feature *on top of* an orderly universe – a "super natural" entity. Thus any time God reaches down into the universe, it constitutes a violation of the rules, like tilting a pinball machine or upsetting the game board. God has the same properties as the pieces, but comes from a different set, as though outside was just like inside, only bigger. But this was precisely the sort of thing that traditional creationism denied.

Firstly, we cannot imagine the universe as existing without God in the picture. We wanted to know why there was something rather than nothing, so we invoked an odd cause to deal with the problem. Non-Christians may prefer an infinite regress of causes, and I respect that axiomatic choice, but they must not mistake the Christian worldview as that infinite chain *plus* God. For many of us the universe simply does not make sense as a stand-alone entity. Instead we see it resting on God as first cause and foundation. God exists below nature, because without God, the universe would have no place to stand. God is not the cue stick that pushes the balls around the table; God is the table itself. The table frames the balls and makes them behave in a consistent manner. This is what the idea of a Supreme Governor and Unmoved Mover means.

Second, Christians have generally denied that God can, in any sense be meaningfully absent within the game. Every piece, every place, every action occurs due to God's willing it to occur, continuously. This doctrine has been called *occasionalism* and was most notably defended by the Muslim philosopher al-Ghazzâlî. It was largely rejected under the assumption that if God made the universe anew in every instant – if every instant was an occasion for divine action – then we have no reason to believe in cause and effect. With no cause and effect how can we create a scientific view of the universe? I feel, however, that this is an unjust critique. Ghazzâlî argued that we can do science because God chooses to be consistent the vast majority of the time. Though we alone may not be able to cause things to happen, God recreates the universe in a way consistent with history and with our intentions. This is really just a reiteration of creationism, but without all of our attempts to make it historical. It is the exact opposite of Deism, where God created and stepped away. The universe is continuously created and sustained. God, existing outside of time, crafts both time and space. God creates now as well as then. And God, being good, creates a consistent universe, which remains consistent with natural law (as we know it) 99.999999% of the time. God, creating and sustaining everything, can then intercede with miracles, not by breaking the laws or changing them, but by choosing not to enforce them in a particular case. This allows us to understand the laws without insisting that God be bound by them. It allows God to have mercy.

Maimonides in Judaism and Aquinas in Christianity would reject *occasionalism* as crafted by al-Ghazzâlî (perhaps because they misunderstood him as being anti-science or anti-natural philosophy as it was known at the time). They would, however present very similar ideas about continuous creation and God's ability to both cause things directly in the moment and historically through a chain of created causes.

The only major downside to this idea is that it involves God's will in *every* historical event. (Such a position has been called divine providence.) How then can we understand some of the truly awful events in history? This was the very problem the non-omnipotent camp was trying to avoid. I side with Gottfried Leibniz (1646–1716) in thinking that this is the best of all possible worlds; we're just not in a position to appreciate it...yet. Occasionalism, in one form or another provides the best picture of the universe for me, but I can see why it would not appeal to everyone. God cannot cheat, because the rules are derived from God's consistency and not the other way around.

God versus Chance

A subnatural God removes the problem so often faced in science and religion discussions: was X a product of chance or design? If we imagine God acting under the laws of the universe, the question makes perfect sense. Did it happen by chance, according to the laws of nature without the imposition of a will, or was it a result of a choice made by an agent? Once we recognize that the natural laws (including the regularity of deterministic and probabilistic events) come about through God's agency, the problem dissolves. God is responsible for instituting and enforcing natural laws. To set them at odds requires us either to demote God to the status of a citizen, subject to law, or to promote probabilistic regularities to the status of divinity, uncaused cause and organizing principle for the universe.

We can still ask whether an event represents an exception to God's usual consistency, but we cannot ask whether an event lacks God's will. God wills all things, some for the sake of mercy, others for the sake of consistency, which is also a kind of mercy. It would be more difficult, both practically and emotionally to live in a word where prediction was impossible.

One can never use an event as proof of God's status as Supreme Governor. The argument for that lies in there being something rather than nothing. Anything at all, even empty space, would be consistent with such a picture. Miracles, in my view, can only be used as evidence for God in the personal sense. We see God's character in what occurs by God's will. That may be a problem for your concept of God in a personal and narrative sense, but it need not enter into questions of rationality or consistency with science.

UNCERTAINTY

One of the dreams of the Enlightenment was that we might have all of the certainty of revelation without the subjectivity and politics of religion. There was a hope that humans could have the consistency of natural law without the expedient of a lawgiver. Modern science was a big part of that program and has contributed immensely to human success. And yet we have found, largely through science, that the program cannot get us all the way there. The founders of modern science imagined a universe ruled by an omnipotent enforcer, who made and tended the mechanism (or made a mechanism that didn't need tending). They also believed that the enforcer granted us the ability to understand the machinery, being separated from it by our souls, intellects, and/or minds. In the last 150 years we have discovered many cases where no such mechanical consistency can be discerned by science (quantum mechanics and uncertainty). And we gave come to doubt that we hold a privileged place from which to draw such conclusions (evolutionary biology and cognitive neuroscience). This leaves us unable, logically, to make the kind of universal claims we want to. Revelation may grant certainty, but science alone cannot.

Many fundamentalist Christians want science to defend the unassailability of their claims made on the basis of revelation. They do not appreciate that science cannot work that way. Science cannot be used to defend a previously held position, nor does science provide certainty about anything. Science can provide strong confidence, but apparently not for the positions fundamentalists are more publicly ardent about – human uniqueness, special creation, and a young Earth. Worse yet, in turning to science in defense of their theological positions, they have short-circuited the traditional checks on claims of revelation. They want it to provide perfect knowledge without admitting the important and imperfect (because it is human) role of the community in moderating what is and is not considered the word of God.

Curiously, the new atheists and other scientific positivists have fallen into the same trap. They want to deny the existence of miracles or revelation on the grounds that the universe is perfectly consistent. The laws, they say, cannot be broken. They forget that the notion of laws depends on the notion of a lawgiver. Science does not provide unbreakable laws; it provides models. We can have strong confidence in those models based on observation, induction, and logic, as long as we are willing to adhere to the axioms of science. We do not, however, need to subscribe to ontological physicalism (nothing but the physical universe exists). Nor is the idea of a subnatural God, who shows up on a rare occasion, inconsistent with the scientific worldview or the generation of confidence. It's okay to say the rules work *almost* all of the time. Indeed, it often seems necessary to say exactly that.

Traditionally Christians accept the power of a Supreme Governor and the possibility of revelation as an antidote to excessive certainty. We accept that the world is understandable and worth understanding. We also accept that we will not, possibly cannot understand it fully within our lifetimes. There are borders to our observation and our comprehension. They need not be immovable or taboo, but it is perverse to say that they don't exist. If anything, science and Christianity agree in reinforcing our humility. They also agree in reinforcing our ability to cease being ignorant, but only through constant effort. This requires a willingness to be proven wrong every time we interact with the world beyond ourselves. It may involve mutual observables or revelation, but will likely include a community of accountability in either case.

This need not be a problem, but it will require a shift in perspective. If objective and certain truth cannot be used as a benchmark, how do we measure our science, much less our religion for accuracy? We will be forced back upon our axioms about ontology and value. What words have we chosen to describe the world? And what sorts of explanations do we prefer? Such problems cannot be easily solved; they require us to work with non-mutual observables, preferences and agents. From a pragmatic standpoint, I find Anglican metaphysics compelling. It provides an ontology with God and a critical, rational epistemology open to science. It has been effective at helping me understand the world and my place in it.

To what extent is your epistemology open to an absence of certainty? What things are you willing to be uncertain about? Do your axioms aid or hinder you in the process of discovering inconvenient truths? Questions about miracles usually reflect concerns about the reliability of our knowledge in science and religion. For me, it is important to recognize that Christian doctrines were constructed and preserved for the sake of these questions. They are not just modern attempts to defend the inerrancy of reason or revelation.

☙ ✦ ❧

Christians and other theists can often conflate multiple doctrines about God. On the one hand, God is presented as the Unmoved Mover and Supreme Governor of the cosmos. On the other hand, God is seen as a personal savior and actor in the history of the world. Both can rationally be the case, but they find different roots in Christian thought and solve different problems.

The positive assertion that God is the Creator does work metaphysically. It provides an explanation for our experience of an objective world and our ability to understand it, if only to a limited extent. The positive assertion must be balanced by a negative claim: God is not constrained by the world for which we needed an explanation. God is not a normal actor and neither obeys nor breaks natural law. God is the reason for the law, both in an ontological sense – God explains why the law exists – and in an epistemological sense – God explains how we come to know the law. As C.S. Lewis has said: "I believe in Christianity as I believe that the sun has risen: not only because I see it, but because by it I see everything else."[69]

Miracles have a place in Christianity. They reveal the character of God as a person and as an actor. They do not, however, prove the existence of God as an agent within the universe; to do that, God would have to behave like other agents. Theologians have asserted time and time again that we can speak of God only by analogy to created things; God is similar but not the same. This makes "God" an important boundary marker for knowledge rather than a proper name.

Some post-Enlightenment thinkers have pursued a form of radical certainty. Secularists have hoped for a universe with universal laws, but no lawgiver and no enforcer. They seek rules so secure that they cannot be broken as well as absolute certainty about those rules. Science, however, fails to provide any logical or empirical reason to believe such regularity exists. We advance in science precisely because we come to it with prior axioms of order, intelligibility, and progress. Christianity provided these elements in the early days of modern

[69] "Is Theology Poetry?" lecture to the Oxford Socratic Society, 1944.

science by making an appeal to a Supreme Governor, who upheld the law but need not follow it. I can imagine accepting, *ad hoc*, each of our axioms without a governor - many people do – but they remain profound ontological and axiomatic commitments and I, personally, find them uncompelling without an appeal to revelation of some kind. What is more, I think modern science denies us certainty of any kind. We are left either at the mercy of a God, who can break the rules, or at the mercy of evolved brains that can never guarantee true knowledge. Both force us to abandon such rigorous certainty as we might hope for.

Within Christianity, similar movements tried to limit the freedom of God to behave in unpredictable ways. The rise of papal infallibility in Roman Catholicism and scriptural inerrancy in Fundamentalism both attempted to regularize revelation in a way that would remove our dependence on social cooperation and provide a bedrock of certainty without all the mess of ethical and political constraints. Both movements hit their stride in the late 19th century in opposition to the rising tide of secular certainty described above. Historically, however, Christians have avoided this kind of dogma because it stops further inquiry. Certainty is not possible in this life, but faith is. So we take the philosophical notion of God as a solution to the philosophical problems (consistency, ontology) and leave the personal notion of God as a solution to the resultant emotional problems (frustration with inconsistency, theodicy).

The apparent contradiction is softened, if not completely eliminated, by a realization that both claims are negative. On the one hand Christians deny that God is bound by natural law; God transcends nature. On the other hand, Christians deny that God is only an impersonal regularity in the world; God interacts personally. The resulting tension leads us to believe – or perhaps forces us to recognize – that the world will always be greater than we can conceive. Certainty, if it can be had, will be had in the context of unprovable axioms, political communities, and imperfect ways of knowing.

CHAPTER 15
The Human Condition

In the last two chapters, I spoke about the Christian cosmology, how we look at the totality of the cosmos, understanding both the apparent order and the boundaries to what we know at a basic level. Ideas about God and creation provide necessary context for how Christians come to understand the world, including science. Now I want to turn to humans and how we look at ourselves. Once again, ideas about value and meaning will be tied into basic axioms about the world, not to sneak them in uncritically, but in an attempt to elegantly deal with questions of reality, knowledge, and value.

Theologians have dealt with these matters in a variety of ways, but I would like to start with a question. How are we to understand people? Any theory that deals meaningfully with the world must make account of the personalities we encounter on a daily basis. A huge portion of our attention is devoted to interactions with our neighbors.

When I introduced reason in chapter three, I said that all forms of rationality require some notion of free will. My ability to actively choose a good argument over a bad one or to choose an accurate model of the universe over an inaccurate one depends critically on my having a say in the matter. But who exactly am I? Likewise, when I introduced science, I said that mutual observables were important, things that you and I can see equally (or close enough). We reason about our observations together. That presumes some parity between my ability to sense the world and your own abilities. Finally, when I spoke of things science had trouble with, I spoke of choice and agency in the world. Can I identify myself as a locus of change? Even if people are fully determined by physical laws (as I believe they are not), we nonetheless view them as convenient focal points for changing the course of events. What is the nature of those focal points and how do they relate to other objects in the universe? What value do we place on them, and is there a difference between my locus and yours?

Hopefully by this point I have convinced you that those are significant questions, the answers to which will shape the way we reason about the world. They include important aspects of value and agency that fall outside the realm of mutual observables and therefore can only be touched tangentially by science. At the same time, we must fit them in with our concepts of cause and effect, matter and energy – into our physical universe. Ideas about persons inform our ability to do science just as much as science informs the way we look at persons. There is no science without scientists and we will need some notion of who they might be. Christians have been using science, as well as other forms of reasoning, to deal with these questions since at least the second century.

The Unit of Choice

Chapter seven looked at the units to which science reduces the world – atoms and forces. Christians begin with another unit – souls. As with creationism, it is important to start with the most basic version of the doctrine before adding on to it. The concept of soul asks us to believe that there is such a thing as an individual person, with unique value and unique preferences, who makes choices in the world. This individual has properties like a tiny unmoved mover (it makes things happen in unpredictable ways) and like a collection of matter (you can touch it), but neither of those perspectives really sums it up. A soul is just the best way of talking about the sort of thing, like ourselves, we can interact with, the sort of thing that prefers and reasons and makes choices.

A soul need not be irreducible. Some readings of Genesis suggest that souls can be decomposed into material dust and divine breath. Aristotle had some idea that souls could be thought of as self-perpetuating patterns, but patterns that had no existence outside the matter in which they were active. Many Christian thinkers, including Augustine of Hippo and Martin Luther, seriously considered the possibility that your soul was made up of pieces that had broken off from the souls of your parents (*traducianism*). At the most basic level, a soul should be seen simply as a unit for the sake of explaining the world. We generally don't consider it reducible, simply because we cannot currently see how its properties can be reduced. And it is a tremendously useful idea, one which helps us reason about behavior and value.

Though a soul may be reducible, there are some specific reductions that Christians reject. The soul is not the same thing as a brain, or any other part of the body. We think this is true for a number of reasons. First, a living body appears to have the same number and order of parts as a dead body, but we're confident that the interesting aspects of soul are present in the first and not in the second. So the matter involved is not enough to understand preference, choice, and reason. Second, people can lose parts of their body, even parts of their brain without losing the ability to prefer and choose. Sometimes we think that their reasoning is impaired, but this can also be said of many people with whole brains. Thus, it would be difficult to identify exactly one organ or part of an organ with our idea of soul. Increasingly, biology and psychology have revealed how radically our whole body chemistry and external environment impact our preferences and choices. Note that it would be irrational to claim an absence of free will and then locate that absence in the brain. If we are automata, then we are radically integrated automata. We are whole bodies that act.

Historically, philosophers have speculated on the location of soul or souls throughout the body: usually in the head, in the heart, or in the abdomen. In the 20th century it became popular to associate the soul just with the function of the brain, but we are coming to understand that neurons near the heart and stomach also impact our thinking, not to mention the hormonal signals that travel throughout the body and the impact of microorganisms living on and in us. The brain may be necessary for a human to have a soul, but it does not appear to be sufficient. Nor can we imagine a human without other physical features.

Christians, drawing on Hebrew tradition, have almost always associated souls – necessarily – with bodies. We've insisted, though, that modeling souls as only bodies or only brains was not enough; we have never been able to identify how bodies produce preferences and choices. An "appeal to ignorance" would claim that we do not know how bodies produce preference; therefore, bodies do not produce preference. That is not where I am going. Instead, I appeal to practical necessity. Our model of a universe filled with particles and forces fails to provide the necessary tools for dealing with people. It does not easily allow us to understand and work with preferences and choices. It does not give us a locus for them. We need souls, therefore, or some other model that deals with these questions. People require us to think in terms other than physical bodies.[70]

Nor is the soul the same thing as the conscious mind. Our preferences and behaviors frequently arise through no intentional process. Automatic bodily functions, subconscious desires, and conditioned responses all affect our footprint on the world: our dispositions and actions. For the last few hundred years, philosophers have placed a particular emphasis on human minds, hoping to use them as a way of explaining human uniqueness. More importantly, they have seen them as proof of our connection to God and as justification for our ability to understand the world. As I mentioned in the last chapter, that endeavor is starting to break down. Our minds may not be enough to grant certain knowledge of anything. Meanwhile, other animals, even plants and fungi, optimize their interactions with their environment in ways quite similar to human "problem solving." Ants, for example, herd aphids and cultivate fungus. A mind, like a brain, may always be associated with a soul, but it is unclear exactly how.

We feel confident that newborns and the senile still have preferences and make choices, despite the fact that we cannot communicate with them to find out if these are a product of mental activity. There is something to the human self that we just do not understand in terms of physical bodies and forces. Modern biology as well as ancient doctrine encourage us to distinguish the soul from the physical brain and from conscious mind. They are undoubtedly related, but figuring out how will require a great deal more work and curiosity.

---

[70] It is not even clear that *bodies* can be reduced to particles and forces. "Body" as the spatial extent of an inanimate object, perhaps a crystal, seems easy. We arbitrarily pick some trait – composition, density, color, etc. – and call all the connected bits with the trait a body. "Body" as a biological concept turns out to be extremely difficult. Most commonly we turn to functions, like metabolism and survival, but both involve processes that transcend our common sense bodies. Where does your body end and the products, by-products (waste), prostheses, and parasites begin? More cells in your "body" have non-human DNA than "your" DNA.

Soul Value

Perhaps more important than the ontological question – do souls exist and what are they made of – is the question of values. Christians assert that every person has value as a self, rather than simply as a body or a mind. Numerous ideologies have attempted to reduce humans to organic automata or intellectual engines, but Christians reject them as overly simplistic. Physical wholeness and mental soundness should not be treated as evidence of a better or more valuable person.

Each of us has preferences for the way the world should operate. Set aside the question of objective values for the moment and simply consider subjective values. Christians begin with an understanding of personal preference and agency and project those onto others. To the extent that I want and choose for myself, so too do others want and choose for themselves. Over the centuries, Christians have debated free will. Do we have more or less control? Nonetheless, we find an important insight in recognizing that others have the same level of control we do. To value another person is to recognize in them the same agency (ability to move the world) or passion (being moved by the world) that we see in ourselves. We are all different with respect to mental and physical capacity, but we are all the same in respect to our souls. That sameness grounds most modern ethical systems. Whether you use the Christian foundation – axiomatic souls – or some other, the way you treat people depends critically on who else you view in a class with yourself.

Soul Existence

What is the soul? It is the unadorned self. It is the you that is not reducible to mind or body, but nonetheless has an impact on the mental and physical world in which you find yourself. Unfortunately, the concept of selves is so fundamental to the way we look at the world, I am not sure I can meaningfully communicate about it clearly. In some ways it is axiomatic. Descartes thought his own existence was self-evident. Indeed, he thought it was one thing, if not the only thing, he could be absolutely sure of. How could I write to you without some notion of a me and a you who can communicate? For good and ill, these entities do not map well onto our scientific picture of the universe.

First, the experience of being me defies mutual observables. The interior experience of observation can be expressed in words, but we are never sure we have expressed it accurately. How do I know that you and I are both experiencing the same thing when we talk about an object being "red"? Philosophers call these internal experiences *qualia*. Observers are not necessarily interchangeable. In order to get there, I will need to either assert it axiomatically or derive it from some other axiom. I can minimize the number of kinds in the universe (ontology) by saying you and I are both examples of the same kind. In fact, I have to do just this sort of thing for the word "mutual" in mutual observables to have meaning. The category of observers, however, simply will not go away – at least not if we are to do science. The concept of soul does this work for me. It is not necessary for science, but some appeal to observers as a category will be.

What category or categories do you use when you speak of the beings that observe, feel, prefer, choose, and reason? How broad or how narrow are you willing to make it? Can all humans reason? Can some non-humans reason? Is it possible to prefer without choosing? Is it possible to choose without reasoning? How often do these things occur? I could ask countless more ethical and epistemological questions, but will leave you with just two, both of which I believe have a profound impact on our discussion. Whose preferences do you consider worthy of your interest? Whose arguments and conclusions are worthy of informing your reason?

Second, questions of preference and choice require us to think about more than one potential future, while science only observes one actual past. How are we to make sense of our intuition that paths through time split? Is the apparent dichotomy just an illusion and only one future exists? If that's the case, why do we feel so confident we can choose between them? Science can do nothing with the path not taken, which philosophers call *counterfactual* because it runs counter to the facts we observe. Even if we reject the idea of value (one path is better than the other) we are still stuck with a question of why we think there are two paths at all.

Do you think there are multiple possible futures? If so, on what do you base your conclusion? Do you control which path you take? Can others control your path? If you believe in only one possible and actual future, how do you understand your preferences for one over another and your experience of choosing between them?

Third, questions of preference and choice require a model of value. Whether we consider it objectively real or simply the product of individual preference, what do we mean by saying one outcome is better than another? If it is objective, we have not found a way to reproducibly observe value. If it is subjective, it fails the mutual observables test and some method other than science will be needed. What method will we use? We need of some concept that will allow us to model human preferences and choices – our own and others'. Science alone simply cannot do the job. It may at some point in the future, but I have my doubts, because the question is framed in a way that requires categories alien to science: qualia and counterfactuals.

Soul Purpose

Christians deal with this dilemma by stating that souls come in the image and likeness of God – the Unmoved Mover – with all the ambiguity that entails. It collapses two tough agency questions into one. My ability to create one actual outcome out of multiple possible outcomes (if I have one) is a smaller version of God's action creating existence out of non-existence. It also collapses the multiple questions of individual preference, into a categorical question – what does it mean for souls to prefer – and a normative question – is there a standard preference, perhaps God's preference, against which all other preferences can be judged. Let me reiterate. This is not an elimination of the ontological and epistemological problems. It is, rather, an attempt to cut them down to a reasonable number so that we can proceed. The doctrine of souls does this elegantly. Souls are the minimal unit of choice and preference, having these abilities as images of that which chose and preferred the cosmos (over nothing).

This book focuses on how we change our minds, so I have avoided diving into all the other functions which souls might and do serve in Christian theology, some based on revelation, others on other types of reasoning. I want to emphasize the epistemological work that souls do in relation to our understanding of creation and a creator. They allow us to assume that my experience of the world and your experience of the world are sufficiently similar for us to compare notes and share models. They also lead me to believe I should not value my own observations too much over those of others who share access to the same universe.

Eternal Souls

Another aspect of the Christian soul has to do with eternal life. As with the Unmoved Mover, I encourage people to think of this, not as a historical statement, but as the assertion that something is going on beyond the normal boundaries. The Christian doctrine of souls provides hope of a life after this one, but that falls out as a consequence of its primary work. Souls represent that aspect of humans which persists through movement in time and space. I am the same soul that existed in the past and the same soul that will exist in the future. My past choices affected my present self and my present choices will affect my future self. Christians affirm that we have an existential ability to navigate in the world. This ability goes beyond the mechanical sequence of events, which we model in the physical universe. We associate it with our being in the image and likeness of God, rather than being composed of atoms or adapted to our environment. The three are not mutually exclusive, but they are distinct and have distinct effects on our being.

Christians believe that humans transcend the physical atoms and forces that go into our bodies. This transcendence gives us an ability to think objectively about a world that cannot fully contain or constrain us. Such belief can – and often has – led to overconfidence about human reason, and I think that is a real temptation. I am not convinced we may know anything absolutely or dogmatically. At the same time, the idea has tremendous power to motivate curiosity and science…when tempered by humility. Human transcendence is not the same as divine transcendence, so it should not be taken as the ability to know fully (at least in this lifetime), but it is analogous to it. It should be taken as admitting the possibility of true and unbiased knowledge.

Human transcendence also gives us the ability to prefer in a special kind of way – to choose between possible outcomes and impact future events. Human dignity (the respect due to all humans) comes from this ability to experience, to prefer, and to choose. I am not convinced that such human transcendence rules out the transcendence of other creatures, though that position has been popular among Christians. Anglicans have been among the most speculative in this regard, never denying the transcendence of humans but occasionally granting other animals similar status. Humans can form strong bonds with dogs and other animals. This suggests that dogs may form bonds with one another and even with God. Thus, I would emphasize that I am speaking of transcending the physical – or at least scientifically verifiable – universe, rather than transcending our "animal nature."

Turning Around

Our ability to choose and cause change in the world has profound implications for morality – particularly in light our imperfect knowledge. We feel compelled to judge actions – both our own and others' – on the basis of our preferences. Throughout history, humans have reflected on this disconnect. "I do not understand my own actions. For I do not do what I want, but I do the very thing I hate." (*Romans* 7:15) How are we to make sense of being able to do a thing, wanting to do a thing, and yet not doing it? More importantly are we capable of changing preference or action so that they agree?

I believe this to be a central question for any philosophy, particularly because it forms the foundation of epistemology. If knowledge is to mean more than our current state of thought – if it has anything to do with accurate or desirable models of the world around us – it must invoke an ability to choose one model over another, one way of thinking over another. If belief is to mean more than pre-programmed action, it will require some sense that we influence the propositions that influence us. I do not say control, for I do not think we are in complete control of our belief systems. Nor would I say our belief systems fully determine our actions. Rather, we live in that strange world of counterfactuals where a person can change their mind and so change themselves in a profound way.

Folk psychology, the default beliefs humans hold about the state of their minds, has been surprisingly hostile to this notion. Every era of history appears to have its own determinism, claiming that no real agency exists.[71] Humans simply follow the script. In

Antiquity this script was written by Fate, the goddess who predetermined events, or by "necessity," which we would now call physical laws. In the Middle Ages and the Renaissance, the script was written by the stars (astrology) or God (Providence). In the age of the Enlightenment we turned to more mechanical models and have recently settled on chemical, genetic, neurological, or ideological determinism. In each case the central premise is simple: you have no independent control over your actions or preferences. You simply do what you have been programmed to do – like a robot. The persistence of this belief and the variety of its justifications leads me to think it has not been proven by recent science any more than it was proven by 18th century science or 13th century science or earlier models of reality.

Determinism reflects an axiom about choice. It has to do with whether we allow true agency – unmoved movers – into our model of the world. Science must be silent on a question of counterfactuals. What other options for reason do we have? It would be inconsistent for you to defend determinism, for in defending it you presuppose you (or I) might believe otherwise. Determinism can be logically consistent but it defeats all rational argument. Argument presupposes you have a choice between models of the universe. With no access to your internal experience, I cannot prove that you have preferences and choices. I can only assume that beliefs, preferences, and choices work within you to generate your behavior as they work within me to motivate mine.

---

[71] For the sake of this discussion, I will speak of agency and determinism as two axiomatically opposed notions about choice. Agential choice requires some component not fully forced by the environment and history. An agent "could have done otherwise" in the classic definition, whereas an automaton must follow a program. Philosophical determinism refers to the absence of such agency.

Note, philosophical determinism is not the same as physical determinism, a now unpopular scientific theory that everything in the universe is predictably forced by past events such that a complete knowledge of the present state of the universe would be sufficient to predict the state of the universe at any point in the future. We now know that many physical processes obey probabilistic (technically stochastic) rules whereby the outcome of a large number of events may be reliably predicted, though individual events may not. In any case physical determinism is a testable scientific theory; philosophical determinism is axiomatic.

Christians have largely appealed to common sense on this issue. "Of course you have choice." Christian philosophers, however, generally appeal to the soul as the locus, if not a full explanation of such activity. Preference and choice abide there. Meanwhile, the physical body, environment, and history all impact the choices the soul makes.

Truth and Consequences

Christians have argued that everyone has choices; therefore, making bad choices represents a failure of some kind. Sam Harris has recently made the argument that we should do away with the notion of free will. He thinks the whole idea of a bad choice is scientifically untenable and does little more than justify our desire to punish one another. He thinks that belief in free will leads to violence.[72]

His is not a scientific claim. Counterfactuals cannot appear in the provisional worldview of science, so there is no way to measure whether we have access to alternate paths or not. Harris cannot prove a lack of will; he simply asserts that there is no scientific evidence and, thus, the thing must not exist. But, let us grant Harris some metaphysics that allows him to rule out free will on the basis of scientific reasoning. Science has proven our wills far more constrained than we thought they were. Perhaps at some time in the distant future, we will have done sufficient experiments to see how every action was predetermined by its environment and history.

A far more dangerous chasm opens. Harris' science argument is a knowledge argument. Harris is also making a belief argument: free will leads to violence. He thinks we are inclined to severity in our legal (and extra-legal) responses to behaviors we don't like because we blame the culprit and want to punish them. We think not only the action (choice) must be dealt with, but also the intent (preference). For Harris, the deliberation of juries, judges, and politicians must be softened by the realization that the guilty party was guilty unwittingly. Their actions were determined.

This deals with the actions of transgressors, but fails utterly in speaking to the society that punishes. Mercy in itself requires preference. It requires that authority figures in society do something

---

[72] Sam Harris. *Free Will* (Free Press, 2012).

other than respond with their default beliefs about retribution. Vengeance is completely natural. Indeed, studies show that individuals primed with a belief in determinism (no free will) are more likely to treat others poorly.[73] The hanging judge is neither more nor less responsible for his choice than the murderer. Both are accountable for their choices or neither, but you cannot have one without the other. If determinism is true, no benefit could come from believing in determinism or free will. Preferences for law or mercy, if they exist at all, have no impact on the actions of individuals. On the other hand, if we do have some element of free will, then our belief in free will helps us to exercise it. Harris' argument for determinism fails both as knowledge and as belief.

Repentance

Christians have a much more nuanced picture of choice. In truth a great deal of variety appears. Reform theologians lean heavily on Providence and predestination, making them very similar to Harris in principle if not in the details. Anglicans, as I said, have a high view of reason, which leads us to value the role our souls play in decision-making. We are prone to many errors, biases, and prejudices; we have imperfect knowledge; and yet we can make the best of the evidence we have in the formation of right beliefs.

The Christian doctrine of repentance both emphasizes and reinforces our ability to pick between possible beliefs. The Greek word found in the New Testament is *metanoia*, literally changed thought or afterthought. *Metanoia* reflects our ability to reflect on our own beliefs, then reach in and change them. The process is not easy, but it can be done. Humans undergo conversion; axioms change. The word *metanoia* has been translated as repentance or penitence, from the Latin "to regret," though those words have picked up a host of other connotations in modern usage. Originally it simply meant to turn your thought around – to recognize and fix an unsatisfactory state of mind.

---

[73] Baumeister RF, EJ Masicampo, and CN DeWall. 2009. Prosocial Benefits of Feeling Free: Disbelief in Free Will Increases Aggression and Reduces Helpfulness. *Personality and Social Psychology Bulletin* 35(2):260-268. For further details of related issues, see Daniel Kahneman's excellent book *Thinking Fast and Slow* (Farrar, Straus, and Giroux, 2011).

The power of true *metanoia* represents a profound belief commitment. To think you can change almost requires that you do so in an intentional manner. How can such an idea not be beneficial, even essential for reason? We speak of robots as being rational rather than emotional. (Consider Data on *Star Trek: The Next Generation*, or the robots of Isaac Asimov or Karel Čapek.) Automata are not even rational; they are automatic. We never speak of computers as rational because we know they cannot reason. They process data, inputs and outputs, without ever choosing the more rational option. Bad computer input leads to bad computer output. Humans possess the strange notion that there is a way to make the output slightly better, without changing the input. Some added force of preference for the truth leads to objectivity, sensibility, or just "reason."

Folk psychology can also support ideas about choice. Like determinism, choice represents an axiom about the world, a commitment to counterfactuals and preferences. Christians ground their ideas of choice in a soul, the seat of such activity. And, though the soul cannot explain the notions of preference and choice by reducing them to simpler phenomena, it nonetheless creates a language by which we can talk about them – a language consciously grounded in non-physicalist ideas of the world. It highlights that choice happens at a boundary of the known. Just like the strange fundamental particles of subatomic physics (e.g., quarks) souls can be a category useful in explanation without being fully understood, or even unambiguously "real." They represent a different sort of thing, which nonetheless helps us form coherent, useful explanations.

Souls have duration in time and even transcend time. They formalize the idea that our self is somehow a persistence of memory, preference, and identity. They are always found associated with bodies and minds and help us interpret and predict the behaviors of those bodies and minds. Above all, they are capable of change. As unmoved movers they are not fully predictable on the basis of environment and surroundings but can be influenced to become better or worse. They form the primary unit of choice in the world – not just embracing beliefs and effecting behaviors, but influencing them. Repentance makes souls both interesting and practical. It provides a lever, by which we can make the future significantly different than the past.

Character

More than changing our conscious mind, we can change thy types of choices we habitually and unconsciously make. The Christian idea of character holds that souls may be conditioned to make better or worse choices.

Providence and occasionalism, each emphasizing God's absolute control over events, must be balanced with repentance, the role of individuals in changing their minds. For most Christians, salvation is a forgone conclusion. Our ultimate destination in heaven or hell as well as our favor in God's eyes rests solely with God. This concept of salvation was emphasized in the Protestant Reformation under the tag line "salvation by grace alone." Grace simply means free gift and it suggests we have no control over the process. This turns out to be the traditional and Roman Catholic viewpoint as well, but different times and communities emphasize it in different ways. Augustine and Calvin emphasize the role of the believer in accepting the gift. Aquinas emphasizes the role of human reason in aligning itself with natural law. Each tradition balances human and divine influence in a unique way.[74]

For Anglicans, salvation is in God's hands, but individuals may be *sanctified*. The process of human choice can lead to souls with better beliefs, better choices and actions. Better, here, means more representative of the goodness and order of God in Creation, but not more deserving of grace or salvation. Engaging and improving our reason provides one of the best ways for humans to pursue sanctification, hence the importance of rational pursuits in Anglican Christianity. Our ability to be saved and our ability to reason exist in parallel. God determines the first, but we have the ability to show God's grace by developing the second. As always, I am not claiming

[74] A small minority of Christians explicitly believe that our actions can determine whether or not we are saved, whether we go to heaven or hell. The idea has been called works righteousness, justification by works, or Pelagianism. (Note Pelagius probably did not think this way, but Augustine accused him of doing so, hence the name.) All three have been rejected in very strong language by the vast majority of Christians. A larger minority of Christians are *crypto-Pelagian*, they know that salvation comes by grace alone (based on scriptural and traditional evidence) but believe that they are justified by their works (and feel compelled to act in certain ways to avoid eternal punishment).

that only the doctrine of sanctification can justify reason. It is only one way to do so, but I find it fits well with both science and the pursuit of clearer thinking.

Faith Seeking Understanding

Once we start thinking of character and sanctification, or if you like rationality and intellectual formation, we can talk about how to harmonize choice and preference. We can set up feedback loops. Do your preferences lead you to make choices that lead to outcomes you prefer? Do your choices shape your preferences in ways that give you greater control over your choices?

This sort of feedback loop has often been associated with science. The iteration of hypotheses and observations follows the same pattern. You might be tempted to say that I am importing science into religion when I compare the iteration of science to the iteration of character building. That, however, would not fit the historical evidence. The founders of modern science were embedded in a Christian culture that said God empowers souls to do science. Ideas about order and intelligibility came first; we must say, then, that science imported the pattern of awareness, reflection, repentance, and amendment from religion.

Many religions do not practice this type of feedback. Many Christians appear oblivious to external influences, feeling constrained by dogma and authority to neither question nor change. I am not claiming that all religion or even all Christianity has been iterative or good for reason. Instead, I want to convince you that the question of self-improvement arises within a worldview. Religions, in helping us construct such worldviews, shape how and whether we think the process works. They may be dogmatic or encourage creativity. They may be progressive or eternalist. They may be pro-science or anti-science.

Whether we identify these questions of axioms and world-view construction "religious" or simply "philosophical," they impact the way we think, reason, and interact with others. My own fondness for Anglicanism has much to with its use of reason. Anglican theology has historically contributed to open ended critical thinking and modern science. My appreciation for Judaism and Tibetan Buddhism springs from a similar source. Conversely, my distrust of dogma makes it harder for me to understand Christian Fundamentalism and Wahhabi Islam. I have preferences when it comes to reasoning and preferences when it comes to religion. Those preferences have been shaped by – and continue to shape – my beliefs.

We may improve ourselves. Specifically, we may improve ourselves through reasoning. The proposition is neither trivial nor self-evident, and yet it has a huge impact on our actions and identities. In the remainder of the book I will explore systems of thought, action, and community that work to integrate preference and choice. That is not the only function of religion, but it is the one that concerns us most when we ask how to play well with others, when playing the game of reason. For now, I will leave you with three examples of the type of feedback I'm suggesting.

First, directly philosophical feedback can be seen in the motto of Anselm of Canterbury (1033–1109). "Faith seeking understanding" has often been misunderstood by those who define faith as "belief based on authority" or "holding true without proof." For Anselm faith was an act of will; it meant preferring God and being in relationship with God. The love of God leads to learning about God. Learning about God, in turn leads to a greater love. Anselm saw faith as a process of aligning our choices, our preferences, and our picture of the world with the underlying order of the cosmos. For him, there was a feedback loop, in which faith led to knowledge and vice versa through the process of contemplating God and creation.

A more concrete example of feedback between preference, choice, and action can be seen in the *examen* of Ignatius of Loyola (1491–1556). Ignatius founded an order of priests and brothers called the Society of Jesus, commonly called the Jesuits. They practice daily meditation using a five-part exercise: openness to God, reflection on the day, awareness of your emotions and God's presence in the events of the day, prayer arising from one feeling or event, asking God for guidance about tomorrow. The examen encourages regular thought about the relationship between choices and preferences.

Third, we can see communal feedback in the accountability groups of John Wesley (1703-1791). Wesley encouraged Christians to meet weekly with a small group of friends, who would hold one another accountable to their common preferences. This provides strong social pressure to conform to community standards, but it also allows members, week by week, to remind one another of personal goals. Modern research has shown that we are far more likely to follow through on promises made publicly.[75]

I have only sketched the history of iterative thought in science and Christianity here. Christopher Beckwith traces recursive thought back in time through European Christianity, Central Asian Islam and Buddhism in *Warriors of the Cloisters.*[76]

☙ ✦ ❧

The process of choosing cannot be separated from the individuals and institutions in which the choice takes place. Reason, choice, and preference must be associated with the physical form in which they appear, but cannot currently be explained in physical or scientific terms. Christianity, using ideas of souls and repentance, provides a conceptual framework in which to understand and improve decision-making. That framework created a template for the iterative process of observation and hypothesis that drives the scientific method. The two can and often have been separated, but doing so should raise questions. Why and how do we think iteration works? What category contains the entities that do it and what faculty do they have for carrying it out? Can robots do science? Can computers? How about non-human animals? There are many people, for whatever definition of people you may choose, who think they cannot do science. They see themselves as incapable of arriving at truth by use of their reason. Worse still, they see themselves as out of control of their own beliefs, preferences, and choices. These questions matter profoundly to the way you and your neighbors act.

I believe science is compatible with many forms of religion. The two can even reinforce one another. Anglican Christianity and many other faiths uphold a worldview that empowers and encourages me to pursue truth, both in science and in other ways. Science, in turn, helps me think critically about whether my knowledge and beliefs bring me closer to an accurate understanding of God and creation. For me, they must be integrated.

The media often presents religion as a set of dogmatic propositions upheld by authority. Instead, let me suggest that religion involves beliefs, communities, and practices for reinforcing *and*

---

[75] See *Nudge* by Richard Thaler and Cass Sunstein (Penguin, 2008).

[76] (Princeton University Press, 2012).

changing belief. They facilitate conversion and provide common rules for evidence when using all of our rational faculties, not just revelation. Epistemology turns out to be something more than a mindset; rather, it happens at the intersection of preference, choice, and action, of personal and communal meaning making, of norms for thought, behavior, and society. In order to deal with this vast constellation of forces, religions have had to take a big picture approach, looking at the way all of these factors change us. Religious groups have engineered change in the way we look at the world, consciously and unconsciously, for good and for ill. Whether you look at these questions as religious or not, I'd encourage you to think critically about how your own beliefs about learning, deciding, and cooperation impact what you think about the world.

CHAPTER 16
Religion in Practice

How do religions work? I've spoken rather extensively about the knowledge and belief propositions present in religion. After all, most of our religion and science debates revolve around questions of knowledge, belief, and reason. I think it would be a mistake, however, to think of religion only in these terms. The major religions I have mentioned all exist with a variety of goals and a variety of practices. The epistemological goal of knowledge will only be one of these; it's worth taking a look at what other things might be going on in religious communities that impact reasoning. I want to return now to different ways people define and characterize religion: what I call the three realms of philosophy, practice, and politics.

Several authors have noted these parallel aspects of religion. Most recently, I encountered them as belonging, believing, and behaving in the works of Phyllis Tickle.[77] Significantly the various authors disagree about which of the three elements is essential to Christianity and which should come first. Some argue that right action (behaving) comes from right thought (believing), others that right thought only arises from right action. Still others say we must allow people to belong to a group before we expect them to accept its norms and models.

As catchy as the three Bs are, I have chosen to recast them slightly. I use them in a slightly different way, particularly "believe." Instead, I will speak of philosophical, behavioral, and social aspects of religion, or more alliteratively as philosophy, practice, and politics. I also diverge in making no claims about the priority of one over another. I see all three as interrelated, though in this chapter I want

[77] She mentions this in *The Great Emergence* (Baker Books, 2008). Tickle sites John Wimber as perhaps the earliest to use belonging, believing, and behaving. The terms also appear in works by Diana Butler Bass, Robert Webber, and Alan Kreider.

to focus on how others have used each one as a definition of "true religion."

Philosophy and Right Thought

Religion deals with intellectual propositions. Those propositions can be historical or doctrinal as we often see in church creeds. They can also be more broadly philosophical, including the ontology of Thomistic theology (two creations) or the epistemology of Christian Fundamentalism (scriptural inerrancy). The philosophical definition of religion claims that true followers are those who think the right way. The word *orthodoxy* comes from the Greek words for properly aligned opinions and has come to mean correct thought. A similar word, *creedal* refers to those groups, particularly churches, who subscribe to a particular statement of doctrine or creed.[78] In recent years, churches that define themselves by the set of propositions they affirm call themselves confessional or confessing as well as orthodox or creedal. Confusingly, the Eastern Orthodox Churches do not define themselves in this way, as we will see below.

During the Reformation and the Enlightenment, orthodoxy was extremely popular and denominations frequently arose around creeds. We can still see this in several Protestant groups. Lutherans observe the *Augsburg Confession* (1530), Southern Baptists adhere to the *Baptist Faith and Message* (2000), and most Presbyterians subscribe to the *Westminster Confession of Faith* (1646). These creeds set forth the common beliefs of members of the denomination and are normative for membership. In other words, to belong is to agree (mentally) with the doctrines of the church.

Alternatively, the "ecumenical creeds" (Apostles', Nicene, and Athanasian) predate such heady belief. They represent a view more focused on how beliefs shaped behaviors and communities. Many

[78] Curiously, the word "creed" comes from the Latin word *credo*, which means to believe. Historically both words had more to do with devotion, giving of your heart, than intellectual assent to a proposition. Thus the original use of *credo* favors my definition of convictions with consequences. Nonetheless, the word has come to have a very heady, intellectual flavor in modern English and "creedal" Christians favor right thought. Karen Armstrong traces the history of creeds and the evolution of the word "belief" in her book *The Case for God* (Thorndike, 2009).

Christian communities, sharing this older focus, think philosophical definitions of religion flirt with *Gnosticism*, the worship of knowledge or the belief that knowledge can save you. So, despite the current popularity of philosophical definitions in religion, they are not common to all religious groups, nor even to all Christian churches.

Throughout the book I have focused on epistemology, ontology, and other philosophical statements; therefore, I may appear to lean toward right thought in my own definition of religion. This is not the case. Being an Anglican, I recognize the weight of all three aspects of religious identity. As philosophical definitions are very popular, and as I have spent so much time talking about them, I will say no more about orthodoxy here, instead turning to practical and political definitions, first as brief sketches, then in more detail.

Practice and Right Behavior

Religion also deals with practice, including how we relate to others and ourselves. This would be a behavioral definition. Throughout history, we can see examples of large-scale religious change arising in revolt to overly intellectual models of faith. Both the Christian *scholastics* and the Islamic *mutazilites* valued reason very highly and attempted to defend creedal statements using philosophy and natural science. In both cases, the appeal to "secular" thinking caused trouble. The Protestant leader Martin Luther com-plained that scholastic theology allowed human reason too free a rein. Both he and John Calvin argued that our reason caused us to question too much the revealed truth given to us by God. Salvation, they said, comes not from thinking things, but from accepting God's grace – over which we have no control. Both argued that religion had been corrupted by philosophy and should be re-grounded in revelation, relation to God, and the practice of faith. In Islam, al-Ash'ari (874–936) turned away from the intellectual traditions of the mutazilite theologians. He asserted that many things in religion could not be understood – most notably who goes to heaven. These things lie beyond human reason and we must not spend too much energy trying to unravel them. True Islam lies in obedience to God, not understanding of God. Asharite theology has long been the dominant strand in Islam.

The revolt against rational intellectual religion tends to result in a mystical or dogmatic anti-rational focus (still centered on reflection and the intellect) or a more behavior oriented definition of religion. We can see examples of both in Christianity and Islam.

Behavioral definitions of religion have been referred to as *orthopraxy*, a Greek word for properly aligned action. Advocates of orthopraxy argue that you can tell whether someone is a true Christian (or Hindu…) by how they act – a very common argument in the mid-twentieth century. I go into greater detail below, but for now remember that for many "actions speak louder than words." Some people define religions by their behavioral patterns rather than their philosophical assertions.

On the other hand, there are those who say this kind of religion is too *pietistic* or oriented toward works righteousness. For them the focus on behavior demonstrates more care for presentation than for content. Such critics attempt to shift religious identity to a more philosophical or political focus.

Politics and Right Relationships

Finally, religion has to do with identity and authority, how we constitute ourselves as societies. This would be the political or social definition. Many religious groups transparently associate membership with ancestry or social status. Hindus, Jews, and Confucians all have very strong political components to their religious identity, as do Roman Catholics. Historically, most people were born into a religion when they were born into a community. They constructed their worldview according to the norms of their society and few options were presented. This may reflect a failure to think about the topic. Equally, it may reflect a conscious decision to value membership over intellectual assent or behavioral conformity.

Many Christians, Muslims, Hindus, and Buddhists identify themselves as part of their "religious" community long after consciously setting aside beliefs and practices. You have no doubt met "lapsed Catholics" and "secular Jews" or at least encountered them in popular media. Many people carry around the culture long after they have left the religion by any philosophical or behavioral standard. Many groups define religion by descent, location, nationality, or status.

I know of no word meaning right association, but the concept should be familiar. I speak more about the details below. Some people consider your community to be more important than anything else (e.g., "my country, right or wrong," and "blood is thicker than water"). Some groups define themselves by relationships independent of our other categories. In an age of intellectual definitions and universal religions, it can be hard to use the word "religion" in this sense. Membership may be unconscious or even against your will. Nonetheless, this perspective exists alongside the others and has impacted all major religions.

Opponents argue that this category refers to cults of personality or social clubs, but not "true religions." For the moment, I am not interested in the normative claim, but only description. Such groups exist and are frequently labeled "religion" by both insiders and outsiders. Right association arguments appear again and again throughout history.

Each definition has its own strengths and weaknesses. All three interact in interesting ways, reinforcing or competing within the consciousness of a particular religious group. To my mind, no picture of religion would be complete without all three, and no critical approach to reason would be complete without understanding how each impacts our worldviews. Once we give up reasoning alone, we must take on limitations to the things we can say and the ways we can say them. Communication requires common norms. It's not a question of whether you think for yourself, but how thinking together constrains and broadens the things you think about.

Religion as Behavior

"Actions speak louder than words"

Three types of action mark out three aspects of religion as behavior: social justice, purity, and liturgy. No group cares exclusively about one and neglects the others; instead they always balance the three. Often, however, one type of action will stand out in their language and self-identification. Often one type of action is used rhetorically to define who is in and who is out.

Social Justice

A social justice emphasis highlights the importance of how we treat others, particularly those who are disadvantaged or outside the community. How are you treating the poor? How do your actions impact the environment? Only those promote justice are considered true members of the group. In response to the creedal dogmatism of the Enlightenment, many mainline Protestants (esp. the social gospel movement) and many Catholics (esp. the liberation theology movement) have stressed our social justice obligations. Thus, this focus will be familiar to most Western readers. Historically, we can cite Francis of Assisi (1181/2–1226), who reportedly told his followers, "preach the gospel; use words when necessary." Social justice has to do with our actions in relation to others. Advocates consider right action essential to right belief and right relationship, which they see as flowing from it.

Many Evangelical Christians have argued that too much attention to social justice denies the importance of a personal relationship with God and obedience to God's will. For them our tendency to sin corrupts our ability to reason about how we should behave. We must instead follow the rules set down by God without deviation. Such belief has profound implications for moral reasoning and their willingness to incorporate epistemology and science when reading scripture, shaping preferences, and setting standards. This divide generates some of the greatest tensions between the different branches of Christianity as well as contributing to miscommunication about science and religion.

Purity

A purity ethic asks where you stand in relation to the proper order of the cosmos. Christians think of it as living in accord with God's word or will or simply as righteousness. Do you keep yourself unsullied by the world? Do you observe the cleanliness, dietary, and sexual restrictions proper to a believer? Do you associate primarily with other pure people? Membership rides on your ability to keep yourself separated from corrupting influences. Orthodox Jewish rigor in keeping kosher and avoiding work on the Sabbath should provide a familiar example. You can also see a purity ethic in Mormon prohibitions against alcohol and caffeine, Baptist prohibitions against dancing, and the segregation of men and women in countless groups. Proponents consider purity to be a necessary first step in right living; it creates an environment in which alignment with the unseen order is possible.

Groups that emphasize purity often claim guarantees for their knowledge of the rules. Some form of revelation, tradition, or authority provides certainty about what the standards are and how they should be interpreted. Because conformity to the standard is so important, it must also be unambiguous. Appeals have been made to the inerrancy of scripture, the perfect transmission of doctrine, or the infallibility of a particular leader. All purity definitions rely on some epistemology to establish and interpret standards.

Those who focus on social justice or liturgy may accuse purity followers of being legalistic. In Christianity, this has been associated with Pharisees, who were criticized in the Gospels for having purer outsides than insides. In Islam, the concept is called *taqlid*, or blind obedience to the opinions of others without understanding. No one person sits entirely in one camp, but the words they to describe morality help reveal how they reason about morality. Purity means a focus on actions required to align yourself with the cosmic order.

Liturgy

Liturgical emphasis highlights the ritual actions of faith.[79] It's not just about you and your personal behavior. Morality requires that the community perform certain rituals that properly orient individuals, groups, or the larger world. Does the community meet regularly? Do you pray regularly, using the appropriate forms? Do you tithe? Only those people who fulfill their ritual obligations belong. A liturgical emphasis may be inclusive – all who participate belong, regardless of other issues – or exclusive – certain individuals must play particular roles – but always requires communal norms and common action. The central role of the Divine Liturgy in Orthodox Christianity, the place of the Haj within Islam, and Buddhist meditation practices all

[79] Membership comes from participation in the "liturgy." The Greek literally translates as public works. Liturgy represents what people do together, but tends to emphasize ritual and religious action. Liturgy is not just the work of the people, but also those things done for or in the presence of the people.

indicate a liturgical focus. Proponents almost always argue that morality lies in the doing. Like the purity camp, they focus on the means and methods, rather than the ends, but like the social justice camp they focus on connections, rather than divisions.

Opponents of the liturgical camp worry that the rituals of the community will not be enough to reach the real world. Social justice calls for an engagement with the world that may not be available with pre-set plans of action. Purity calls for a personal commitment, which many think can only be found in private and spontaneous devotion. The community and the tradition, they say, cannot do the heavy lifting for you. "Liturgy" has become a bad word in many non-denominational Christian churches, where it is considered to suppress a personal connection with God.

As an Anglican, I favor the liturgical emphasis, though I recognize the importance of all three types of morality. The Wars of Religion raged across Europe in the sixteenth and seventeenth centuries. Social and economic forces had a large impact, but at the forefront of public consciousness was a debate between Catholic morality – generally communal and liturgical or social justice oriented – and Protestant morality – more individual and purity oriented. In England and Scotland, the wars finally settled down with what is known as the Elizabethan compromise. Queen Elizabeth (ruled 1558–1603) and later King Charles II (ruled 1660–1685) said that the people could be Protestant or Catholic in philosophy as long as they all came to church on Sunday and used the Book of Common Prayer as a script for worship. Liturgy in worship became normative for civil society. Anglicans favor common methodology, not only for worship, but for moral reasoning, scriptural interpretation, and government. We work best when working together. We need commonly agreed upon rules and, though the rules can be changed, everyone benefits from a coherent, transparent, and well-crafted (even poetic) script. No doubt this shines through throughout my arguments about thinking fairly. We benefit from reasoning by the same rules, even when we don't come to the same conclusions.

Convictions with Consequences

We can never fully separate morality and philosophy; our thoughts influence our actions and our actions influence our thoughts. Our ontology (e.g., who is human?) and epistemology (e.g., how can we learn about value and preference?) impact the way we treat one another and the way we treat ourselves. They shape our definitions of community: who is in and who is out and do we treat them differently? Still, we can see how some branches of Christianity came to be defined in terms of behavioral expectations. Similarly, many Muslims look at concepts like *zakat* (almsgiving) and the moral commands of the Qur'an and say that Islam is primarily defined by its moral imperatives.

One should also note that Christian crusades and Muslim jihad, though antithetical to modern Western values, also represent norms of practice in particular communities. By saying behavior relates to morality, I am not claiming that the norms of religious practice have always been good. Rather, I am saying that the ways in which we differentiate good actions from bad are tied up with our understanding of religion. Religion has to do with beliefs and belief systems formed in the context of a community. I have no illusions that religion is always a force for good.

Orthopraxy and behavioral definitions of religion should be appealing to empiricists. After all, one cannot look inside individual minds and souls to see what they think, prefer, and believe. One can judge them by their actions. We can observe practice and use it as a measure. How many people go to church on Sunday or Mosque on Friday? How many Muslims observe *halal* and *zakat* restrictions? How many Christians feed the poor and tend the sick? Behavioral definitions, however, will always run the risk of ignoring the transcendent elements of faith. Protestant Christian theologians decried salvation by works because it seemed to deny God's agency in salvation. Faith should be about a relationship with an *unseen* order and practical definitions can easily start to function without that unseen element. Behavioral definitions also risk missing the forest for the trees. Religion appears in groups, not just individuals operating by individual standards, but complex societies with moving parts. How many Jews are necessary for communal prayer? How do the Hindu castes relate to each other? How are Catholic priests changed by their ordination and does it allow them to do things other people cannot do?

Whatever religion you claim – even if you claim no religion – it is worth asking how you distinguish good from bad behavior. What rules do you use? Do they apply equally to all people, or do different people have different roles to play? How did you come to think this way and can you change the way you think? Do others play a role in that process and, if so, how?

RELIGION AS SOCIAL STRUCTURE
"One for all and all for one."

Our final model for religion invokes social order. Religions, as we experience them, usually involve social structures: communities, authorities, group activities, and group property. People do religion together. American individualism has led to an increase in "cafeteria religion," the idea that one can pick and choose which aspects of faith one wants and self-assemble a spiritual life. As the term implies, such self-determination has been frowned upon historically by the major faiths. The word heresy comes from the Greek verb to choose and has always carried the meaning "to choose for oneself" apart from the community. I think it is safe to say that most of what we associate with the word religion happens in a communal setting.

Perhaps the communal aspect of religion is what modern Americans find most unsettling. Why should I allow others to make choices for me? Why should I give up self-determination in any aspect of my life? Anti-religionists like to point out instances when authority has been abused in the history of religion – perhaps forgetting the cliché that "power corrupts." Power structures set up the possibility of abuse, regardless of where the power comes from. Religious authority represents one of the more dramatic forms of power, but it is not the only one.

The First Vatican Council (1869-1870) set forth a very clear definition of religion in terms of social structure by stating that all those who do not accept the primacy of the Pope are not part of the church. The church becomes a property of the central authority with all others belonging only insofar as they are connected to that authority. This communal and hierarchical model appears most clearly in the "magisterium" or teaching authority of the church leaders. The idea of religion as social structure matches well with the Renaissance concepts of feudal authority that shaped many Roman Catholic institutions.

Christianity need not be so hegemonic; nor, indeed, is today's Roman Catholic Church. Members of the faction supporting papal power have been called *ultramontanists*.[80] Over the past millennium there has been a gradual accretion of power in the papacy. In some ways this peaked with Vatican I, though in other ways, John Paul II concentrated even more power in Rome. One of the most famous catholic alternatives, called *conciliarism*, holds that ultimate authority comes only from a council of bishops assembled. This faction held sway briefly in the high Middle Ages, though elements of it can be seen in Vatican II. Like any other faith community, Catholicism does not form a monolithic whole. Individuals and factions exist. Each holds a different view of how the church should be structured, but they all believe that structure to be important.

This political naming extends into the modern age in the names of mainline Protestant denominations. *Episcopalians* viewed bishops as the highest authority – arguably valuing the conscience of individual bishops over the conscience of the bishops assembled in council. The word "Episcopal" comes from *episcopos*, the Greek word for overseer, commonly translated from the New Testament as "bishop." *Presbyeterians* viewed bishops as unnecessary. For them, the highest authority and political power was the local minister or elder (from the Greek *presbyteros*). *Congregationalists* did not even accept that authority and insisted the church authority resides only in the congregation assembled. All three groups currently have representative and democratic leadership, but with proportionately more or less power assigned to bishops, presbyters, and congregations within each system. Other Christian churches operate in other ways. The Quakers, for instance, decide by consensus. All these examples show strong evidence of social construction of the faith, even though the details differ.

Religions such as Christianity and Islam, promote the idea that one's faith is a matter of choice, but many other religions hold a more restrictive view. Hinduism provides a beautiful example of a fixed social structure. The Hindu caste system integrates social position and religious membership. Your birth dictates your status. Judaism does something similar when it attributes Jewish identity to

[80] The word "ultramontanist" arose in France during the Protestant reformation. It referred to Papal loyalists who saw religious authority as originating from Italy, beyond the mountains.

children with Jewish mothers. Membership comes from belief (exemplified in the *bar/bat mitzah*) and from practice (shown in circumcision and the keeping of *halakha*), but a strong cultural identity exists independent of either. People refer to themselves as culturally Jewish. The same can be said of any number of other faiths. For some, cultural identity *is* religious identity. According to many schools of thought (including physicalist determinism), you have little or no control over your religious affiliation. Believers in the social definition of religion are more likely to expect members to follow religious norms because they belong, whether or not they agree.

Critics of the social definition of religion argue that it asks the wrong questions. Evangelicals worry that it does not provide a concrete enough connection between the individual and the divine. Individualistic cultures, like the U.S., complain that corporate faith denies the individual conscience. Believers in the philosophical definition of religion see faith as a property of the mind and a personal prerogative. Believers in the behavioral definition see faith involving necessary ends or actions with non-conformists riding on the efforts of the "true believers." In each case, communities seek to exclude those who do not line up with their definitions.

In and Out

The question of inclusion and exclusion proves particularly important for the definition of religion and may tell us something interesting about the role of the scientific worldview. We have seen how worldview and metaphysics shape who we treat as our neighbor. When the Israelites settled in Canaan, they exterminated the local population. Critics of Judaism and Christianity have pointed out that the commandment "thou shalt not kill" must not apply to non-Israelites. It begs the question of whether, and to what extent, ethical rules apply to non-members. A parallel can be seen in Islam, where Muslims and non-Muslims have different rights and responsibilities under the law. It makes a difference whether or not you belong to the in-group. In theory, the New Testament advocates treating all humans as neighbor. In other words all people deserve to be treated as though they were members of the in-group. In practice, we see that Christian groups usually treat other Christians better than non-Christians and other members of their own sect better than non-members. I advocate for the ideal – the theory of inclusion – in my own tradition, but recognize how often we fail to achieve it.[81]

Ontologically, inclusion can be a wonderful thing: all people are equal in the eyes of God, all people have the same rights, and we must treat them all the same. Ethically, inclusion can be extremely troublesome. If everyone has the same rights, do they not also have the same responsibilities? If anyone can become a member, why haven't you? I did not understand this problem at an emotional level until I visited Samoa. Samoans are wonderfully generous and inclusive and I laud their ability to care for people. If you live on a small island, it takes work to feed everyone. Lone individuals fare poorly and everyone has someone to whom they can turn. At the same time, the system of allegiance gives chiefs and pastors immense power over the people they patronize. Individuals feel keenly the responsibility they have to family and society. Women and sexual minorities can be trapped by the system and abuse arises when leaders take advantage of their power. Living on a small island, dissidents cannot simply move away. The interdependence of the people makes it very difficult to complain or change the system. Thus ethical challenges arise from universal inclusion. It is not enough to assert or enforce the ideal; communities must work out the consequences and guard against abuses.

We see these same issues writ large with Christianity and Islam. Both are universal religions – anyone can be a member. Both can claim a desire to convert the whole world. If you have a better truth, a better ethical system, and a better social structure, why should you not share it with the world? They try to take care of everyone. But what about those that don't want that kind of care? What about people with other religions or other identities that do not find the view better from the inside? The ability to include everyone can easily

[81] Christian countries, both Protestant and Catholic, differentiated by religion under the law up until the 19th century. Nationalism and human rights philosophy began to erode these distinctions. It should be noted that human rights philosophy in the Enlightenment drew heavily on Christian natural law theory. As with science, the historical pedigree does not entail necessity – one need not be Christian to believe in human rights – but if one does not use the natural law foundation, we must ask what other foundation we will put in its place.

be interpreted as a need to include everyone, and an excuse to use extreme measures to do so.

Lest we consider this a solely religious phenomenon, I'd ask you to consider capitalism. The use of money and ownership in understanding almost all social interactions can be alien and troubling to people brought up in communal or socialist countries. Once you allow anyone to join, you almost always create penalties for not joining. The mistreatment of Native Americans by European immigrants provides a great example. First the Europeans forced local tribes to reimagine land as property (to be owned) and then they refused to recognize their property rights. Talk to anyone who has moved from a socialist country to a capitalist one and they will tell you about the disorientation and disempowerment of discovering they have to account – literally account financially – for their preferences. Largely, I see the shift to capitalism as a good one, but I also note that it represents a society level choice made by groups. Individuals cannot opt out and they cannot survive without taking on capitalist behaviors and identities (owner, consumer, worker,…). All communities must negotiate membership and boundaries, and this is always challenging.

Questions of in and out form the core of social and political definition of religion. The issue spans all three realms, drawing on and impacting both philosophy and practice, but shapes social structure in a truly profound way. Authority figures of all types tend to be the keepers of boundaries, with common rituals that reinforce a sense of inclusion (or exclusion). Religion makes little sense without some element of how people construct and maintain social groups, how they bring people in and send people out. This same communal aspect has been praised as "radical hospitality," "in-clusion," or "acceptance" and derided as "hegemony," "assimilation," or "colonialism" but in every case we see the formation of a larger body out of individuals. The extent to which you find this wonderful (or disturbing) will depend on how much you value community and how much you value individuality. From my perspective good religions will be reasonable in asking these questions explicitly and in balancing the needs of the group with the needs of individuals.

Authority

Whenever we attribute faith to a group, whether in the form of creeds, practices, or communities, we must ask who has the power to speak for the whole. Who maintains consistency for the larger organism? Who remembers and keeps the tradition? Who defines norms, sets boundaries, and enforces restrictions? These functions take the shape of authority and each of us can identify numerous examples, whether or not we have belonged to their religious community. In the United States, the pastor, priest, rabbi, and nun may be the most familiar, but imam, mufti, monk, and lama are slowly infiltrating the national consciousness.

Religious authorities help define most religious communities. While a few religions truly do operate on purely egalitarian consensus, even these tend to attract persons who carry the tradition's stories, who organize communal rites, and who are available to answer questions. All societies create authority figures to preserve the norms of the group and facilitate collective problem solving. They recognize the diverse gifts of their members, assigning different tasks to different people. Religious societies follow the same pattern. Those with talents for organizing, managing, defending, or producing often get chosen to be leaders.

If we believe in transcendent, unseen realities, then we must also believe that some people will be better qualified to mediate between the seen and the unseen. Religious leaders may be chosen for apparent talent in this area. How they do so differs depending upon your philosophical assumptions. Surprisingly often, religious leaders are chosen for more immediate reasons including intelligence, charm, and patience.

Once again, we must never assume these communal decisions are made without reason. In order to survive for more than a generation, religious authority structures need to provide real service to the community. When looking at a religious authority structure, it will be important to ask not only how it works, but why it works. What need was the role created to fill? What needs does it actually fill? How does it relate to the larger structure? Can the authority be questioned or displaced? If so, how and by whom? No doubt many religious authorities – and many secular authorities – act as parasites, siphoning off resources without providing a return. Nonetheless, some will provide services not immediately apparent. We can judge their worth, but we need to be careful if we expect to do so using the best criteria.

What boundary keepers exist in your life? Who defines the bounds of community, consensus, and rationality? Whose opinion matters to you in questions of value and inclusion? Are their preferences transparent or hidden? All of these issues arise when judging the health of religious communities, indeed communities in general.

SCIENCE AS RELIGION

I have paid particular attention to the philosophical definition because, in these areas, we see the greatest overlap between religion and science. Religion entails epistemology; it requires normative statements about how we know things. Scientific methodology, by making strong epistemological claims, will necessarily interact with religious philosophy. Some partisans want science to take over all the philosophical functions of religion. They believe that scientific commitments to mutual observables, symmetry, hypotheses, and iteration should be the normative – if not exclusive – epistemology for all humans. Along with these basic principles, they may also import reductionism, physicalism, progressivism, and a host of other ideological commitments. I am not convinced that those ideas serve us well in setting up standards of practice and politics. Nor do I think they form the best standards of philosophy as they are often intentionally blind to consequences. Science, at least in principle, favors rigorous knowledge over effective belief (though these are not fully separable as we will explore in the next two chapters). In any case, we must pay close attention to how and why we set the standards we do, and how and why we enforce them. Philosophical considerations alone are not enough for religion or any other society. Social structures and ethical norms must be established, transmitted, and maintained.

As I write this book, I hope you will share my appreciation for a diversity of reasoning styles. More than that, I hope you will come to appreciate that religion, in all three of its aspects, contributes to how we understand reality and use reason. Our actions and our social structures contribute to the way we see the world. No matter how much philosophical, practical, and social cargo of religion we toss out, we must have metaphysical constructs that allow us to operate. Eliminating religion would not eliminate the constructs, but it would eliminate almost all of the careful, systematic, and thoughtful ways we have found for generating those constructs. Those who ask for the end of religion are really asking for metaphysical disarmament. They don't want us to be critical of our creeds, our practices, and our authority structures in any way other than the way their own metaphysics dictates.

Religion creates worldview. It fosters beliefs using the tools of thought, discipline, and community life. Without question these implements have been used poorly at times. People have utilized evil means, sought bad ends, and formed unhealthy relationships. They have also created the very value systems we use to judge what is evil, what is bad, and what is unhealthy. Religions help define our place in the world. They establish a sense of cosmos, an ordered whole that includes both what we see and what we do not see. They place us within that whole, giving us meaning, purpose, and connection to the world around us. And all of these activities are intimately tied to our ideas of what exists, how we generate knowledge, and how we form belief.

Science has an important place within these processes of worldview formation. It can be one of the stronger and more influential tools, but it will never be able to expand beyond the philosophical aspect of religion, at least not as a methodology. Science, as I have presented it, does not give us preferences, though once we have established preferences, it may help us decide how to achieve them. Neither am I convinced that the current culture of science provides the best tools for achieving those goals scientists agree on: accurate models, progressive knowledge, and the power to predict the consequences of our actions. One need only look at the increasing cost of scientific journals to see that our process of peer review is highly problematic, if not profoundly broken.

The culture of science might give us our preferences – even if scientific methodology does not. The individualism, physicalism, reductionism, and progressivism of modern Western culture and science might be worth pursuing. But, once we allow this philosophy to determine our preferences – to the extent that it determines our values, morals, communities, and authority structures – it would have become a religion in and of itself. It would need to establish gate-keepers and enforcers making value judgments beyond the realm of the scientific method. It would be prone to all the same errors and abuses as the older social structures. Is that truly what we want?

☙ ✦ ❧

In this chapter, I laid out three common aspects of religion as we see it. Religions have philosophical, practical, and political dimensions, none of which operates independently of the others. Unsurprisingly, religious people throughout history have struggled over which aspect should be considered the most important. As observers, it will be our responsibility to appreciate the argument each is trying to make. Too often partisans both for and against particular religious positions have presented us with a false dichotomy. "Either you believe in X or you have no faith at all." "Either you do X or you are not really one of us." "You're either with us or you're evil." It is rarely that simple. Religion operates in a number of realms, and no one area is completely separable.

Think about how philosophy, practice, and politics interact in your life. What communities are you part of and how are they organized? What actions do you take on a regular basis? What do you think you know about yourself and your surroundings? In the last section of the book, I give my own suggestions for how to fruitfully integrate these three aspects of life and community in a way that promotes solid reasoning. You can view this as integrating faith and science or simply thinking carefully about world and your place in it. For my part, careful reasoning has made all three aspects of my life more fulfilling. It has also allowed me to better align my preferences and choices. Science and Christianity have both been indispensible in the process.

CHANGE

CHAPTER 17
Power over Nature

What role does power have in our models of the world? How do our ability and desire to control our environment – both through prediction and technology – affect our philosophy? Metaphysics has been heavily influenced by questions of efficacy – what works. The next two chapters look at the philosophical and ethical implications of this relationship.

For the last few centuries, science has promised greater and greater control over the natural world – and delivered on those promises. Supporters of science have justly pointed out the immense benefits of engineering and architecture, medicine and manufacturing, instruments and armaments. These skills and tools provide leverage for humans in dealing with the physical world and have improved the standard of living for humans around the globe. Science produces results.

Phil Dowe, as many others before him, has suggested that modern science is intimately tied up with a concept of dominance over nature.[82] At first I was dubious about this notion, thinking that power is more part of scientific culture than an essential feature of science itself. The more I read about the history of science, however, the more I became convinced that from the time of Francis Bacon onward, scientists have been judged on their ability to predict and compel natural events. Perhaps it is more central than I thought. Let me lay out both a contemporary and a historical argument for the place of power in science.

I want to tread carefully here. Rhetoric about science and religion frequently confuses normative and descriptive claims. They need to be separated if we want to think critically. This chapter will explore the descriptive claim. Do more powerful models trump less powerful models in the practice of science? How does the criterion

[82] Phil Dowe, *Galileo, Darwin, and Hawking* (Eerdmans, 2005), pp. 57-81.

of power relate to the aesthetic of science? It seems uncontroversial to say that science and scientists care about results. They aim to create knowledge that gives us a better idea of how we impact our world. That goal is accomplished through an iteration of observation and hypothesis that carefully records discrete effects of discrete actions. Exercising power over our surroundings in a controlled way generates powerful knowledge. Thus the scientific epistemology uses power. We know that scientific epistemology and ontology work because we can test the knowledge they generate.

The next chapter will look at the normative claim, whether we can jump from epistemology (how we know) to axiology (what we value). Does the factual claim – science produces power – support a preference claim; should we value power? Should we value models and methods that give us power over those that don't? In particular, should we value (support, fund, perpetuate) the people, policies, and institutions that generate the most powerful knowledge? And, how does a preference for powerful knowledge relate to other preferences we might have?

Epistemology and Power

Ask any advocate for science why science is so important; they will all give you the same answer. "It works." Science provides knowledge of the world in concrete ways that allow us to change things. Even the examples have become somewhat standard. How has science improved the world? It has given us indoor plumbing and antibiotics. Longer lists usually include electricity, medicine, and telecommunications, but the message is always the same. The world is better because of science and that improvement can be demonstrated through the technologies science produces. The progress of science, mentioned in chapter six, comes part and parcel with the idea of iteration. More observations and hypotheses lead to better observations and hypotheses and all of this produces better knowledge. Science is good because it produces what it promises, knowledge of the world.

Here comes the interesting part. How do we recognize it as *knowledge*? How do we differentiate between good reasons to think something true and bad reasons to think something true? The scientific method as I have presented it is an epistemology, a way of coming to know things or a way of justifying our beliefs about the world. To say science produces knowledge really doesn't give us enough information. After all, astrology is also epistemology. Many people have claimed (and still do) that they know things about our personal lives based on observation of the stars and planets. They justify their beliefs on the basis of astrology exactly as astronomers justify their beliefs on the basis of astronomy.

Hopefully you find this statement somewhat offensive. I do. And yet I also recognize that it is strictly valid grammatically and logically. Both astronomers and astrologers make observations of celestial objects, apply a few axioms about the relationships between objects, and come to conclusions. Both are doing epistemology *of some sort*. Both arrive at conclusions about the world that they think are justified. In my mind, the difference comes from reliability – the power to make accurate predictions consistently. The *a priori* assertions of astronomy – about symmetry, simplicity, fields, etc. – allow astronomers to reason from sky watching to cosmology, galactic formation, stellar fusion, and hundreds of other topics. They can predict the positions of stars and planets in the sky every night and pinpoint planets, asteroids, and comets well enough for us to send robots to them. The *a priori* assertions of astrology – holism, the effects of major and minor houses, the influence of the planets, etc. – do not allow astrologers to reliably predict whether you will come into a great deal of money or find love.

This is not just a subjective choice between axioms. There are bad axioms. There are very bad axioms. "The universe is unintelligible." "Humans cannot know anything." "We cannot communicate." All three of these are discussion stoppers and, I believe, reason stoppers. We need a way, then, to be explicit about how we choose between epistemologies and the axioms upon which they are built. Questions about whether science produces knowledge and whether science produces "better" knowledge will rest upon this kind of argument.

If we say science is the search for knowledge and justify science by saying it produces knowledge, we're talking in circles. They only way to justify any epistemology is to measure the confidence it produces against some *external* standard of truth. Arguments against "reasoning" through revelation almost always follow these lines. "Show me evidence." We require back up proof, at least once in a while, to confirm that our way of knowing works. We think that magic, astrology, and extra-sensory perception (ESP) don't work because we have measured them against science, but what do we measure science against?

Again, I have to be painfully explicit. Science *does* work and it *is* justified. I have not set up this argument to convince you that science has no support. I have set it up to establish that science does have a support and we should be clear about what it is. It is not enough to say science works because "science." Nor can we simply say that science is the pursuit of knowledge. Many methodologies, from the ridiculous to the sublime, pursue knowledge. We must figure out what standard we have for saying scientists actually find knowledge.

I have come to think the way I do about the scientific method (epistemology) and scientific culture in order to deal with this very question, which turns out to be a matter of value. It is not value *within* the scientific framework, but value *for* the scientific framework, which motivates scientists. We value truth, an agreement between the models in our heads and some external reality. We value methods that lead us toward truth, and we judge those methods by their ability to help us interact with the world. The principles of hypothesis and iteration explicitly link our beliefs about the world to repeated observations. Thus a successful hypothesis must predict some future event that we can observe. Even better, the most successful hypotheses will allow us to make something happen in the world. Experimentation and technology are neither more nor less than doing something to the world with the hope of getting a predictable response.

In short, the scientific gold standard for knowledge is power. Does it allow me to anticipate and control my environment? The statement "knowledge is power" is a cliché, and we normally argue from the former to the latter; any time you know something, that knowledge gives you power over it. I am suggesting that science reverses this relationship; anytime you have power over something, that power constitutes knowledge. Science places the highest value on knowledge claims that allow us to anticipate and manipulate the physical universe. It's not surprising that this mindset has led to increasing power. No philosophy could do it better.

I am skeptical of string theory, multiverse, and many worlds hypotheses in physics precisely because they – at present – have no relationship to power. They may at some point in the future be borne out by observation. In the meantime, they are lovely theory and philosophy, but only tangentially science. Elegance is not enough. Indeed, choosing based on elegance apart from power would eliminate the very important difference I see between science and other ways of knowing.

One must ask whether this equation of power and knowledge holds for every epistemology. Perhaps power is a value not only for science, but for humans generally. Many philosophies suggest so, but I think we have other options. In particular, I would hold up models of knowledge as unbiased communication between two or more subjects. Within Christianity, this includes the idea of mystical communion God. Within Buddhism, it includes perfect meditation, the attachment and aversion free appreciation of a situation. Even within scientific culture, I think there is a notion of observation without pre-conception that fits the bill. If you are uncomfortable calling these knowledge, then ask yourself why. The first two, at least, have longer historical claims to the words "knowledge" and "science" than does our modern concept.

I don't want science to seek these other kinds of knowledge. I like the fact that science does what it does so well. I want all people, but especially scientists, to be aware that this quest for power can be part of a larger set of goals. The power criterion works, but it should not be the only criterion present when we construct our models.

Ontology and Power

The question of supernatural entities has relevance to scientists because science provides so much power over the natural world. To many people "natural" has become synonymous with "observable to science" or "amenable to scientific observation and technological control." On a purely personal level, the supernatural seems like an affront to the progress of science, which so far has made great strides in understanding. I admit of this feeling myself. Why can't science, so helpful in our understanding of the physical universe, be helpful also in our understanding of the greater cosmos? In what ways might scientific methodology be used to understand things like preferences, souls, and values?

Such reasoning has fatal flaws. First and foremost, the utility of science comes from its limits. It deals with mutual observables, things all humans see equally. Science is something we do together and it distinguishes itself from non-science and pseudoscience by the careful application of common principles of reasoning. We test our hypotheses not only against our observations, but also against the observations of countless others. Delving into things which different people perceive differently presents problems.

It would be easy then to simply split the cosmos into the natural (scientific) realm and the supernatural (theological) realm, much as Aquinas did. Scientists, however, can point to the rapid expansion of science. Daily we discover new ways of looking at the world – ways that represent subjective experiences, such as happiness, in terms of objective observations, such as dopamine levels. The myth of progress within the scientific community generates a frontier attitude wherein the unexplained is a challenge. Scientists always seek to colonize and expand "nature."

This leads to a position known as "God in the gaps," when theologians claim that religion exists to explain the things that science cannot yet touch. It comes with the implicit idea that science will eventually reach everywhere, leaving religion with no more point. While I firmly support the expansion of the scientific frontier, I deplore a parallel religious retreat. Religions are in the business of describing reality, creating common knowledge, and explaining relationships. For me these areas can be, indeed must be, informed by science, but they also require serious commitments outside the bounds of the mutual observables. They have to do with values, choices, and people. They also have to do with the foundational metaphysical work that makes science reasonable in the first place. How do we deal with math and imagination and possible futures? These questions dramatically affect our ability to do science – and they cannot be observed or induced. Religions do real work for people and part of that work will never be replaced by the scientific method. I adhere to the philosophical axioms inherent in the scientific method and many of those present in the scientific culture precisely because they fit with my beliefs and practices as an Anglican Christian. Admitting my humility, I use the tool at hand to help me understand reality, but I do so for the sake of my religiously moderated goals.

As with any tool, science has its limits. You may be familiar with the saying, "to a man with a hammer, every problem looks like a nail." I find this particularly applicable in the case of science. Because science has been so incredibly successful as a tool for gaining power over the natural world, we want to use it everywhere. We want to redefine all problems in terms that science can handle. It remains possible that we will one day achieve this goal. Perhaps science will one day expand to explain all things. It also remains possible that I will never need to face another home improvement problem that cannot be solved with a hammer. I doubt it. At best, we know that science will not provide all knowledge within our lifetimes. At worst, some things will never be explained by science. Either way, for the foreseeable future we must use other methods of coming to knowledge – from *a priori* reasoning to revelation, from dialectic to deduction.

Pretend for a moment that science did explain everything, with all knowledge of the physical universe available to us and definitive proof that nothing else existed. What then? We would still need to determine the purpose of our lives, choose how to use our knowledge, and come to terms with our existence within this perfectly explained world. Knowledge and power do not automatically produce meaning and purpose. Knowing that dopamine and oxytocin cause my attraction to someone in no way helps me determine what to do next. Knowing that my heart will fail does nothing to aid my fear of dying. Knowing that I have been conditioned by centuries of genetic evolution utterly fails to help me cope with existential angst. In every case, science tells us something interesting, but doesn't tell us all we really want to know.

I like the metaphor of a toolbox. Science for me is a hammer, tremendously useful and something I pick up whenever I have a project. My religion operates more like a toolbox; it provides a whole suite of tools tailored to individual tasks. More than that, Christianity provides a house to fix, schematics to plan the repair, and fellow workers. In that context, the hammer represents only one piece of the bigger picture. So, even if science were capable of ex-plaining everything, explanation does not fill all my needs.

Does Christianity? Does my religious faith provide for all the needs in my life? An interesting question, and one I am happy to answer. No. It does not provide a complete comprehensive plan for my life, but, like a toolbox, it has compartments that help me identify what might be missing. Religions provide a language for talking about meaning and purpose, as well as epistemology, ontology, useful behaviors, and community.

The project of understanding reality and our place in it has been going on for thousands of years. I want to draw on the experience of countless ancestors who have asked the same questions before me. Who am I? What should I do? When did it all begin? Where do I belong? How do I respond to the situation I find myself in? Jesus of Nazareth, Mohammed, Siddhartha Gautama, Lao Tzu, and countless others have given us answers to consider.

I don't claim that all religious answers are right. Many are wrong and some are extremely dangerous. And yet, as a scientist, I would be ridiculed for coming to a conclusion without at least skimming the relevant literature. Why should these questions be any different? How can I pass up countless pages of potential answers to my questions, answers that have proven satisfying to millions? I believe everyone should be familiar with a variety of options when it comes to belief systems. We should teach at least the basic outlines of Christianity, Islam, Hinduism, and Buddhism in school, and be introduced to belief systems that would reject all of those. Religious leaders – theologians, pastors, scholars, etc. – need an even deeper knowledge of the alternatives so that they can think critically and teach about why one might be better than the others.

Like science, religion happens in groups. Scientists use the experience, observation, and reason of hundreds of scientists, technicians, and engineers when coming to conclusions. Religious professionals likewise use large communities to do work that cannot be done alone. As in science, religious communities have standards for whom to trust and whom not to trust; they have authority structures.

If we are to be pragmatic with regard to power (again, I do not think we must) at least let us judge religious structures on the basis of whether they deliver. It would be irrational to toss them out *a priori*. We must ask whether religious philosophies produce powerful knowledge, whether religious practices empower participants, and whether religious communities accomplish things that could not be otherwise done. We must ask why religious authorities hold the roles they do within their communities. What do they provide? A critical part of answering these questions will involve asking those who follow them.

For me, religious structures help create a comprehensive worldview (including epistemology, ontology, and axiology), they help us define our priorities, and, if they work right, encourage us to assess how well our needs are being met. Rational religion requires nothing less.

☙ ✦ ❧

Modern science invokes power as a criterion of success, perhaps the chief criterion for success in the pursuit of knowledge. Good knowledge is knowledge that allows you to understand and control your environment, to predict the consequences of your actions in the physical universe. As we think critically about reasoning in religion and science, it will be important to think about how this preference for power relates to the central methodology of science. I believe it is both necessary to the scientific method and central to scientific culture. Power to do – and power to predict the outcome when we do (or refrain from doing) – provides the gold standard in science as epistemology.

Is powerful knowledge our only goal? Or even our chief goal? Relational knowledge presents one alternative, though we might also consider knowledge that leads to peace, curiosity, or stability as alternate criteria. Undoubtedly knowledge as power will indirectly serve our other goals; it allows us to accomplish things in the world; it allows us to do work. In the next chapter we'll look at how this preference for power fits within a larger axiology and whether it competes with other criteria as we create belief systems for navigating the world. We will also look at how social structures regulate and integrate our ability to exercise power and produce powerful knowledge.

CHAPTER 18
Power Plays

Power plays an interesting and important role in our understanding of science, religion, and nature. If we start by thinking only physical things exist (ontological physicalism) and assume that one of the primary functions of knowledge is power over nature, then we start to see all things through the lens of the power they give us. This interpretation of religion appears again and again in modern rhetoric. Both opponents and supporters of religion have argued that religious philosophies, practices, and politics are chiefly about gaining power. Similar claims have been made about science. It can be hard to tell when we want power for the sake of knowledge and when we want knowledge for the sake of power, particularly when the two are so intimately related – as they are in science. Is knowledge always power?

We now turn to the normative aspects of this relationship. How does a preference for powerful knowledge reflect on science as a moral endeavor? Scientists produce power. I want to be very clear that when I speak of scientists preferring power, I'm not talking about serious men in lab coats trying to take over the world. I am not saying that scientists prefer to have power. I am saying that scientists prefer to produce knowledge that gives people power over their surroundings. It's a very different notion. Most of us find this second version less problematic morally, but that doesn't make it value neutral. We need to think about how this power fits into our lives.

Along similar lines, it may be worth comparing scientists with religious leaders in terms of how they produce and regulate powerful knowledge. One way of modeling communities is to look at the functions of individuals in particular groups. Some thinkers have argued that religious leaders' primary function is to regulate power within societies that believe in supernatural power. They provide tools for working with the principles and powers that rule the world. Modern scientists, they argue, do the same thing, but they can deliver on their promises in a way that religious authorities never could. For these thinkers, religious authority is just a series of bad beta-versions for real authority, authority based on power over of the natural world. This story of human progress through (and to) science sees the hammer as the perfect tool; all other tools are no more than poorly crafted hammers.

I find this story of human triumph uncompelling. I like screwdrivers and I like the insights Christianity provides into agents, choices, and preferences, not to mention a hundred other aspects of my life. I worry that our society – being focused on power over nature – has forgotten other goals. We fight over who has the best hammer and neglect the need for other tools entirely. We fight over who has the most accurate, powerful knowledge without pausing to ask if that is really the knowledge most important to us.

Scientists possess some of the knowledge producing and verifying functions once given to priests (wrongly or rightly). Some of our loudest debates about science and religion come from shifts in society around trust. Who do we go to for effective knowledge about the world? Who do we trust to guide us in right thought, right behavior, and right community? People get upset because more than abstract knowledge is at stake. Philosophy, practice, and politics are intertwined, and we cannot change one without changing the others. We should take care when adjusting our metaphysics because doing so impacts all these other areas of our lives. This is no excuse for complacency; quite the opposite. It is a plea that we be rational – or as rational as possible – about the rules and structures that underlie reason. Often that means changing our default settings. Critical thinking means considering both the knowledge and belief aspects of the things we hold true.

Power and Dominion

The idea of knowledge as power has roots in Christian religion. Many strands of thought within the monotheisms have encouraged us to think of our relationship with the universe as one of master to slave. The metaphor of God as king can easily be coupled with the idea of humans as God's viceroys, ruling over nature.

Francis Bacon, the father of empiricism, had this to say about knowledge and power:

> "[I]f a man endeavor to establish and extend the power and dominion of the human race itself over the universe, his ambition (if ambition it can be called) is without doubt both [...] wholesome and [...] noble [...]. Now the empire of man over things depends wholly on the arts and sciences. For we cannot command nature except by obeying her."[83]

He considered dominion to be the proper role of humanity and the arts and sciences to be our way of attaining that dominion. Speaking of empiricism, his most famous work, *Novum Organum*, ends with a statement about humans' relationship to nature.

> "For man by the fall fell at the same time from his state of innocency and from his dominion over creation. Both of these losses however can even in this life be in some part repaired; the former by religion and faith, the latter by arts and sciences. For creation was not by the curse made altogether and forever a rebel, but in virtue of that charter 'In the sweat of thy face shall thou eat bread,' it is now by various labors (not certainly by disputations or idle magical ceremonies, but by various labors) at length and in some measure subdued to the supplying of man with bread, that is, to the uses of human life."[84]

By the labor of science, we may regain the control we lost in the fall. This version of Christian theology explains both the efficacy and the cost of science. For Bacon, science was noble because it empowered, and difficult because of original sin. He saw Christianity providing a mandate for scientific progress to the ends of human control of nature. We can see how a philosophical statement (about the relation of humans to nature) and a value judgment (about the goodness of human power) were incorporated from Christian religion into scientific culture. I do not personally subscribe to this picture of Christianity or this picture of Christianity and science. I simply want

---

[83] Francis Bacon, *Novum Organum*, Book 1: 129. Spedding translation (Taggard and Thompson, 1863).

[84] Book 2: 52. The internal quote is from Genesis 3:19.

to point out its prevalence in the thought of Bacon and other pioneers of modern science.

Power as value arises necessarily from the definition of the scientific method. The ability to predict and manipulate the natural world forms our standard for judging hypotheses. Remember our aesthetics of utility and fruitfulness. Historically, this moral/practical commitment comes from Christian religious philosophy, though we can see how this type of dominion might be equally valued within Islam and Judaism and many atheist philosophies. I'm less concerned with its presence than with its primacy. Do we seek power for its own sake or for the sake of some greater virtue, such as compassion, obedience, or service?[85]

Bacon's theology includes another person with dominion over humans just as we have dominion over nature. This supremacy of God provided a moral level by which to challenge the power of tyrants (natural law and human rights). The theistic God can be a prop for service as well as dominion. I worry about the consequences of too fully embracing our dominion without also embracing our dependence on a higher power. Christians are asked to subordinate the will for power to a will for love. The greatest commandments are to love God and to love neighbor; therefore, power in and of itself will be sinful when not directed to those ends. I suspect that a Muslim theologian would agree, saying that Islam calls for obedience to God's peace and order. When we seek power to bring all things into alignment with that peace, only then do we serve God. When we seek power for its own ends, we practice idolatry.

In the absence of such external concerns, science produces a rather one-dimensional value system. Within the context of a larger community of faith, the value of scientific knowledge and power can be turned to good. It can also be turned to evil. Religion does not make science good, but neither is science alone good. It requires value orientation, like most things in life. The presence of religious values does not guarantee good ends. It only guarantees systematic and communal thought about what those ends should be. Both

[85] Alternatively we might say knowledge is a virtue in and of itself. This, however, simply brings us back to our epistemological question. What constitutes desirable knowledge? If we use power as our utility function in judging knowledge, can we really say that we seek knowledge in the abstract?

theists and atheists can be tempted to focus too much on power and control.

Ask yourself what your ends are and where they come from. Why do you value scientific knowledge? Do you actually use scientific knowledge for the ends you describe? In other words, does scientific knowledge line up with belief for you personally and for you as a member of specific groups? When an "atheist" argues publicly for some value – perhaps broader access to health care and education – ask how they came to see that as valuable. When a theist argues publicly for the same thing, ask the same question. Above all, look for agreement between the stated moral justifications and the stated actions.

All of which brings us to the question of dominion within theology. I am not qualified to speak for many philosophies, but I can say a word or two about Christian thought on the matter. Baconian dominion represents one school of thought, albeit a very popular one among Enlightenment Christians. It was slowly built from the Middle Ages onward. For centuries, many Christians placed a divide between humanity and the rest of creation. Perhaps the most influential thinker on this topic was Thomas Aquinas, who separated the creation into physical and spiritual realms. Humans were unique in having a spiritual soul in a physical body, thus we were at the pinnacle of the physical world. We share in the spiritual properties of the angels. The human body appears at the top of the physical creation, making us the proper rulers over all things on Earth (and yet subject to things in heaven). Aquinas introduced an ontological line between humans and other animals, a line that has profound consequences for Christian moral theology.[86]

Christians have considered several other models for the place of humans in creation. Two prominent historical trends can be seen in the book of Job and in Celtic spirituality, both of which emphasize the limited role of humans within nature. We represent only one aspect of God's creation and not the culmination of it. These theologies seem more amenable to the scientific idea that humans exist as one among many animals. I find this to be one of the prime reasons for Christian diversity when it comes to evolution (and the common descent of humans among the apes). Evangelicals and Pentecostals

[86] I discuss this idea in more detail in Mix, LJ (2016) Life-value narratives and the impact of astrobiology on Christian ethics. *Zygon* 51(2):520-535.

are more invested in theologies that contrast humans with the rest of creation. They worry that scientific arguments conflict with authority-based arguments on the matter of human uniqueness. Catholics, Orthodox, and Anglicans, on the other hand, draw more heavily on theologies that highlight God's pervasive favor for all of creation, often in ways that marginalize or even ignore humans. From this angle, the idea of common descent reinforces a theology of human integration with all life. Of course, none of these traditions is unequivocal, but I want to highlight one way in which theological and scientific arguments are concretely interacting. I also want to point out how the differences are fundamentally ontological; they have to do with the definition of "human."

Recent theologians, dissatisfied with dominion theology for scientific as well as moral reasons, have returned to earlier traditions in hopes of producing a less human-centered theology.[87] These systems provide important metaphysical positions capable of dealing with questions like global warming in moral terms.[88]

Power and responsibility go together. Science provides us with one but not the other. That important moral question requires far more words than would fit here. Nonetheless, we can see how the power to do what we will forms an important, possibly essential element in any moral system. In science we come to an understanding of the natural world capable of making concrete, definite, and lasting changes to our environment. I would like to see a parallel, rational and communal process of reasoning about which changes we want.

The Professional Power Broker

Science gives us power over the physical world; does anything give us similar power over the non-physical world? Do any religions provide us with tools that really work? Critics of religion – from Jewish prophets to modern secular scientists – delight in pointing out religious practices that have no effect. What can idols give you, they ask. It's a

[87] Sallie McFague represents an excellent example of this type of thinking.

[88] They have arisen primarily within schools of thought that are behavioral in their definition of religion and, therefore, most appealing to progressive Christians. Yvonne Gebarra has made some attempt to move this in a more social direction, while Jon Sobrino investigates more philosophical aspects having to do with good and evil.

good question. Each religious person needs to ask whether or not they believe in unseen realities and what, if any, impact those realities have on daily life. If power is your only value, this will be the all and all of the religion question. For many of us, there is more to life than power over the physical environment.

Most religions make claims that they help people transcend physical reality. Christianity stands out in this regard, as sacramental acts provide an "outward and visible sign of an inward and spiritual grace." Most Christians believe that human actions have spiritual and subsequently physical results. Transubstantiation and healing prayer are good examples. Defenders of religion frequently appeal to the practical benefits of joining: "Look, my God can do X and yours can't." The scientist in me screams. The theologian asks whether the claim holds up or not. In this book I avoid answering the question; it should be enough to challenge you to do so for yourself. What standards do you use? How honest are you in using them? As with the knowledge/power relationship if we say that a religion is good (preferred either by ourselves or God) it's worth asking what we mean by that. What makes it good?

Another question arises when we look at the people whose work provides power over the world. Religious power has become deeply entrenched in the model of religion as social structure. Leaders frequently claim access to, power over, and better knowledge of the unseen order.

Modern consumer culture likes to measure things in terms of value added and this shows in how we look at religious institutions. Do we think of religious authorities as supernatural service providers? If so, they need to be judged on the basis of the service they provide. Can they perform works – healing, revealing, removing demons? Progressive Christians (in the modern liberal sense of "progressive") may consider themselves more enlightened, seeing religious leaders as social service providers. Do they lead, empower, and facilitate? These questions are different, but still service oriented. I like this second model better than the first, but am still troubled by the commodification of religion. It seems deeply invested in power, dominion, and productivity. We value people because they give us more control or make us more effective.

No matter how you look at it, the service provider model will start to favor scientists. After all, scientists provide great utility –

medicine, engineering, computation. If the purpose of a priesthood lies in their ability to control the world, then scientists make great priests. Our societies are increasingly led by pragmatism, materialism, and consumerism.[89] If you place the highest value on power over the physical world, scientists and engineers can provide that power.

The Professional Catalyst

An alternate model of the religious leader has been that of mediator – someone who opens up communication. In this model, the free exchange of ideas between the seen and unseen has higher value than power over either. The leader reveals the unseen and activates connections. Like chemical catalysts, they speed up reactions, but are not consumed in them. Often their action is extremely subtle, but things work better in their presence.

Bill Countryman has suggested that the role of priest is to be a guide in the borderlands between seen and unseen realities.[90] I might add that sometimes the unseen is simply beyond the horizon – it need not be invisible. Some religious leaders work to help people feel their way through the rough patches between here and there without claiming unique access or unique knowledge. Gil Stafford argues that good religious leaders listen in a way that helps people to hear themselves better. This listening also creates a quiet space in which people become better observers; attentive silence rather than active interference.[91] Catalyst, guide, and listener are alternatives to power broker as we think of the role of leaders. Indeed, some of the most successful "scientists" have been those individuals who mentor, co-ordinate, and find funding for others, rather than using the scientific method themselves.

I believe that scientists improve society by the power they provide. I am in favor of more science spending, more science education, and more science communication in the U.S. and around the world. At the same time, I think we desperately need more and better catalysts – mediators between humanity and the unseen order,

---

[89] Materialism may refer to either the ontological commitment that only physical entities exist – physicalism – or the ethical commitment that it is good to own more things. As both apply in this instance, I will leave the ambiguity.

[90] *Living on the Border of the Holy* (Morehouse, 1999)

[91] *When Leadership and Spiritual Direction Meet* (Rowman and Littlefield, 2014)

seekers after that order, and observers of the process. I think we need more mediators and moderators who build healthy, open communities. I hope to recall a model of religious authority that has little to do with power and everything to do with communication – with helping each person see the things that do not appear equally to all. We must learn to live together and that means reasoning together about what we know, what we believe, and what we prefer.

Scientific Authority

It can be reassuring to think that science only reflects statements generated by sense data. The empirical monopoly on information presents a picture of an ordered and orderly world in which we need only go and see for ourselves. Everything can be proven, and indeed I can do this myself. Alas, science does not operate so neatly. Like every other culture of knowledge and almost every other method of reasoning, science relies heavily on authority. We must rely on the word of others if we hope to appreciate the vast array of data currently available. We must recognize the role of boundary keepers, rule makers, goal setters, and referees.

The most obvious example of scientific authority comes in the form of peer reviewed scientific journals. Each new study cites tens, if not hundreds, of articles previously written on the subject. These articles give context, provide justifications, and relate new data to previously accepted knowledge. Modern science depends on this deep interconnectedness of different research endeavors. Scientific authorities appear in the structure of universities, companies and laboratories. Oversight and regulation arise every time a project receives funding; and science has become quite expensive.

All of which forces us to ask: how is scientific authority constructed? What makes one researcher trustworthy and another less so? The primary criterion appears be one of reception (a method used for judging the authority of Christian leaders for two thousand years). Is this person accepted by the community as legitimate? Each individual scientist judges her colleagues. Many minor and not-so-minor conflicts arise between individuals, but the sense of the group reflects the opinions of tens or hundreds of people. When judging a colleague, scientists ask a number of questions. Are they able to secure funding? Do we approve of their methodology? Do they attend the right conferences? Do they have a degree from a reputable university? Do they publish in well-respected journals? Above all, we want to know whether their results allow us to manipulate the world around us. We want to see that they have been tested and approved and reproduced. In practice, each scientist exists within a network of trust and reciprocity that may or may not have sufficient resources to do cutting edge research. Peers and funding determine who can make the necessary observations, what observations they make, and whether anyone will listen.

For me, science has a healthier relationship with authority than many religions. This is not because authority is less valued, but because the construction of authority is more transparent. Authorities can always be questioned and are almost always challenged to defend their positions by presenting both observational data and a clear defense of their reasoning. They usually only respond to challenges by other authorities, but the system is set up competitively to insure challengers appear, especially when controversial claims arise (e.g., Martian life).

This stops anyone from accumulating too much power when it comes to shaping communal models. Abuses occur, as they would in any social structure, but there are methods for correcting them. For example, one particularly powerful reviewer can stop certain types of articles from being published. Say the most influential person in a small field wanted to squash a new avenue of research; they could do so by negatively reviewing articles and proposals related to that avenue. Of course, if it's a good experiment, many researchers will want to use it and an alternate journal will pop up. The same thing happens with research. It can be blocked for a few years, even a few decades, but if it produces results then new funders will appear to support it. Within the scientific community, it can be frustrating to see these small abuses of power, but from an outside perspective, the society corrects itself quite quickly. In my experience, science can turn around fairly substantially within a decade, while religions often take a century or more. Honestly, we wouldn't want it to change faster than that.

In chapter 21 of his book *Descent of Man*, Charles Darwin cautions against accepting new observations too readily. "False facts are highly injurious to the progress of science, for they often endure long; but false views, if supported by some evidence, do little harm, for every one takes a salutary pleasure in proving their falseness: and when this is done, one path towards error is closed and the road to truth is often at the same time opened." Accounting for absolutely all the data is important to scientists, meaning the incorporation of false data can be extremely damaging. We want to ensure that only carefully conducted experiments find their way into the common discourse; otherwise we may spend decades trying to explain things that never really happened. Sometimes even sense data – received on authority – will need to be tossed out if we cannot repeat the experiment and the results are too novel. Early attempts to reproduce odd or suspicious data can save much trouble. Journals scrutinize the work of new scientists more closely until they have shown the skill and sensibility to produce reliable data reliably. Similarly, once the reputation of a scientist has been tarnished on the basis of faked data they find it difficult to recover credibility.

My goal has been to show how large a role authority plays in science and how politics and practice shape even scientific knowledge. We can imagine other scientific cultures and have seen many in the history of Europe. For centuries, scientific data only became widely circulated if you were rich or had an aristocratic patron to fund both experiments and publication. The modern system is more open, but doesn't necessarily reflect a truer incarnation of the scientific method. Instead it is a different scientific culture and we must continually ask how well it fits our preferences.

Sometimes debates about religion and science come from competing power structures. Take a close look at the communities represented by various authorities. For whom do they speak and on what basis are they credible? Whom do they allow to check their work and what's at stake for them in being right. Does their position impact their standing with others?

I've presented a fairly rosy picture of science – the ideal to which scientists aspire – because I think it is that ideal of transparent, selfless, communal work that makes science so successful. It is not about escaping metaphysics, but about doing the metaphysics well. Axioms, deduction, and authority all play critical roles. Science rests on a foundation of preferences that cannot be defended scientifically, but they do need to be defended. Thus, I evangelize for the type of philosophy – for me an explicitly religious philosophy – that sets the ground rules for good science. It can also set the ground rules for other aspects of our lives.

☙ ✦ ❧

Power plays an important role in how we interact within communities. It has been intimately involved in the culture and method of science for hundreds of years. Science produces knowledge and we tend to judge our knowledge by the results it can provide. Power though, represents only one kind of knowledge. As individuals and as groups, we will need to assess how much powerful knowledge is worth and how we value it in relation to other kinds of knowledge – knowledge of ourselves, our place, and our purpose. Power alone can be a dangerous thing, but power in the context of meaning can lead us to the kind of world religions have dreamed of for millennia.

As a society, we can ask how we want to spend our resources. What is the best balance between activities and how can we achieve that balance? Scientific and other communities should think critically about the types of authority structures that meet their goals and the beliefs that promote their preferences. For me, religion is not a luxury item, a priority once our primary needs have been met. It plays an integral role in the production, maintenance, and updating of worldviews. It promotes communication and community formation as well as serving as a repository of historical knowledge.

Before reading the last few chapters I hope you will pause for a moment to reflect on what religion and science mean to you in light of this discussion. Which individuals and communities shape the way you ask questions and the way you answer them? What role do authority figures and power brokers play? What are the rules by which you reason and, we must always ask, who gets to referee?

CHAPTER 19
New Knowledge

We live in a complicated and confusing world. From the beginning, humans have struggled to understand the world around them, both in terms of the physical universe and in terms of a larger meaning or cosmos. We create models to help us deal with it all. These models give us power. They also provide comfort by making the universe more understandable and our own place in it more definite.

For good and ill, each one of us holds on to our models of the universe with great tenacity. Whether or not we like our perceived place, we want to know about it. Perhaps it saves us from despair. Our tenacity – our tendency to hold fast to the models we form – makes it very difficult to change our minds. When should we do it? Why should we do it? And, perhaps most importantly, how should we do it? Science gives concrete, definitive answers to these questions, at least as regards our models of the physical universe. We should change our model whenever we find a better way to explain the observations we and others make. We should change our minds because finding a better model gives us more power over the world around us. The scientific method provides a clear epistemological structure for reframing our model of the physical universe.

We have seen that science, as currently constructed, values power in terms of predictions and progress in terms of ever increasing power. One can easily construct a value system where scientific culture continuously adapts in ways that provide for the most rapid progress toward physical mastery. But what if we want to challenge that goal? What if we want our science to serve other purposes? What if we want accuracy more than power? What if we want good communication, or selfless behavior…or happiness? In short, how do we decide if physical power satisfies?

Richard Hooker wrote a passage that profoundly shapes my own view. In the preface of his *Laws of Ecclesiastic Polity*, he writes, "Nature worketh in us all a love to our own counsels. The contradiction of others is a fan to inflame that love." Once we have decided something is true, it can be terribly hard to change our opinion.[92] Worse yet, we often use arguments against our position as an excuse to cling more tightly and to search harder for support. Noting this, epistemology and related metaphysical propositions become more than just philosophical speculation. They become the tools for intelligently, systematically, and reasonably changing our minds.

Chapters two through sixteen explored a range of options for how to think and how to change. They set forth common tools of reason and how they can be applied in scientific and Christian epistemology. In chapters seventeen and eighteen, I reflected on the role power structures play within communities of inquiry and how they shape knowledge and belief. Now we turn to practical suggestions: concrete ways for assessing and updating our knowledge. If reasoning about the world is a game, these are the strategies I use to play the game well.

MODELS

Knowledge evolves and so does our concept of knowledge. Root level epistemology shapes our images so pervasively that it can be hard to see, but more has changed with time than simply our thoughts. Our very concept of knowledge has changed as well. In his book *The Order of Things*, Michel Foucault argues that knowledge changed radically between the 15th and 19th centuries. We went from seeing order as something within objects – essential organizing principles – to seeing it as the best way to view the world – an imposed field of meaning – to seeing it as the ways in which individuals manage their interactions with the world – pragmatic schemes present in the observers.

One of the great challenges for discussing reason will be to recognize how different people think about order. Renaissance philosophers favored participatory knowledge. We only understand by interacting, uncovering correspondences between patterns in the thing and patterns in ourselves. Knowledge was sympathetic: like a

[92] This concept has even been demonstrated scientifically; for examples see Kathryn Schulz *Being Wrong: Adventures in the Margin of Error* (Ecco, 2010) and Robert Cialdini, *Influence: Science and Practice* (Allyn and Bacon, 2001). pp. 52-97

wax mold, you formed your concepts by shaping them around the thing itself. Enlightenment philosophers favored absolute knowledge. We understood things by appealing to one perfect perspective – usually God's. Knowledge was the right way to see the world. After the Enlightenment, we became skeptical of a perfect perspective and started talking about our individual perspectives. Knowledge had to do with how we labeled a thing and fit it into the models in our heads.

These are three radically different systems of reasoning. Our ontology changed as order moved from something in the world to something true of the world to something said by us. Meaning and purpose used to be present within the things we studied, waiting to be discovered. Now we see them as constructed in the minds of observers. Our epistemology changed as well. The balance shifted from revelation and deduction toward observation and induction.

As we read commentary on science and religion historically, it will be important to keep an eye on these differences. Much commentary on Christian knowledge comes from the Renaissance and before. It presumes no objective separation between observer and observed. Indeed, it favors closeness. Most of the early development of scientific reasoning occurs in the Enlightenment, when scholars thought they were discovering the fundamental rules by which the universe was governed. Their thinking betrays a trust that the rational observer can completely separate herself from the object of her study – being completely unbiased and impartial. The observer was expected, quite literally, to take a God's eye view. I embrace a more modern perspective, one that emphasizes models.

A model is a smaller or simplified version of the thing it represents. I believe we each carry around a toy cosmos, a model of reality that we use to navigate the world. The first step in changing your worldview will be to recognize that the toy is not the thing itself. A gap exists between the way you think and the way the world is. Only by allowing the possibility of error – the possibility that you might be wrong – can you reason about what is right.

Statisticians speak of parameters and statistics. The parameter is a real property of the thing you're observing, such as the percentage of people who voted for Barrack Obama. The statistic is your estimate of the parameter based on a limited set of data. If you polled 500 people on election night, the percentage of people polled who voted for Obama would be an estimate of the national parameter. Scientists emphasize the need for data to drive hypotheses. Zen Buddhists emphasize *mushin*, usually translated "mind without mind," or the ability to perceive something without pre-conceived notions. Both encourage us to distinguish between our models and the world they reflect.[93]

By holding our models lightly, by not becoming too attached to them, we prepare ourselves to receive inconvenient facts. At first this may seem antithetical to the earlier pictures of knowledge. Looking back, we tend to see them as more confident than ourselves, more certain in asserting a single opinion. Partly this comes from our perspective. The farther you go back in time, the fewer people had the ability to record their thoughts and the fewer records actually remain. More importantly, however, we must recognize that confidence has shifted location. In the Renaissance, thinkers were certain that the order existed, but more skeptical of our ability to participate in it. They emphasized our alienation from God and the created world. This alienation limited our ability to see clearly. Yes, the organizing principle for the universe was present in scripture, and interpreted by the church, but never held perfectly by an individual. In the Enlightenment, many thinkers posited perfect order in the mind of God or in the laws of nature, but they also recognized a distance between those cosmic orders and the people who sought them. Physical laws are only our imperfect attempt to describe the eternal laws. They became better through more observation and

[93] To be explicit, I think we operate *as though* we had such a toy cosmos. The truth appears to be closer to this: we use a number of heuristics, most of them unconscious, to project outcomes based on our circumstances. These heuristics are not mutually consistent, as they have developed (through evolution and conditioning) to tackle specific problems using minimal data to produce acceptable responses. So it would be more accurate to speak of dozens, If not hundreds of thought processes, each revealing a number of unexamined propositions regarding the relationship between things in the external world. My *model* for all of this – my simplified picture – is a single toy cosmos. It incorporates and balances all of the many propositions about the world and how they are represented to the conscious awareness in a way that allows us to speak succinctly about ridiculously complex operations. It also encourages us to think about all of them in a systematic way, open to critical examination and updating. I am aware of the complexities, but choose to focus on those aspects appropriate to the problem at hand – rational worldview construction.

communication, but were never conceived as personal possessions. Only in the modern period did we begin flirting with the claim that our minds might contain truth. Only in the last few centuries has truth been objectified as a relation between our state of mind and the state of the cosmos. I will not argue that that shift is either good or bad, only that it is quite recent. It would be anachronistic to project it onto historical concepts of revelation or objectivity.

I propose we export the hopeful uncertainty of science into all realms of knowledge by embracing the idea of models for all areas of knowledge. Our worldview is only a toy version of the world itself. As I discussed in chapter fourteen, I do not find this to be an imposition on Christianity. Instead, I find it both historically and morally falls out of Christian theology. Similar arguments have been made in all the major religions. There is a gap between the thing itself and our picture of it. Only by taking conscious control of our picture can we hope to improve it.

THE GAP

Philosophers have long known that a potential gap exists between the world and our understanding of it. Everything we touch, taste, see, smell, or hear comes to us mediated by our senses. These wonderful mechanisms we use for perceiving the world give us a slightly filtered picture and it can be difficult to tell just how significant that filter might be.[94] "Visible light," for instance, represents the range of wavelengths humans can see. Not surprisingly, those wavelengths correspond to the right energy to make chemical changes in our eyes. Other species have different light receptors and literally see the world in a different light.

Once we recognize a difference between our model and the actual world, we need to ask how to bridge the gap. Plato was deeply suspicious of direct observation, indeed of the changeable physical world. He argued that no true knowledge comes through our senses. Such a skeptical view of empirical reasoning may seem utterly foreign today, but it demonstrates the long history of asking the question. Hume and Kant were the most prominent Enlightenment thinkers to question our ability to perceive accurately, but they were not alone.

[94] I talk about the biases inherent to humans in *Life in Space*, chapters 5 and 19. Francis Bacon calls them *idols of the tribe* in his book *Novum Organon*.

As the West largely turned to empiricism as the dominant way of knowing, the question would not go away.

Most scientists think the gap between understanding and the thing understood is small enough to be crossed by observation. Ernst Mach (1838–1916) presented an alternative. For Mach, the gap was too great to say anything meaningful about things in and of themselves; we can only make models that successfully predict future observations. The approach has been called *phenomenalism* because it says science predicts experienced phenomena instead of detailing reality. It is close to the philosophy of Osiander from chapter twelve. Science and most religions have to deal with the question of whether the models we have are in some sense true or simply useful.[95]

The phenomenalist position expanded in the early twentieth century with discoveries in quantum mechanics. Werner Heisenberg demonstrated that some things simply cannot be known. For any photon, we can determine the position or the momentum, but we cannot be precise about both. If we multiply the uncertainties (the margin of error) for the two measurements, the result will be greater than a fixed value.[96] Similar relationships have been found for a number of other paired physical properties. Human knowledge can only go so far. That realization led many scientists to give up on pinning down reality and focus on making accurate predictions. You need not give up on (objective) realism completely; I suspect most scientists hold to an imperfect realism. They know that limits exist, but believe we are usually close enough to ignore the difference.

Quantum mechanics gives us another wonderful example of the difference between models and reality – the Bohr atom. Niels Bohr once proposed a model of the atom in which electrons orbit the nucleus. They zip around the core protons and neutrons the way that the Moon orbits the Earth.[97] It tells us a number of things about atoms and electrons – things we find incredibly useful – and for that reason, every chemistry student learns about the Bohr atom and every chemist and physicist talks about electron "orbitals." Unfortunately, the model is wrong. We cannot track the electrons precisely

---

[95] Alistair E. McGrath discusses this in more depth in *Science and Religion: An Introduction* (Blackwell, 1999) pp. 61-67

[96] This value has been determined to be h-bar over 2.

[97] Technically, the Rutherford model suggests that electrons orbit, while the Bohr model has them travel in circles of discrete size.

(uncertainty principle again) and we now know that electrons occur probabilistically around their nuclei. Rather than being in one place or another, they exist potentially until interacting with an observer or another particle. The "reality" is much more confusing than the Bohr model. So, the Bohr model is useful, even if it is not strictly accurate.

The fantasy author Terry Pratchett sums it up beautifully in the words of his character Ponder Stibbons. In explaining a complicated bit of reality, Professor Stibbons says, "That's a very graphic analogy which aids understanding wonderfully while being, strictly speaking, wrong in every possible way."[98] We must ask ourselves how seriously we want to take the models of the universe we use. Part of this decision will be based on our certainty about the model. How well does it make predictions? How well does it line up with other models in our heads? What reasons do we have to doubt the evidence of our senses? Part of the decision will be based on how we feel about the impact of the model. Does it do what we want our model to do? Does it make life simpler? Does it improve our interactions with the world around us? It turns out that science is also deeply invested in belief; the work a proposition or model does for us affects whether we think it is true.

We need to be self-conscious about the value judgments that inform our knowledge, even in science. How do we balance accuracy and utility in our models? The question parallels the discussion of scientific simplicity in chapter seven. For me, the answer rests with my desire for open-ended learning. For me, the love of God calls for a love of creation and understanding of it. I judge my understanding, however, not solely by the power I have over a thing, but my ability to see it clearly, appreciate it for its own sake as well as mine, and learn more about it. Being skeptical of perfect knowledge, I think there is always more to learn about every thing. Thus my preference will be for those types of knowledge that promote the acquisition of further knowledge.

I generally seek models with a level of complexity that allows me to learn more – simple enough to work with, complex enough to keep me curious. That level can only change with time; as I come to understand things more clearly, I'll want more detailed models. This preference can make me, and most Anglicans in my experience,

---

[98] Terry Pratchett, *Making Money* (Harper Collins, 2007) p. 216.

difficult to pin down. Knowledge exists in the process of coming to greater knowledge. Any truly final answer would stop us from learning more and that would be a shame.[99]

Knowledge and Confidence

How do we measure our progress toward truth? Statisticians use the word confidence in a very particular way; they attempt to quantify the trust we put into a particular statement. For example, one might hear about a recent poll in which 78 percent of voters (plus or minus three percent) favor proposition X. What exactly does that mean? It means that the pollsters are aware of their own biases: they have only asked a small group of people (a sample or subset) and projected their results onto the whole population. Knowing that the sample and the whole don't have exactly the same preferences, they estimate how different the results would have been with different random samples. Generally 78 plus or minus 3 percent means that the statisticians believed that if they repeated the experiment (the poll) 20 times, then in 19 cases the results would be between 75 and 81 percent. Ninety-five percent of the time, the results would have come out as they did; therefore they can report a range of numbers (75-81) with a confidence of 95 percent. The percentage is called *confidence* and the range a *confidence interval.* Confidence is usually reported as a percentage with 100% meaning certainty and 0% meaning complete skepticism. The confidence interval reflects the range of values for which you are confident at a given level (most often 95%).

The math may not be intuitive, but the concept should be. There are many things we know with near absolute certainty. I can say definitively that I am writing this while sitting in my office at home. I can say without fear of contradiction that I am a mammal, a human, and a male. These statements come with very high

[99] Theological readers may dismiss this as contrary to C.S. Lewis' views on truth. In *The Great Divorce*, Lewis critiques a theologian more interested in the journey than the destination. This is not my point. With Lewis, I think the target is moving. In the same book, Lewis speaks of the vastness of heaven and our ability to move ever higher up and deeper in. Perhaps in heaven, God and the world stay still long enough to be known. In that case, I'll be happy to lay down my quest, "to know fully as I am fully known." In this lifetime, I will continue under the assumption that I am imperfect and must chase after truth.

confidence. On the other hand, if you were to ask me to tell you the exact amount of money in my bank account, I could only give you a rough estimate. Were I to produce an exact number, it would come with a lower confidence. Ask me to draw out the chemical structure of deoxyribonucleic acid, and I could probably sketch something, but it would have even lower confidence. I can be said to know all of these things, but I have a different level of confidence in each. The statistical number attempts to quantify that confidence.

As we look at the variety of human knowledge, we can ask what gives us confidence and how do we assign it. Different people weight things differently, but all of us begin with a set of inputs that need to be incorporated. The question of rationality deals with how consciously, conscientiously, and consistently we make these judgments.

Knowing the Rules of the Game

Models and confidence allow us to be self-conscious about the way we move from the things we experience to our accounts of the world and truth within it. The more commentaries I read on reason and related ideas like objectivity, the more I realize that people are concerned about thinking well. It can be hard to say exactly what premises and practices go into "good" thinking, but we generally agree that we should bring all of our powers to bear, as much relevant experience and critical thinking as we can. I support axioms that give us access to our own process of reasoning. I believe in transparent epistemology; it produces results. And, it provides a way of looking under the hood when things go wrong.

✦ 1. Know your axioms.

My first piece of advice for thinking clearly is to be conscious of the propositions that go into your worldview formation. Learning always begins by paying attention. We learn to play music by attending to the mechanics of the piano, violin, etc. Only by practicing can we improve; only when the fingering comes naturally can we focus on the melody. We learn to play sports by attending to the rules of the game and limits of our bodies. Only with practice can we move on to strategy. Both music and sports admit of "naturals," people who became good unconsciously. In both, the true experts, the best of the best, will tell you that this is not enough. Mastery comes from practice and self-awareness. Reason must be the same. We need to practice reasoning if we want to do it well. We need to think about the tools we use.

Many, if not most, of the premises we start with come from observation and authority, but even those must rest on fundamental propositions. How do we bridge the gap between the self and the world? How do we bridge the gap between the self and other thinkers? Without committing to such answers, at least provisionally, you cannot claim rational knowledge. I have spelled out how concepts of God and souls work for me in both characterizing and bridging the gap. What answers work for you?

✦ 2. MINIMIZE YOUR AXIOMS.

Reasoning must start somewhere. I've taken the philosophically unpopular position of emphasizing *a priori* claims because I want a model I can work with. The cosmos may be eternal, but my picture of it cannot be. My picture has to fit within my consciousness.

If I had a Platonic or Enlightenment view on knowledge, I could say that the order exists elsewhere and I only participate – I enter into the realm of ideas. So I will admit the possibility of eternal knowledge. My participation can be eternal, but my conceptualization – my formation of a model – still needs to be limited. Once I start talking about it – once I attempt to share it verbally, or even reflect on it – I have to fit it into a discrete package. Further, most of us feel even the participation will be limited in this lifetime.

As I have a more modern view on knowledge, it's simpler for me to say that our model is not the thing itself. It's a toy. Our goal will be to get it to do the most things with the fewest moving parts. We don't want it to break. We want to be able to change as many things as possible in response to a world where we constantly learn new things. Personally, I want to be open to new possibilities and new relationships and that means not overloading my system of thought. Every axiom should do something.

In martial arts we call it minimum effort for maximum effect. In science, we call it elegance. Medieval Christians called it simplicity. It's not the same thing as parsimony (less is better) because we want to accomplish something and we are balancing the pragmatic goal with the aesthetic preference. If you can identify the preferences you start with, you'll be better able to pursue them. If you keep those preferences minimal, you'll be better able to achieve them.

Let me reiterate. Less is not always more. I'm not arguing simplicity for simplicity's sake. I am arguing simplicity for the sake of progress toward whatever goals you set. Epistemology, like any other endeavor, can be maximized if you can keep sight of where you are going.

✦ 3. MAKE YOUR AXIOMS AND PREFERENCES TRANSPARENT.

I am deeply committed to communal reasoning. I believe in forming knowledge with other people. Sometimes that means coming to the same conclusions; sometimes only sharing the process. In both cases we benefit from being able to identify the axioms of others. So often we hide our thoughts, even from ourselves. Genuine dialogue around science and religion – or anything else – can reveal as much about our own thinking styles as it does about others'. Conversation forces us to articulate how we justify things to ourselves. By making your axioms transparent you can make it easier for others to figure out if they agree with you.

This is not always the best rhetorical strategy. Sometimes we want to convince others that we are right or that they should act a certain way. When competing for resources, you may be more successful by misrepresenting your preferences, by leading people to think you reason differently than you actually do. If this is your perspective, I would advise you to be doubly careful to identify your axioms so you can spin them intentionally. Knowing them helps you keep them hidden. Ethically, I would say we have very different outlooks. I prefer more data, more perspectives, and more critical analysis of my thinking. That means I will act to encourage honest communication. In the long term, honesty wins out, at least from an epistemological perspective.

✦ 4. PRACTICE YOUR LOGIC.

Logic is not a philosophy, but a discipline. We often see a new skill, like juggling or playing a musical instrument, and think "I want to be able to do that." We want someone to show us how, little knowing the hours of practice that go into doing these things well. The term *kung fu* has come to mean martial arts in the West, but it carries with it a long history. Originally, it meant anything done well through care and practice. In Chinese, it still carries that flavor and may be applied to any hard won skill, from cooking to acrobatics to meditation. Confucian thought emphasizes the importance of *kung fu* in all things. Not everyone needs a college level education in logic, but most people enjoy it more and use it more effectively when they practice. A little stretching of the mental muscles, a few challenges, and a good sparring partner will go a long way.

We are skeptical of those who practice logic. We might accuse them of "casuistry" or "sophistry," two words that suggest being clever is better than being right. The first comes from moral reasoning about hypothetical cases, used by the Jesuits to train priests in hearing confession. "How would you deal with this type of sin?" The second is much older and refers to professional teachers of rhetoric in Ancient Greece. (It was also a school of thought.) Both groups were accused of caring more about argument than truth.

The challenge for any rational person will be to achieve mastery of logic without losing sight of truth. They must grow proficient at seeing the connections between ideas and communicating them persuasively. Whatever your true goal – and remember that is one of the more contentious issues – you will be served by being able to think about it and express it clearly.

Any type of problem solving will do, including crossword puzzles, making a budget, or mastering a video game. We find greater challenge, though – and for me, greater reward – in puzzles that push us to reason in new and difficult areas. Do you ever talk with your friends about moral puzzles, either hypothetical or real? Do you argue about politics and religion? I don't mean paired monologues with each side asserting a position; I mean genuinely trying to understand what motivates them to assert the things they do. Personally, I'm fond of martial arts and obstacle courses, where I am forced to reason both mentally and physically.

Good logic requires discipline, training, and repetition as well as decent instruction. You don't need a black belt to be any good at it, but you do need to think about what you're doing and recognize that the most important skills, the most delicate applications, and the most profound results only arise after years of practice. Good logic comes from applying your principles in controlled, often fake situations, so that when you really need them, they're there for you.

✦ 5. Clarify your deductions.

I have not spoken too much about deductions, as they have become less popular in modern thought. Often it simply means logically necessary conclusions. If you use deduction as a synonym for logic – or logical conclusions about specific things based on general principles – then the last rule should be enough. If, on the other hand, you subscribe to ideas about rationally necessary truths – things we may know by reason alone or reflections on our own process of reasoning – then it will be important to identify explicitly what they are. Is this really an *a priori* truth about the universe, discovered by reflecting on reflection? That's what Descartes was going for with "I think; therefore I am" and what Kant was going for with his "categorical imperatives." Looking back, we now know that they both had ontological axioms about how minds worked, separate from the physical world, that made those deductions work for them. More recently we might consider commitments to eternalism, progress, or symmetry. Are these necessarily true? Are they necessary assumptions for us? Are they simply convenient axioms? And how do you defend the claim that they are one or another? By clarifying what we mean by deduction and which deductions we are allowed to make *before we have to make them*, we can be more rational thinkers and more effective communicators.

We live with the bizarre notion that we are all playing the same game. The rules for rationality, truth, and success were handed out before birth and, if you didn't get them, then you have missed something. Worse still, as we all feel this way, most of us are too scared to talk about it.

I want to communicate. I want to reason in a way that reveals inconvenient truths and nurtures better relationships. I want to have a worldview that works for me and for others. To do those things, I'm going to have to learn to talk about rationality in a rational way.

In chapter nine I suggested skepticism when looking at the rules of reasoning. It can be easy to accuse others of playing the game without a net, without obeying the rules of reason. We should ask who made the rules and why we should follow them. Here I want to take one step further. I want to ask you to set up rules for your own game, talk about them, and see how people react. It's so easy to critique someone else's metaphysics, because it is a tricky business. The world defies explanation much of the time. It can be so much harder to open ourselves to critique. You can craft a metaphysics – ontology, epistemology, and axiology – you can be proud of, but it will take time, hard work, and humility. We will both be better off for having had a real discussion about the games each of us are trying to play. We might even find we are actually playing the same game.

Having established the rules, let us begin to play. In the next chapter, we look at the gathering of new experiences.

CHAPTER 20
New Experience

Our worldviews change when we encounter new things. New sensations, new ideas, even new emotions can trigger a shift in the way we look at the world. Whether you embrace change or try to avoid it, whether you are a physicalist or believe in something more, you are constantly comparing your toy cosmos with the things you encounter. That comparison provokes one of four responses.

Affirmation. The new experience supports what you already think to be true. It reinforces the way you look at the world and the ways you interact. Affirmation explains why it can be harder for people to change their minds as time passes. The weight of evidence and positive reinforcement for their models increases. Every time you see people stop at a red light or stop sign it affirms your understanding of traffic laws.

Updating. The new experience fits reasonably well with your picture of the world, but requires you to shift things slightly, adding new details or a new rule. Perhaps you are driving in Quebec and come across a sign with a red octagon, saying "*arrêt.*" By observing people's behavior and by analogy with English signs, you decide the word means stop. You've updated your understanding of the rules, but the basics remain the same.

Dissonance. The new experience does not fit. You can discount the experience – ignore it – or change your model of the world to accommodate it. A minor dissonance might be a green stop sign, a penguin crossing, or the first time you see a roundabout. You ask yourself if this is a regular occurrence – something you need to be prepared for in the future, or just a fluke. A major dissonance forces you to stop for a moment and question the experience. Imagine a person zooming down the highway without a car. You mentally paint a motorcycle into the picture or you reassess your friend's claim to have a jetpack. Dissonance means discarding something, the new input or some aspect of your model. The more we have to discard, the more uncomfortable the event is.

Breakdown. Occasionally, dissonance is so painful that something breaks. In extreme cases, we block out the negative experiences, denying or even forgetting an event. More than revising it, we shut it off from conscious memory. If our worldview fails in a way that prevents basic functions (eating, sleeping, …), we can pro-tect ourselves with amnesia. This is well documented in cases of severe trauma. Extreme updating, on the other hand, changes one or more of our basic propositions about the world, usually an axiom or something held very firmly on the basis of authority. In other words, we have a conversion experience.

For me, rationality means allowing myself to experience new things, while keeping the updating as comfortable as possible. It means recognizing times when dissonance should be dealt with by doubting the event, but never doing so without some justification. It means looking for times when conversion may be desirable. This chapter looks at good ways to handle updating and deal with dissonance. The next will tackle the difficult questions of conversion, particularly important when dealing with religious knowledge and belief.

Exploration

One motto for scientists could be "see for yourself."[100] Nor is the idea foreign to Christianity. Jesus repeatedly says "come and see" and Paul writes "test everything" (I Thessalonians 5:21). Sadly, we cannot test everything. The world is too big and our desires too broad for us to see and do all things. But that doesn't mean we can't try. Science and Christianity have taught me to love seeing for myself.

[100] The Royal Society, perhaps the oldest organization of scientists in the modern sense, began in London in the 1640s as "a Colledge for the Promoting of Physico-Mathematicall Experimentall Learning." It has included many prominent scientists, starting with Robert Boyle, and including Isaac Newton, Edmund Halley, Carl Linnaeus, and Charles Darwin. Their motto is "*nullius in verba*," often translated as "see for yourself" or "take no-one's word for it." It might be more accurate to render it, "by no one's word", as it comes from Horace's *Epistles* (I.1) and reflects freedom from authority in life as well as learning.

When confronted with new experiences, I ask, can I do it again? Sometimes the answer is "no," but it amazes me how often we fail to ask. We associate rationality with clear thinking, but also with the curiosity necessary to challenge our thoughts. If an experiment works, will it still work if I try it out on the other side of that hill? If the proposition makes sense to me, will it also work for others? I give myself chances to be wrong.

I frequently give students this advice. There are two kinds of ignorance, visible and invisible. Visible ignorance is much more painful, but at least it's over quickly. With humility it gives us the chance to be corrected. Visible ignorance is vincible ignorance; it can be conquered. None of us can know all things, but by exploring we can learn more tomorrow than we do today. By talking about what we know – and more importantly what we think we know – we find that other people have different knowledge. Some of it will affirm our worldview, some of it will require us to update, some we will find dissonant. The gap between our model cosmos and the real cosmos, however, cannot be crossed passively. It will take work to climb over the hill and see what there is to see. It requires a sense of adventure. This kind of exploration can also save us from stressful breakdowns. When we consciously seek out that which is foreign, we learn to handle the shock better; often we can meet it on our own terms.

Dogma is associated with institutions, and a need to maintain stability. It should not necessarily be associated with religions. That entirely depends on the preferences the religion promotes, the epistemologies it endorses, and the value it places on constancy. Science is uniquely suited to encouraging curiosity, based on the balance of skepticism and hope it borrowed from Christian theology at a particular time and place. But science, too, can go wrong when our collective thinking traps us in a conceptual corner, as it did with both circles and eternalism in astronomy. You never know which of your ideas will become dated. That is the delight and terror of exploration.

We limit our exploration. Sometimes we stop exploring because of limited resources. Sometimes we do it for our mental health; more change would be too emotionally difficult. Learning is not everyone's top priority. It is worth asking where you rank it. What are you willing to learn more about? And what things do you care about enough to re-evaluate? How far will you go to be more confident? These questions require serious reflection on our personal motivation. They require a type of reasoning that cannot be done using only observation, logic, and induction. But we can think carefully about them. And we can apply observation, logic, and induction as we think. Every once in a while, we can step back and measure the amount of time we devote to study.

Above all, we must not fall into the trap that symmetry presents us. Sometimes the world is not uniform. Sometimes the grass really is greener on the other side. Why not see for yourself?

CONSISTENCY

Having seen and having encouraged new experiences, what do we do with them? Science adds value to our reasoning by setting an example of how to use hypotheses and observations together. With a simple experiment – like the poll mentioned in the last chapter – we can form a hypothesis – 78 percent of the electorate (plus or minus 3 percent) will vote for proposition X – with a fixed confidence level – 95 percent. With that as a starting point, we can actually repeat the test 20 times and see whether or not our confidence interval was appropriate. This new set of data, 20 times bigger, will give us a more precise reflection of reality. If we did our work right the first time, then the confidence interval will shrink. Using a larger sample, we can speak about the whole body of voters more confidently. Normally science proceeds in this fashion with increasing confidence as more and more data accumulates. The directed accumulation of data with revised hypotheses and refined confidence goes by the name *Bayesian reasoning* after Bayes' Theorem in statistics.[101]

Most of the time, science provides a gradual approach to knowledge. The more we know the more confident we are. Each observation shifts our confidence a little bit until we believe one hypothesis is true (or the best option available) or we are convinced that we need a new hypothesis. Sometimes new data shows that we have been doing the experiments in a biased way. It reveals that things differ from our expectations in an interesting way. Maybe proposition X increases Medicare benefits and we've only polled in retirement communities. They might not be representative of the

[101] Thomas Bayes (1701–1761) was a Presbyterian minister as well as a natural philosopher and statistician. He was also a member of the Royal Society.

entire country on this issue. A better experiment – polling in a mall, perhaps – might radically redefine our confidence, making us aware of questions we failed to ask before. Induction requires us to constantly ask whether our sample is representative of the whole. Bayesian reasoning allows us to speak concretely about how new data updates our model. Sometimes it increases or decreases the confidence – relative to the quantity of new observations. Sometimes it identifies other options we had never considered.

We can easily calculate the probability that something will occur, if our model is correct. This "data given the model" or formally the *likelihood* measures the probability of observing something when you know exactly how it works. If I think a coin is fair and I see it land heads, I'll say it landed heads with a 50% likelihood.

This is rarely what we want to know. We usually want to know whether our model is correct based on the data we have – the probability of "model given the data." If I flip a coin 5 times and it comes up heads every time, how confident can I be that the coin is fair?

Bayes' Theorem provides a logical proof that the two probabilities are related. The probability (model given data) is proportional to the likelihood (data given model) times the *prior* – how confident I was in the model before the experiment. The details can be hard to follow, but in summary, it requires me to list what I think the options are and then measure the data against all of them. It highlights the subjectivity of my confidence – I never know that I have the right priors. It also tells me exactly where my priors are and how much work they are doing relative to the data.[102]

According to Kuhn's model of scientific progress, scientists spend most of their time updating models by the gradual shift of confidence. More data always leads to better confidence and better models. Our models approach reality, getting closer and closer, but always having a little bit of room between them. Kuhn calls this "normal science." On rare occasions, we experience a paradigm shift, when our prior (initially *a priori*) ideas about the models change

[102] A school of thought among philosophers of probability and philosophers of science called *frequentism* denies such subjective probabilities are useful. They are only willing to use Bayes' theorem when all the possible models are known. They either refuse to speculate on the probability of models in other cases or assume their axioms and *a priori* probabilities are necessary and self-evident.

radically and the standards have to be reset. The shift from eternal to evolving species was one such shift (Charles Darwin). The change from an eternal to an expanding universe was another (Edwin Hubble). New evidence made a whole new model possible, even probable in a way that no one could have accounted for in advance. The commonly accepted model broke and we replaced it with another.

The drive for increased confidence experienced in normal science always calls for bigger and bigger data sets. We quickly discover that one researcher, one lab, or even one institution would be incapable of generating all the data necessary. I credit this drive to know more, the exploration and communication it fostered, for the great success of modern science in teaching us inconvenient truths. I see no reason that it cannot proceed the same way with our larger models of the universe. Encountering new abstract concepts, new people, and new values forces us into a more conscious awareness of our models and how they work.

A Warning

So far this chapter has presented a rosy view of new experiences. The world is worth knowing and knowing more is always better. Were this uncontroversial, I think we would all be much less conservative. And, were it undoubtedly the case, I would be much more optimistic about the Enlightenment dream of unbiased knowledge.

New experiences can be dangerous, and not just because we might break our worldview. First, we can misinterpret what we see in ways that give us too much confidence – or too little. This is why we must be so careful about our axioms and how they affect the things we observe. Second, our experiences condition our behavior as well as our models. They can change our beliefs, even without passing through our conscious mind. A small benefit in knowledge may not be worth a major cost in belief.

Possible Harm to Knowledge

If confidence comes from the weight of evidence supporting your claim, balanced with the evidence against, then it matters what evidence you allow in. We frequently look for just one counter-example to show that a general rule does not apply universally. Much ink has been spilt (and voices raised) over whether there are any organisms with traits that could not have evolved. Just one example of an "irreducibly complex" trait would be enough to show that evolution is not the only force at work in shaping living things. We might also consider a closed system that produces energy. A "perpetual motion machine" defies our current understanding of thermodynamics. Just one example would be enough to demonstrate that what we thought were universal rules have exceptions. Yes, we want to work to prove ourselves wrong, but no, we don't want to lose confidence unless our evidence is reliable.

We set up standards. Throughout this book, I've proposed standards for how we judge the quality of our evidence. Exploration requires preparation. It takes knowing what sorts of experiences we want and what sorts of experiences we will accept. Do you have to see for yourself? It's a solid standard, but it will stop you from knowing most of what there is to know. You will have to rely on some authorities. Which ones work for you?

On the other hand, how do you deal with things you can see but others cannot? All of us experience illusions and misperceptions, even with something as straightforward as vision. How are we to deal with more complicated perceptions, using expensive technology, one-time occurrences, and complicated phenomena, not to mention harder cases of moods, abstract entities, values, and memory?

One of the reasons I feel so passionate that science must be a methodology of mutual observables is that it provides a clear standard. Other definitions – including science as the search for truth, science as the study of the physical world, and science as the study of natural causes – fail to specify the unique quality of science. Mutual observables are not the only form of evidence, but they are definite and discrete. They allow us express clearly what we mean when we say "science gives me confidence that…" They allow us to say beforehand exactly what sort of evidence to seek. Epistemological precision makes science powerful.

This is also why I will argue so strenuously against attempts to make science the all-in-all of knowledge. That would mean either ignoring all other types of evidence (including personal experience, consequence based arguments, and revelation) or shoehorning them in. In order to preserve the power of science, I must also preserve its specificity, the transparency of the epistemology.

Science needs to exclude some forms of experience, not counting them as evidence. Other epistemologies make the same move. Some exclude predictions of the future. You only know the present. Some exclude reports by outsiders, or claims to knowledge unrelated to some central aspect of their model. Most epistemologies require acceptable evidence to be framed in a particular language. The language of knowledge in Europe was Latin for centuries (then French, then English). We think of language as non-essential, and yet, when it comes to common construction of knowledge, what the community knows, it really matters what the majority can access (and what leaders can access).

What languages do you speak? What types of experience are you willing to count as evidence? Are your rules consistent and transparent? What checks stop you from accepting only the claims that support your position and rejecting all others?

Possible Harm to Belief

A more difficult issue arises when we think about effects new experiences can have on our beliefs – thoughts that change our behavior. Being bitten by a spider at age 8 might prevent you from becoming an entomologist. Or it might drive a lifelong interest in insects and arachnids. When teaching and learning, I try to pay attention to the way experiences encourage or discourage further learning. And I look at the ways they impact other behaviors.

I have learned a great deal from watching students learn about microbiology. I can write a fact on the page: Your "body" has more microorganisms than human cells. It's true, your frame hosts a vast ecosystem of bacteria, protists, even tiny insects. Alternatively, I can introduce students to the idea by showing them in the lab. We take a sample from the surface of their cheek or elbow and place it on a sterile plate of nutrients. The microorganisms rapidly grow on the right nutrients so that you can identify them with a microscope. The lab provides much stronger responses. Students remember longer and attach emotions to the idea: usually fascination or fear. A little microbiology often makes people scared of germs and far more careful about cleanliness. A lot of microbiology (six years or more for a PhD) leads them be less careful. The bacteria are there anyway. Why worry? The relationship between experience and belief is important.

Knowledge about bacteria and beliefs affecting your cleanliness are not quite the same. I can change student beliefs with a few very scary pictures of flesh eating bacteria without helping their knowledge in a significant way. Or I can give them tons of evidence about metabolic pathways without changing a single action later in their lives.

As we think carefully about reason, we want to be aware of how beliefs are shaped alongside knowledge. How do those two processes match up with our preferences? Sometimes it may be necessary to bypass knowledge altogether in pursuit of our goals. At other times we will go out of our way to integrate the two.

Reason in Action

Reason is not static; nor are knowledge and belief. Each requires that we engage with the world we are trying to model. We play the game by rules based on our epistemology, axioms, and preferences. We seek out new experiences to make our models work better and to learn something about the universe beyond ourselves. In doing so, we separate out those experiences allowed by and for particular types of reasoning. The word "data" captures this distinction. We do not call every experience data, only those experiences acceptable to our epistemology. The word appears most frequently in science, where data means mutually observable sense experience and instrumental readings (which must have mutually observable outputs for us to use them in science). The word also appears in computer science, where data simply means input for a program, regardless of how it was generated. Because the rules for acceptable evidence in other epistemologies are less commonly known, I'd be hesitant to use the word outside these contexts without some very clear explanation. Bearing that in mind, I can propose several ways to get new data (whatever your standards) while minimizing the dangers.

✦ 1. Observe. Repeat.

When possible, see for yourself. Most of the truly profound moments in life only happen when you go looking for them. This is not to say that you will have the experience you were looking for. The benefit comes from finding things you didn't expect and never could have predicted. Science encourages us to see for ourselves, but so do many religious philosophies. Models with more data are more accurate and more powerful – remembering that not all experience constitutes data. It's good to look at the world, and even better to look at the world in hope. Come prepared to gather data. When something interests you, think about how it could tell you something new. Think about what aspects of the experience you can repeat and what aspects you can share.

Shared experience makes for better, more transparent reasoning. It allows us to compare our own vision and model with those of our companions. When we agree, it makes for more confident knowledge. When we disagree, it provokes us to look more carefully.

After an observation, observe again. When hearing about observations, observe again. As a Christian I see no point in having senses if we don't use them. Use them consciously, not just to navigate the world, but to find out new things about creation. Perhaps you have a different religious background, but hopefully you share my love of finding things out. We downplay the emotional importance of curiosity in science and Christianity. Perhaps this comes from our Enlightenment sensibilities, which tell us that the thoughts of an abstract mind should be preferred over the emotions of a physical body. I agree that our emotions provide unreliable data (from a science standpoint) but they also motivate data collection. They move us and thus have a profound impact on our belief.

When reasoning, few activities have greater reward and lower cost than observation. Think about whether observation can provide you with the data you want. And, when in doubt, try.

✦ 2. Refine observations.

Like reason, observation is a skill. It improves with careful practice and can be aided by reflection and instruction. Thoughtful reporting will also improve the quality of data. You can make observation more efficient and effective.

The easiest way to improve observation is to attend to details. Train yourself to notice things beyond your normal interests. Often we focus on solving a problem at hand instead of keeping our minds open to all the input available. I like expanding my perception by reflecting on things I normally would not. What type of floor am I walking on? What are the words to the song that's playing in the background? What font is that on the sign? Those are just a few random questions that we usually think of as trivia or esoteric knowledge, but they represent things in daily life the most of us don't notice.

You can find people who make a study of just about anything. If you are curious, there is always more to learn and more people willing to share – if you ask nicely. Familiarity with multiple disciplines provides insights unavailable to those who stick with only one. Each discipline has different areas of focus and different ways of asking questions. My own ways of thinking have broadened immensely by working with scientists on the question of life in the universe (astrobiology). By talking about the question of life with geologists, chemists, astronomers, and a host of other experts, I've learned to ask the questions in ways that biology never provided. How does the range of energy produced by the Sun impact the types of life chemistry we see on Earth? (Both human vision and photosynthesis occur near the peak frequency for our star.) Beyond the natural sciences, social sciences have spurred me to look at the social dynamics of reason. Who has the most influence on my standards of data and why? (My thesis committee had a disproportionate impact, because of strong opinions, frequent interaction, and status.) Martial arts has also shaped my willingness to ask questions in different ways, encouraging me to attend to my goals and the goals of others.

Some disciplines are, no doubt, better at observation than others, but a breadth of observing and reasoning styles should highlight for you what your own preferences are and give you suggestions for improving them. At the most trivial level, we can think of observation exercises like "spot the differences" in the comic section of your newspaper or observation games with kids. My niece likes to punch whoever is sitting next to her if she sees a yellow car.

We practice observation with kids and don't have to stop as we grow older, though it can be fun to explore more obscure areas of observation and knowledge. (Is there a difference between the letter shapes in this book and those used in the last book you read?)

Tables

One great observational technique associated with science is the table. In truth, this is a way of refining classification. Because it organizes observations and encourages us to look for particular things, I will mention it here. Any type of data can be consolidated into a chart that relates one observation to another. It requires some notion of regularity in the things we observe, so it will add another layer of prior assumptions, but the right regularity will show us exactly where the missing observations are. Roger Bacon (1214/20–1292) is credited as one of the first great table makers, but the idea really took off after the Renaissance. The success of the periodic table was as much a victory for tables as it for reductionism. When we can imagine bits of knowledge coming in sets, our psychology drives us to complete the set. This can be a tremendously useful way of motivating people to learn more.

✦ 3. QUESTION AUTHORITY.

We have looked at numerous issues related to authority in science and other epistemologies. Appeals to authority can be valid within a rational system when the authority is justified. We cannot do all the reasoning by ourselves: neither observation, nor revelation, nor logic nor any other of the techniques I have introduced. In our individualistic society, we may be tempted to think we set our axioms by ourselves, but even that turns out to be an illusion. The language of our communities – the words we use and our comfort using them – shapes us. To unthinkingly reject a model is no more rational than to unthinkingly accept it; and you have to start from somewhere. So even axioms happen in community. Authorities will exist and we must appeal to them if we are to deal with any type of knowledge beyond daily experience.

We need not deal with authority uncritically. I have praised scientific authority as an example of transparent epistemology.

Science uses a system of peer review in which data is judged by trained observers and checked by trained peers. The data can, in theory, always be checked against reality by an independent observer. More confidence is placed in those who have produced more observations, better theories, and portable solutions to problems. Of course, that statement represents an ideal. Still, science represents one of the most transparent and fixable systems of authority available. Scientists hold leaders up to standards of accountability and productivity and they maintain the ideal. As with axioms like symmetry the ideal can do work, even when we know it to be imperfectly realized.

Religions have their own standards. In Christianity, leaders are expected to be compassionate, knowledgeable, and productive. They may give up personal status or property or reproduction in order to wield institutional power. These expectations are usually transparent in the way they are established, but not in the way they are maintained. For me, it is important that all authorities be accountable to the standards they profess, through transparent evaluation. Their dictates should be challenged on whatever metaphysical grounds they manage for their communities. If something is "Bible based" I want to know how. Here too, I can see for myself. If a claim comes from "tradition," I want to know who said it, why, and when. I want to know whether there was dissent at the time. Here Judaism shines as a brilliant example of transparent authority. Rabbis are accountable to Jewish scripture – the Tanakh (roughly the same as the Christian Old Testament), the commentaries, and their peers. They encourage their congregations to know the same materials and defend their positions with the same, well-established rules for debate. They are required to attend schools and maintain their education. As with science, the ideal is not always met, but it is transparently pursued.

This epistemological clarity in Rabbinic Judaism arises because the Rabbi's authority is clearly rational in concept (teacher or sage), but also relational in practice (within communities of scholarship and practice). Other religions place more weight on a leader's other abilities (effective leadership, ritual skill, etc.). In those cases, the philosophical aspect of the religion may give way before practice or politics. But even in those cases I would encourage clear expectations. Know what you expect from an authority figure and ask how you would help them achieve that expectation. Know the areas in which you will allow them to give you confidence and shape your belief.

✦ 4. KEEP MULTIPLE MODELS.

Let your conscious mind do what your unconscious processes already do: work with multiple models. I favor conscious consistency. I think the attempt to reconcile our models forces us to ask the difficult questions, explore reality, and reason better. At the same time, I recognize that a perfect system is usually beyond my grasp. Two models may be necessary to accomplish two different tasks. Light provides the classic example: some properties of light make it appear to be a wave, while others make it appear to be a particle. Each model can be useful when trying to work with light (waves for observing stars, particles for understanding the chemistry of glowing pigments). Recent mathematical models capture some of the benefits of each, but the simpler analogies still work well for us most of the time. It's not a matter of contradictory truths, but of two models working independently for different reasons.

Holding on to independent models while we wait for a better theory allows us to use all the knowledge at our disposal, even when we haven't reached the goal of a unified worldview. It gives us a way to understand and accept the diverse unconscious models we operate with on a daily basis. Sometimes we make the right choices without knowing why, a process often called "intuition." Just because we don't know the process doesn't mean we cannot use the good result. Accepting that we might have two or more models allows us to judge each one on its own merits. We need not accept any model without evidence but, just like authorities, we can think more clearly about why and how they do work for us.

Two flawed maps are better than one, when they are flawed in different ways. Once we have accepted that our worldview is not the world, we can start critically assessing the difference. We can compare one toy universe to another and discover the benefits of each. Eventually we may be able to disassemble both and make a better toy from the spare parts, but we must not do so until we're sure the new toy can do all the things the old ones did. No one wants to lose the features they like.

I have already said I have multiple models – a model of the world based on atoms and consistent with science and another model based on souls and consistent with Christian ethics. One day, I hope to fuse them into a single model. I can't do it yet, but that doesn't mean I never will. Nor does it mean I need to give one of them up. It only means I'm holding onto all the tools I need to accomplish my goals in life.

✦ 5. OBSERVE AND REASSESS AXIOMS AND PREFERENCES.

I fear this piece of advice may be the hardest to follow. Our axioms are comfortable, our preferences dear. Even more than the pieces of knowledge within each model, we cling to the foundations upon which we build them. How could we not? We have limited time, and when you start messing with the bricks on the bottom of the tower, you run the risk of knocking the whole thing down. But we must. Rationality asks that we leave ourselves vulnerable to correction, even in our foundations.

I'm not asking you to be totally open. I may not be the person to judge your axioms or make you reassess your preferences. My questions may not be the ones you need to ask. There will, however, always be standards you can set for yourself, people and practices to which your reasoning is accountable, rules by which you play the game. I am asking you to take a moment every once in a while, figure out what game you play when you reason, and decide whether it really fits the preferences you have for life, knowledge, and belief.

My own rules have changed over the years. My communities and interests have shifted and that means I reason differently than I used to. Overall, I think I have become better at collecting data, constructing models, and understanding the world. I judge my success by the relationships I form as well as the control I gain over my environment. I also judge my success in terms of how happy I am with the state of my worldview. This book has been a wonderful exercise in figuring out why. It has challenged me to be much more honest with myself about where my thoughts come from and what work they do for me.

☙ ✦ ❧

Our experience shapes us. The things we encounter make us who we are. And we, by shaping our experience, shape ourselves. In this chapter, I argued for expanding horizons. It's worth going out of our way to learn new things, to change, and to grow. And yet, I also recognize the danger in this kind of openness, the vulnerability. How can we be sensible about which experiences we seek; how can we best incorporate them into our models of the world?

When we experience new things, they can affirm, update, cause dissonance, or even break our worldview. We benefit from activities that minimize the dissonance but maximize learning. I've suggested a number of rules I use to do just that, but it's worth asking yourself what rules work for you.

All of these processes happen in communities. Authority figures help us moderate our communities and commitments, the rules we have for playing the game of reason. How are your communities of thought set up? Do you trust the authorities and the systems they referee? Why or why not? We always return to questions of preferences and whether or not we are pursuing them effectively – even our preferences for what we prefer.

You may discover, as I have, that your worldview and preferences do not match as well as you would like. In many cases, the path of consciously addressing your own metaphysics – the path of reason – will help you bring the two closer together. The last two chapters contain my advice for taking that road. In some cases it will be a matter of shaping behavior to belief, reinforcing the good habits and defending against the bad. In other cases, it will be necessary to change our unreasoned reasons, the foundations of our thinking. That will require conversion, a resetting of the most basic standards for interacting with the world. In the next chapter, we turn to religious formation beyond epistemology in the strict sense. We turn to the ways in which activities and communities impact our pictures, how our pictures impact our activities and communities, and how all three change our identity. In short, we turn to changes in belief.

CHAPTER 21
New Belief

As I write this book, I struggle with knowledge and belief. I know that writing helps me to align the two. Sharing what I have written forces me to put my values on paper in a way that makes me accountable to my neighbors – and my future self. Others can explore the same ground I have walked. Both personal experience and scientific evidence tell me that simply sitting down and writing will help me in these goals as well as creating connections with others. Still, I find the writing to be hard work, emotionally. I resist and delay. Why is this?

This gap between knowledge and belief has daily importance for most of us. We worry less about metaphysical chasms and more about the simple differences between what we say and what we actually do. What should I eat? Should I work out today? Should I have another drink? We have trouble doing the things we know will make us happy; how can we be trusted to act in the best interests of ourselves, much less others? How can we rationally pursue more sophisticated ideals like love, duty, and justice?

Once we discover such a gap, no matter how small or large, we have the opportunity to do something about it. As with evolution and creationism, many people feel that providing more evidence should be enough. "Let me tell you why eating more is bad for you." "Research shows how much longer you'll live if you exercise." If that works for you, great! I am always in favor of generating better knowledge, with clearer models and higher confidence. Often, however, we need another tactic; we need to change an axiom or a fundamental preference. That change will not occur because of a rational chain of arguments, and yet it would be irrational not to change. There are systems for changing your beliefs when evidence alone is not enough.

THE BELIEF/BEHAVIOR LOOP

Most discussions about reason remain curiously silent about behavior. First, reasoning is a behavior. It is something you do. It takes effort, practice, and skill. Second, reasoning impacts other behaviors. Our conscious thoughts impact the choices we make. Third, and least appreciated, behavior impacts reasoning. The things we think, both conscious and unconscious, are influenced by the things we do. I believe that all reasoning benefits from being tied to actions, just as scientific reasoning is tied to observations.

Our conscious models reinforce and justify the choices we make. We can choose behaviors that work with or against the models, setting up feedback. That feedback can provide affirmation or dissonance. It can help or hinder us in both cases.

Constructive dissonance happens when our models and behavior disrupt one another, helping us get what we prefer without improving our confidence. Christian skepticism about authority often follows this pattern. The Bible contains numerous passages critiquing human religious authorities, from kings[103] to teachers[104] and priests.[105] Human institutions, called churches, preserve and transmit texts that call into question our loyalty to human institutions. The Protestant Reformation and the United States civil rights movement were both times when the conservation of scripture encouraged critique of a conservative social position. The stories told by the establishment undermined the establishment. Scientific skepticism operates the same way: the overall success of science reinforces our belief in the axiom that each individual argument should be critiqued.

Destructive dissonance happens when our models and behavior disrupt one another and the system breaks down. Such events can be

---

[103] I Samuel 8 "you shall solemnly warn them, and show them the ways of the king who shall reign over them."

[104] Matthew 23 "you are not to be called teacher"

[105] Protestants, believing in the "priesthood of all believers," look to I Timothy 2, I Peter 2, and Hebrews as evidence that Jesus' work as high priest means humans need no human mediator between them and God. The Antique model of priesthood, as necessary for communication with the divine, is rejected in one form or another by all Christians. The title "priest" and certain ritual functions are particularly rejected by Protestants, but not Catholic or Orthodox Christians who see their priests as a new type of authority.

harder to identify: by definition, they are short lived. Numerous religious movements have predicted the end of the world and encouraged members to look for it, only to find that it did not occur.[106] Scientists have also predicted catastrophic events, setting up procedures for tracking comets, monitoring volcanism, and following diseases. The differences appear not in the prediction or the vigilance it brings, but how we respond when observations do not bear out our model. How deeply do we have to go in our worldview in order to accommodate the new observation? Or do we choose to ignore it? Several religious groups, faced with failed apocalypses have chosen a new model in which one "world" ended and a new "world" began. They believe the rules of being have genuinely changed.[107] Those of us more committed to symmetry find this solution problematic, but it should be noted that we do so based on our *a priori* commitment to consistency. Catastrophe usually makes us reevaluate.

Destructive affirmation occurs when our models and behavior reinforce one another, but against our preferences. The pairing of addiction and guilt provides a classic example. Feelings of shame can make us want to escape reality, or at least awareness of reality, with drugs. Abuse of the drugs damages relationships and leads to more shame.

Science has fallen into such destructive feedback loops on several occasions. Epicycles were terribly useful; they allowed medieval astronomers to account for their observations without giving up the perfect circles of Aristotelian science. For centuries they enabled natural philosophers by allowing them to continue with a bad axiom about the heavens. Predictability was served, at least in the short term, but truth and simplicity lost out. Whether this was good or bad depends on your preferences, but astronomers generally agree that we are better off now. Circles worked to improve our confidence in the model, but that confidence stopped us from looking for an even better solution: ellipses.

Politics frequently falls into such destructive feedback loops. Fear can strengthen group cohesion and willingness to follow.

---

[106] Shabbetai Zevi, 1648; Millerites, 1844; Charles Russell and Nelson Barbour, 1914.

[107] See note 90. Present day followers of Shabbetai Zevi are called Sabbateans; present day Millerites include Seventh Day Adventists; followers of Russell and Barbour are Jehovah's Witnesses.

Leaders who promote fear of outsiders gain more power over the group. Fear weakens curiosity, making it harder to discover whether outsiders pose a genuine threat. Common action and strong leaders become more and more appealing as the perceived threat increases. Though religions are often associated with this trend, we can see it quite clearly in Communism,[108] National Socialism,[109] and McCarthy-ism.[110] Destructive affirmation occurs in scientific and political communities as well. And, in each case, escaping the cycle requires changing basic assumptions.

Constructive affirmation results when models and behavior interact, reinforcing both according to our preferences. Science as I have presented it does this. A desire for confidence in our knowledge leads to more observations; the observations lead to powerful models; that power brings confidence but also reinforces our belief that curiosity, observations, and scientific modeling will be rewarded. Similarly, Christianity has led me to value curiosity and compassion, which have brought me into contact with increasing numbers of people. Those relationships affirm my belief that curiosity and compassion will be rewarded. Regarding both, my belief in God as supreme governor and compassionate soul has encouraged me to look for regularity in the cosmos as well as attempts to disclose that regularity. The discovery of practical rules for learning and forming friendships affirm my preference for these things and my belief that I might achieve them.

Belief and Conviction

In chapter nineteen, I spoke of measuring our knowledge in terms of confidence. How much evidence do you have? Let us turn to mea-sureing belief. How strong an influence does a particular proposition have on your behavior? How can you tell if your beliefs are getting stronger? Once we know – once we have a way of talking about it – we can intentionally create constructive affirmation and dissonance to shape our beliefs.

Economists, behavioral psychologists, and some philosophers have suggested that the best way to judge the strength of belief is by

[108] E.g., Stalinist Russia with fear of "counter-revolutionaries" and capitalists
[109] E.g., Nazi Germany with fear of Jews, decadent capitalism, and Marxism
[110] 1950s United States with fear of communists

measuring what a person is willing to risk on the assumption that the proposition is true. On a grand scale, we often hear the expression, "What are you willing to die for?" but we can see the same principle on a smaller scale by looking at gambling. I will call strength of belief *conviction.*[111]

How much would you be willing to bet on the flip of a coin? For a long time, it was thought that all people were "rational actors." This "rationality" is not the same reasonable-ness we've been talking about so far in the book. It is, instead only one, very precise kind of critical thinking. "Rational choice theory" assumes that people make their decisions based on a conscious preference for particular outcomes and a clear, if not perfect, knowledge of how choices impact the future. In rational choice theory, preferences are always conscious and knowledge equals belief.

According to this theory, I should be willing to wager anytime the odds are in my favor. For example, a rational bet might be fifty cents for a coin toss. Two bettors each place 2 quarters on the table. One chooses heads, the other tails. Once the coin is flipped the one who chose correctly gets to keep all four quarters. This is called a fair bet because the value of the wager ($0.50) equals the value of the reward ($1.00) multiplied by the chance of getting the reward (1/2). All else being equal, a higher wager would not be fair; you risk too much for what you expect to gain. Rational actors are expected to accept bets only when the odds are even or in their favor. Even though the outcome is uncertain for one flip of the coin, rational strategies always work if the game is played enough times. Whenever the expected reward is higher than the cost, you should play. Rational choice theory makes the assumption that human conviction (what we are willing to wager) matches exactly with human confidence (a calculation of the probabilities).

Recent studies have shown that we are not rational actors. We estimate probabilities poorly but, even when we understand the true chances of success, we still behave differently than probability dictates. Our belief and our knowledge fail to align. Risk aversion demonstrates the situation well. When assessing betting behavior,

---

[111] Statisticians use the term "credence" in a similar way, however I have avoided this as it has specific connotations with regard to philosophy of probability, which I wish to avoid. Further, credence is measured on a percent scale and I don't know what maximum belief would be.

most people are more likely to make a small bet with a smaller payout. Take, for example, two slot machines. The first charges one dollar and returns 100 dollars 1 percent of the time (wager $1 equals probability 0.01 times payout $100). The second charges 50 dollars and returns 200 dollars one time out of four (wager $50 equals probability 0.25 times payout $200). Both bets are completely even, but people are more likely to accept the first, being less willing to lose fifty dollars. Aversion to losing money biases their decision. Humans do not behave as rational actors and confidence does not equal conviction.

The difference becomes particularly important when we look at religious conversion. When I judge whether or not someone is a true believer I will be more inclined to assess their conviction than their confidence. You may say you believe that the little golden idol grants wishes, but unless I see you actually rely on those wishes I will question your faith. On a more popular level, one might judge Christians on whether or not they actually love their neighbor and Muslims on whether or not they actually submit to the will of Allah. Both refer to the border between philosophical definitions (what you think defines membership) and behavioral definitions (what you do defines membership), but whichever way you frame it. It is more a matter of belief than of knowledge. When speaking about religious propositions, we are more interested in conviction than confidence.

Some of my fellow Christians may become anxious about the faith versus works question. Which is more important, what you think or what you do about it? The simple answer to this question will be to say they are inseparable.[112] A more complete answer, however, would draw out our definition of faith. Does faith represent confidence in the truth of a proposal – I am certain because the Bible tells me so – or conviction from the truth of a proposal – I believe and thus accept God's grace. I suspect the most Christians would lean toward the latter. As my simple answer expresses, I admit that faith and action cannot truly be divided. I place both on the side of conviction/belief rather than confidence/knowledge. Still if you

[112] The Council of Trent (Catholic) and Thomas Cranmer (Protestant Anglican) both said that justification comes by grace through faith demonstrated by works. The great "works versus faith" divide in Christianity has always been about how much to emphasize each. To say one camp or another is all works (or all faith) is a false dichotomy.

choose to separate them, the underlying point remains. Conviction and confidence are different, even when they refer to the same statement.

Conviction affects behavior. When I recite the Nicene Creed, I say, "I believe in one God, the Father Almighty, creator of heaven and earth, of all things seen and unseen." I take that to mean that everything visible and invisible has been created by God and fits God's purposes; *therefore* I strive to act with compassion toward all things, without exception. Likewise, I say, "I believe…in the resurrection of the dead and the life of the world to come." And so I talk to and pray for those who have died, believing them to have continuing life and awareness. A very simplistic epistemology would give me 100 percent confidence in the Nicene Creed. I need only adhere to a doctrine that says the Church was infallible in its process of making the creed. Full conviction, on the other hand, will require me to make radical changes in the way I interact with the world. My religion gives me tools to do so.

Tools for Believing

We can take concrete steps to create our own belief. We can use feedback to intentionally raise our conviction in the beliefs we prefer and lower conviction in those we do not. We can join communities that shape us, adopt creeds that change us, and do things that make us into better people.

This brings us back to a definition of faith that I have slowly been building throughout the book. Faith refers to the set of relationships by which we come to believe. It does not refer solely to the propositions themselves, or even the confidence or conviction we have in them. For Christians, faith in Christ means trust in the person of Christ and in his ability to communicate. That resembles, but is distinct from, trust in propositions we know come from Christ. It places the emphasis concretely on our role as knowers and believers – on our epistemology and relationships – rather than on the abstract correctness of the statements in question. It allows God, scripture, and the institutions of the church to be trustworthy in their attempts to reveal without insisting that I am infallible in my ability to receive. I have great confidence that this concept of faith is correct – using evidence from scripture and tradition – and strong conviction –

based on the feedback loops it creates. Faith builds communities in which belief can grow and good beliefs lead to faith.

Not all communities have this kind of faith, not even all Christian communities. Here I speak of the ideal I ought to seek, not the state of religious institutions as I find them. Observation has led me to great skepticism about real world institutions, even as it leads me to hope for them.

There is not enough space here to go into details on the many belief affecting philosophies, practices, and politics. They are far too diverse, even within Anglican Christianity. Such an endeavor requires – and suggests – another book. I can only set out some general guidelines for comprehensive reasoning that provides tools for intentional believing.

✦ 1. CREATE SAFE ENVIRONMENTS.

Dissonance causes stress. Opening up spaces for conversion often means minimizing other stressful influences. Each of us hopes for conversion and increased conviction toward our preferences. To achieve it, we create safe spaces where we will experience stress only in the areas we want to change – stress that pushes us in the direction we have chosen. Strategies for conversion involve surrounding yourself with others who share your priorities and commitments.

This type of feedback can be both constructive and destructive. It softens our emotional and intellectual resistance to new ideas, making us more willing to try new things. It can also lead to stagnation when we become part of increasingly like-minded groups. The challenge is to create environments with just the right level of diversity, neither frightening nor homogenous, to promote positive change.

Professional science provides great consistency and luxury, both in academy and industry. Scientists are surrounded by educated people, with similar resources and backgrounds. They enjoy popular and financial support. I mention this not as a critique, but as a way of reflecting on the regularity scientists enjoy in terms of life and environment. That regularity facilitates a willingness to face uncertainty and challenging ideas.

Religions also create safe spaces for sharing information, challenging ideas, and changing beliefs. Sometimes that comfort will be created with luxury and familiar people. At other times, we use ritual motions, activities, and roles to put people into a receptive mindset, where they can willingly participate in the changing of their beliefs.

What do you find comforting intellectually, emotionally, even physically? Do you ever use those comforts to make it easier to change something about yourself? Can you think of a time when too much affirmation stopped you from making a change you wanted? What is the right level of familiarity for you and do your communities provide it?

Brainwashing

A number of communities, both religious and non-religious, take the opposite approach when seeking to bring outsiders into the group. They will intentionally foster dissonance, even breakdowns in an unsafe setting. The potential believer, feeling out of control, will turn to any authority figure present in the moment of crisis, whether or not a relationship of trust has already been established. As with the politics of fear, brainwashing represents an effective, if unethical way, for leaders to increase their power over the group. I strongly disapprove of this type of activity; it almost always changes people's belief without regard to their preferences. It assumes what is best for them and acts to convert or strengthen conviction without first consulting them about what they want.

Not only does this offend against my ideas of self-determination, I have found it to be flawed as a long-term conversion strategy. Without linking knowledge, belief, preference, and conscious choice, the convert is weak in his belief. Brainwashing leaves him unprepared to deal with future shocks. He has no tools to handle dissonance at a later date; he has no integrated belief system that reinforces belief by linking it to his own choices. I would rather train potential converts to be aware of the process so that they can use it, instead of it using them.

I consider brainwashing and fear-mongering to be the two greatest sins present in modern religion. They actively suppress curiosity and mindfulness.

✦ 2. REPEAT. REPEAT. REPEAT.

Repetition increases conviction by regular affirmation of the belief in question. A mantra said over and over again increases our trust in its truth. An action done over and over again becomes familiar and comfortable. Repetition, though, should not be confused with getting more evidence. Even when it adds no new confidence, repetition still strengthens belief.

In the case of induction, making more observations is not enough. They must be unbiased and relevant. More data, properly collected provides better evidence for a proposition; it increases confidence. Learning something from many, independently qualified authorities also gives us a rational reason to have more confidence.

These are different from simple repetition. Hearing a statement over and over makes us more likely to believe it. Likewise, hearing it from more people or in more ways – regardless of their qualifications – will condition us.

What statements, implicit and explicit, do you hear on a daily basis? Do they strengthen or undermine the beliefs you want to have? Religions excel at repetition-based conviction. Hearing, or better yet saying or singing, the same phrases over and over and over fixes them in your memory. If they are catchy, provocative, or emotionally weighted, you will be likely to repeat them to yourself, even when you don't hear them from others. This process of internalization can be very influential. Explicitly, we repeat prayers, mantras, and creeds that belong to our communities. We set them to music. We share them with friends. We recall them in times of trouble. Implicitly, we internalize the messages coded within communication. We notice who defers to whom, which people are reinforced for speaking up, and which people are punished. We see the way people fit other people into their models.

Traditionally, Anglicans are said to be "soaked in scripture." We read long excerpts in worship and borrow heavily from the Bible in the construction of set phrases for prayer and communication. It is less evident in recent centuries, but English literature draws heavily on the Bible. Milton and Shakespeare both reference scripture almost constantly.[113]

---

[113] For details and for other examples of the Bible in popular culture, see Maggi Dawn's book, *The Writing on the Wall* (Hodder and Stoughton, 2010).

Repetition can also be oppressive. Constantly hearing an ad in the background can make you more likely to think of, and buy, the product. Seeing pictures of a political leader on every building or hearing a political slogan again and again can make you overestimate their power and popularity. Destructive mantras can be harmful in any field, but are particularly dangerous in religion when our worldview is at stake. They can prevent us from even considering alternative ways of thinking or behaving. They can blind us to individuals or whole classes of people.

Which words are most familiar to you? What phrases do you cling to? Are there songs that regularly play in your head? Do you have advertising jingles memorized? These become the bedrock on which we build our metaphysics. Ask yourself what messages are pressed upon you. Ask yourself what lines you repeat to yourself over and over and over and what effect they have. Both as individuals and as groups, we set up environments that reinforce a certain set of beliefs.

✦ 3. SET UP INTERACTIVE SPACES.

The belief/behavior feedback loop usually occurs over long periods of time without our consciously connecting stimulus and response. Teachers can set up interactive spaces where student activities are more immediately encouraged or discouraged. Their goal is to condense the process. Online quizzes have become immensely popular in recent years because they provide feedback for learning. A simple, repeatable quiz allows you to take a test over and over again until you get it right, using repetition and interaction to form conviction.

As a martial arts instructor, I frequently set up situations where feedback is immediate and clear. Physical exercises can provide strong conviction about more general principles, particularly when they involve a student doing something she thought she couldn't do. Attempting to break boards with bare hands and feet quickly shows which students have the right technique. Encountering and overcoming the obstacle on the first attempt (or second) reinforces a belief that their technique is effective and that they can progress in skill. Similarly, encountering a board too early and repeatedly failing to break it generates both physical and emotional pain. It can lead them to underestimate their own powers and reinforce a belief in their own weakness. Worse yet, the fear of further pain creates destructive affirmation. A good teacher knows when the interaction will lead to the right convictions.

This tool, too, can be abused. It's not too difficult to imagine setting up environments that lie – that send false messages about how we interact with the world. Incompetence and occasional malice leads teachers to present difficult obstacles too early or to connect the wrong signals in an environment. Imagine a martial arts student who always competed with women who were more experienced and men who were less. What message would this send about the relative competence of the two sexes? Imagine an environment in which self-destructive drinking is rewarded by social approval. It may be entirely unconscious, but still have an undesirable effect on belief.

✦ 4. FAIL OFTEN.

It's good to recognize the limits of your own conviction, and the only way to find out is to go right up to the edge. We like to fool ourselves about our beliefs. Dissonance is unpleasant, so we pretend that our preferences, thoughts, and actions line up, even when they don't. Because knowledge is different from belief, and because we are not rational actors, we must place ourselves in situations where our true convictions will be revealed. If we think we value charity, we must honestly face our tax receipts and see just how much we give away. If we think we value open-ended inquiry, we must seriously look for uncomfortable ideas and try them out. If we think we believe in resurrection, we must ask how that changes the way we live. In my scheme there are no abstract beliefs, only lived convictions. It's okay to fail. It's even necessary if we want to know what we truly believe.

Failing provides additional benefits. Once we have trusted a person or practice to take us beyond our comfort zone – once we have risked and been proven right – we will have stronger conviction about similar methods in the future. Some of the strongest bonds of trust form when we allow someone else to guide us through fear to success. That trust strengthens our confidence in their authority and our conviction in what they affirm.

For good and ill, belief will always be visible. You may have secret forms of evidence no one knows about. You can hide confidence. You might have preferences and axioms completely unknown to the people you argue with. You cannot hide belief. Your actions keep it on display. This visibility makes hypocrisy a common destructive force in religious communities. When a member or leader sends one message with their beliefs verbally and another with their actions, they undermine themselves and the community. To catch this early, before it can do too much damage, communities often make the cost of entry very high and intentionally push members to the limits of their belief.[114]

I have mixed feelings about high entry costs in religion. On one hand, I recognize that they strengthen the community, the convictions of members, and the chances that they will stay. I also respect the way they test our convictions. On the other hand, the practice reinforces an exchange mentality – if you pay the costs, you can receive the benefits. I find this antithetical to the concept of grace in Christianity. Further, unless you have a very communally oriented definition of religion, it runs the risk of reinforcing political identity at the cost of practical and philosophical elements of faith.

✦ 5. Be accountable to someone.

Making a public statement of belief invites others to judge your integrity. It promote conformity, but it also increases conviction. We are more likely to follow through when we know someone else might be measuring the strength of our beliefs. This strength need not be judgmental. We are moved by the faith our children have in us. We are moved by friends, who may do no more than wag a finger. Simply knowing that another person exists who is doing the math will increase our convictions in things we commit to.

I strongly recommend accountability when it comes to the premises and beliefs we hold most dear. Who asks you if you are living up to your ideals? Christianity takes this accountability seriously, often introducing a formal confessor or accountability group with whom you are expected to meet on a regular basis. If that doesn't appeal to you, friends work very well. Even private journaling and blogging can be effective, if you return to what you have written. You

---

[114] High entry costs also represent a large, often emotionally weighted contribution to the group, activity, or philosophy. Behavioral economists have demonstrated that such contributions increase our likelihood of making other contributions in the future.

can hold yourself accountable. Personal reflection is better than nothing, but social support is even more effective.

This book and you, the reader, can hold me accountable for my ability to reason as I navigate the waters of science and religion. Have I constructed a worldview amenable to both? Is it compelling to you? Will I have the same beliefs about ontology and epistemology ten years from now?

☙ ✦ ❧

We don't always act according to our knowledge, and yet, wonderfully, we can have knowledge of how we act. One of the greatest benefits of religious institutions comes from their attention to what, how, and why we believe. Religious communities and rituals instill in us the kinds of thoughts that reliably shape behavior. They provide tools for conversion, for affirmation, and dissonance. Whatever our thoughts about which beliefs specific religions instill, we must recognize the power religions have and the centuries of expertise they bring to shaping belief, behavior, and community.

Conviction gives us a way to think about the strength of our beliefs, how much they impact our behavior, and how much they impact our identity. How comfortable are you with your beliefs and with the conviction you have in them? What communities, religious and otherwise, have shaped your behavior? What beliefs are they, in turn based on?

This critical question of feedback loops – belief shaping behavior, behavior shaping belief – shows us how inescapable conviction will be for any rational model of knowledge, for any practical epistemology. Even science relies heavily upon the daily success of scientists doing experiments, updating their models, and growing in their power to make predictions. Even in science we must ask questions of belief.

What practices increase our conviction that science works? What experiences might decrease it? When we have disagreements about "scientific" topics like evolution, vaccination, and climate change, we must think about the rules of epistemology and ontology that not only shape knowledge, but motivate doubt and curiosity. Your own belief-behavior loops may differ from those of people around you. How would you find out?

I don't separate knowledge and belief as a bulwark against evidence; I separate them to empower people. It uncovers our differences and helps us take up the tools of rational belief formation. Philosophy, practice, and politics play an important role in how we form our worldviews together. While religious institutions do many other things (e.g., marking rites of passage, organizing charity, funding science, …) they do this one thing particularly well: they allow us to shape beliefs in community and to create community beliefs.

We are constantly assaulted by others who, with good and ill intent, want to change our beliefs without us noticing. I hope that the last few chapters have given you a good perspective on what matters to me, what I prefer and how those preferences are integrated with my knowledge and beliefs. I hope that my example gives you some ideas of what to do (or what not to do). Above all, I want you to have greater control over your own ability to grow conviction. I want the change to be in your hands.

EPILOGUE
Reason Coming Together

The Hill Society had been running for about a year when one of the members said something that stuck with me. We were walking from the Hill to a local pub for dinner and he said, "I'm still an atheist." It was important for him to assert this. He said, "I want you to know I'm still an atheist, but you've convinced me that these are questions we have to ask in a group." I'm not convinced we need to find the same answers, but I have a strong conviction that we must learn to ask them together. Both knowledge and belief are far too important for us to attempt them alone. Both confidence and conviction are too difficult to gain. Or perhaps they are too easy, but shouldn't be. Playing the game of reason in groups allows us to explore a far wider swath of the world than we could alone. Our friends and colleagues play an indispensable role in shaping our thought, our acts, and our identity. Perfect insulation is ill advised, even if it is possible. Though we must reason for ourselves, we need not reason by ourselves.

Our reasoning improves as we become more aware of our own metaphysics. We have a remarkable ability to make sense of the world around us. This can only improve if we use our reason transparently and in community. Science provides wonderful insights about the physical world but it will not be enough to give us a functional model of the cosmos. For that we need more. We need other ways of knowing about people, values, choices, and abstract-tions. We need mechanisms for holding ourselves accountable to the standards we set. We need languages to communicate, rituals to form, and communities to reinforce our models and turn them into actions.

For me, Anglican Christianity provides these things. It helps by respecting the strengths and weakness of modern science and by being open to hearing the wisdom from a wide variety of sources. Christianity more broadly gives me practices and groups integrated with my model. The weekly celebration of a common meal reinforces my belief in a God who justifies curiosity and compassion. It reaffirms my humility in the face of reality and challenges me to actively seek out inconvenient facts. If it really is God's world, how could we not benefit from a fuller knowledge of it? Christianity also affirms my belief that God set things up in a way that I can understand, that my ability to reason can uncover at least some of the mysteries of the cosmos. It works for me.

I do not know what has worked or will work for you, but I hope this book will start a few conversations. I hope it will provoke you to seek better knowledge, better belief, and a better integration of the two. I also hope it will give you a language of reason that can bring you and your neighbors together. I want that kind of understanding for everyone.

SCIENCE AND RELIGION

At their surface, the religion and science debates in the United States represent a dysfunction. We have grown weary of our models and our authority figures. More precisely, we fear losing a few basic axioms (i.e., the world or morality is understandable), and so we try to prop them up, becoming dogmatic about some and skeptical about others. Our society is fractured and many authorities seek to prop up their own power by asking you to distrust all others. We are rightly suspicious of this kind of power play, no matter who makes it. Each of us must learn to reason for ourselves.

At a deeper level our society is right where it needs to be. As a larger community, we are working out a common metaphysics. We are deciding on common rules for how we play the game of reason. We are debating whether words like "natural" and "supernatural" have meaning for us, whether they are effective for communicating our ideas and navigating the world. We are working out the methods we want to use when we foster knowledge and belief. Each of us has our own preferences and our own ways of deciding what works, but all of us work on the problems together.

Undoubtedly, some worldviews are better than others. Some worldviews allow us to reach our goals and some do not. Some value systems lead to happiness, productivity, and enlightenment. Some lead to loving relationships. Others do not. Perspective and accuracy matter. We have good reasons to change our worldview. And we have good reasons to change the worldviews of others. Both personal and social change work best when we are open about the process, when we talk about our goals and expectations. In other words, they work well when we talk about our rules for reasoning as we do. It is not enough to say "I am right" – we should know why we think we're right and explore why others disagree.

We have come full circle. No one reasons in a vacuum. Each of us knows and believes within a context. Structures – intellectual, behavioral, and social – support our reasoning. They, in turn, are supported by it. Having separated knowledge and belief in principle let me now suggest that they are always entangled in practice. It was useful for analysis to distinguish between the evidence that goes into reasoning and the choices that proceed from it. To form a coherent picture, we must see the whole. The web of worldview construction links philosophy, practice, and politics; it shapes knowledge and belief.

☙ ✦ ❧

Abraham Lincoln once said, "If both factions, or neither, shall abuse you, you will probably be right. Beware of being assailed by one and praised by the other." Both scientists and Christians have accused me of undermining their side. Scientists worry that I contextualize scientific knowledge too much while Christians worry that I place too much emphasis on the human aspects of religion. Perhaps both sides have a point. Nonetheless, this perspective has worked for me. And, of course, I'm always open to improving it.

The truth needs no apologist, only a level playing field. I know that science will persist in our culture; it has power on its side. Science generates knowledge, and while that knowledge may be imperfect, for most things it remains the very best our ingenuity can provide. Religion represents a synthesis of thought, action, and community fundamental to human life. Even those who sell science as an alternative are really just advocating for a new synthesis. So religions will persist as well – though there is some question about the kind of religion. Will it be one of hope and critical thought, or a more intolerant, dogmatic faith? Only time will tell.

I believe you have a role to play in the formation of the world. I believe you can make the world a better place by thinking for yourself, but reasoning in groups. Our hope rests in developing an awareness of how the process works, trusting one another, kindly correcting where necessary, and working for a more reasonable world. In such a world I have no doubt that the truth will appear.

ACKNOWLEDGEMENTS

Thank you to Steven Benner, Christopher Clearfield, "Uncle" Mike Kerrick, Ian Hutchinson, Paul Impey, Carole Mandryk, Ethan Mills, Susan Mix, Ted Peters, Matt Quarterman, Paul Stimers, Amy King, Allison Towner, and Louise Williams for reading drafts and giving me comments. Thank you to the students at the University of Arizona – especially the Hill Society and the Canterbury Club – for helping me to understand a diversity of concerns about science and religion. Thank you to the Society of Ordained Scientists for continual prayer, provocation, and support.

ABOUT THE AUTHOR

Some readers will be interested to know my context, others my credentials. This short history allows me to share the philosophy, practices, and politics that have shaped my own story. It also gives me a chance to thank a few more people who have been influential in my life.

SCIENCE

I began a love affair with genetics in high school, where I learned one could do biology without making a mess. Thank you to Sharon Masse and Garfield High School. I studied Biochemistry at the University of Washington, where I received a Bachelor of Science with honors in 1997. Working with Tim Hunkapillar in the Department of Molecular Biotechnology, I studied the use of sequence comparison algorithms in biology. Before and after college, I worked as a DNA sequencing technician with Leroy Hood. Both Tim and Lee are pioneers in automated DNA sequencing. I was a NASA Space Grant Scholar and spent summer 1996 working in the Spacecraft Cooling Systems Lab at NASA Goddard Space Flight Center in Greenbelt, MD. There, I had the privilege of working with Gerald Soffen, who had been project scientist for Viking. He was influential in forming modern astrobiology and he was devoted to including students in all aspects of research.

I earned my doctorate in Organismic and Evolutionary Biology at Harvard University in 2004. Working with David Haig, I wrote a dissertation on the evolution of photosynthetic reaction centers. I am immensely grateful to David for keeping me challenged in philosophy and theory as well. David is a leader in theoretical biology, particularly intra-genomic conflict. While at Harvard, I worked with Joseph Felsenstein at the University of Washington, writing two programs for his computational biology suite, PHYLIP.

I received a NASA Graduate Student Researchers Program fellowship and became involved in the NASA Astrobiology Institute, which had just been founded. As a new community we struggled to communicate and set standards of evidence across the disciplines of astronomy, biology, chemistry, geology, engineering, etc. With a group of early career collaborators, I organized and edited a quick and dirty introduction to astrobiology aimed at scientists entering the field. The "Astrobiology Primer" was published in the journal *Astrobiology* in 2006. (A second, updated edition just appeared in 2016.) The Primer was followed by a popular book, *Life in Space: Astrobiology for Everyone* (Harvard University Press, 2009). I continue to work with the NASA astrobiology programs on communication and strategy, turning recently to the intersection of astrobiology with philosophy and theology.

I taught as an adjunct in the Department of Ecology and Evolutionary Biology at the University of Arizona (2010-2013) and returned to Harvard for a post-doc in theoretical biology looking at the history of definitions of life (2013-2015).

Theology and Religious Studies

I was raised in the Episcopal Church and gained a deep appreciation for God and the church from my parents, Bill and Susan Mix, who were lay ministers, leaders, and youth coordinators throughout my childhood. In college, I explored various denominations and faiths, taking a Bachelor of Arts in Comparative Religion at the University of Washington in 1997. Working with Martin Jaffee, I focused on esoteric traditions, touching on Judaism, Islam, and Buddhism.

After getting my doctorate in biology, I travelled to the Church Divinity School of the Pacific, an Episcopalian seminary in Berkeley, California. Many professors and mentors had a profound impact on me, but Bill Countryman stands out. He helped me appreciate the Anglican perspective and fall in love with the Anglican community. My time at the Homeless Action Center, working with homeless people who experience mental health challenges, was also significant. I went through a several year discernment process with the Diocese of Olympia and, having earned a Masters of Divinity (the professional degree for ministers), I was ordained priest (Epiphany 2008). While at CDSP, I was able to spend time at the Center for Theology and the Natural Sciences, looking at Christianity, Islam, and science.

After ordination, I served as an assistant pastor at Church of the Apostles, a cross-denominational parish in Seattle (2008-2009) and as chaplain to the University of Arizona (2009-2013). I also joined the Society of Ordained Scientists, a distributed order of ministers who also have expertise in the sciences. I speak and preach regularly on science and religion and have also given talks on emerging church, sexual ethics, and evangelism.

My current research brings me back to academic philosophy and theology as I look into what we want when we say we are looking for life. In the 2015-2016 school year, I was a fellow at the Center of Theological Inquiry in Princeton, New Jersey, working on this and related questions in Astrobiology and Society. I maintain a blog with my research, sermons, and reflections on post-modern Christianity «*http://dacalu.wordpress.com*». I also work with the Society of Ordained Scientists to create communities of meaning and purpose around issues of science and religion «*http://ordainedscientists.wordpress.com*».

Martial Arts

At seven, I began studying Taekwondo and martial arts have become a passion for me and my family. I am indebted to Kwang Sik Myung, my primary teacher in Hapkido. A student of the founder, he had a deep love for the art, for teaching, and for bringing people together. I must also thank my brother, Jason Mix. He constantly challenges me, and all of his students, to communal action, active thought, and thoughtful community.

I currently hold a sixth-degree black belt in Hapkido, a fifth-degree black belt in Taekwondo, and a first-degree black belt in Aikido. In 1998, my family and a few friends founded Enso Center for International Arts, a non-profit devoted to promoting awareness, understanding, and harmony through martial arts, healing arts, and community building. I have had the privilege of teaching throughout my travels and have brought seven students to black belt. Each one has taught me more than I can say. You can find out more on the website for Enso Center «*http://ensocenter.org*».

GLOSSARY / INDEX

Different people use words differently. This list includes words I feel are important to this book along with how I use them and where I introduce that use.

☙ C ❧

☙ D ❧

☙ E ❧

☙ I ❧

☙ K ❧

☙ L ❧

☙ M ❧

ଓ N ଓ

ଓ O ଓ

ଓ P ଓ

ଓ Q ଓ

☙ R ❧

☙ S ❧

INDEX OF NAMES

A

B

C

☙ O ❧

☙ P ❧

☙ S ❧

☙ T ❧

☙ W ❧